Wright Morris Revisited

Twayne's United States Authors Series

Joseph M. Flora, Editor

University of North Carolina, Chapel Hill

TUSAS 703

WRIGHT MORRIS
Photograph by Joseph J. Wydeven

Wright Morris Revisited

Joseph J. Wydeven

Bellevue University

Twayne Publishers
An Imprint of Simon & Schuster Macmillan
New York

Prentice Hall International
London • Mexico City • New Delhi • Singapore • Sydney • Toronto

Twayne's United States Author Series No. 703

Wright Morris Revisited
Joseph J. Wydeven

Twayne Publishers
An Imprint of Simon & Schuster Macmillan
1633 Broadway
New York, NY 10019

Library of Congress Cataloging-in-Publication Data

Wydeven, Joseph J.
    Wright Morris Revisited / Joseph J. Wydeven.
        p.   cm. — (Twayne's United States authors series ; TUSAS 703)
    Includes bibliographical references (p.   ) and index.
    ISBN 0-8057-4531-9 (acid-free paper)
    1. Morris, Wright, 1910–   —Criticism and interpretation.
    2. Western stories—History and criticism.   3. West (U. S.)—In
literature.   I. Title.   II. Series.
PS3525.O7475Z95   1998
813'.52—dc21   98-10001
                                                       CIP

This paper meets the requirements of ANSI/NISO Z3948-1992 (Permanence of Paper).

10 9 8 7 6 5 4 3 2 1

Printed in the United States of America

To Rachel and Eric,
and to Alice

Contents

Preface

Novelist and photographer Wright Morris has had a long career as an American artist, his published works extending from the 1940s to the 1990s—half a century of creative activity in fiction, social and critical commentary, photography, and photo-text. Critical response to him has been spotty, but on the whole he has received considerable attention over the years. Still, those of us who admire Morris's work believe he deserves more sustained and concentrated focus, taking into account his examination of the meaning of the American Dream and the obvious aesthetic riches found in his narratives, photographic images, and combinations of the two. This book is intended to provide a new introduction to Morris's work and to encourage critical dialogue among his readers.

To say that Morris is an American novelist is to neglect the emphasis that *American,* in his case, requires. From the outset, as David Madden, the author of the first Twayne book on Morris, asserted, one of Morris's principal subjects was the American Dream; more correctly, perhaps, his subject was American *dreamers,* those men and women who looked west and saw mythic and metaphysical landscapes upon which they imprinted their vast desires for happiness and success. It is characteristic of Morris—and central to his understanding of the American experience—that he transformed a clichéd phrase into something more vital, claiming that "[i]n the dream begins"—not responsibility—but *"irre-sponsibility."* By the time he achieved critical consciousness, Morris saw that the American Dream had been burdened with more weight than it could carry. Having traveled west with their hopes, Morris's travelers looked about and saw that their children's conditions had little connection to the parents' motives.

The America that Morris first wrote about was that of his father (and his uncles)—a place, he points out, where people still walked to get where they were going and where the ubiquitous railroads were first carriers of hope and then potential means of escape. In attempting to make that America his own, Morris turned critical. A high point in his work is that moment when he discovers the nausea hidden at the core of nostalgia, makes elaborate note of it, and turns it into the subject of a series of critical investigations. The sheer range of Morris's imagination, the degree of intelligence and sophistication he applies to complex subjects and settings, is remarkable.

The present work is of necessity a short book. David Madden and G. B. Crump have written excellent comprehensive books on Morris, and I see my work as an addition to, not by any means a replacement for, those studies. I hope that some of my readings of the novels occasionally offer provocative alternatives, despite the occasions when limitations of space kept some discussions shorter than the works deserve. It appears now that most of the essential materials relevant to assessment of Morris's achievement are available. His 20th and final novel, *Plains Song for Female Voices,* appeared in 1980, and after another decade in which Morris took pains to collect and recollect, sum up, and look back in memoir and retrospective shows of his photographs, he fell silent.

This book, then, is a revisitation, a fresh biographical and critical introduction to Morris from the perspective of the closure of his career. It is a fresh survey of Morris's work and a means to view him from a new perspective, attempting, within necessary limits, to take into account Morris's dual artistic preoccupations as writer and photographer. Though I deal with this connection frequently throughout the book, I can obviously make no attempt to be exhaustive. My emphasis is on Morris's fiction, and although he wrote a number of critical books, I discuss them only as they illuminate the fiction. I deal with all the novels but emphasize those I find most important and interesting.

This study is the culmination of my critical examination of Morris's work over two decades: a dissertation completed at Purdue University in 1979 and since then a host of articles, book chapters, reviews, and summations. I am greatly indebted to Morris himself—though wary of critics, Morris has tolerated my questions with characteristic humor, responded patiently to my letters, and allowed me into his home on several occasions, even submitting to an extended taped interview in October 1995. Although a week-long foray into the Morris archives in the Bancroft Library at Berkeley yielded little new information, the experience suggested as nothing else could the vast amounts of raw material Morris processed, especially in the years of his apprenticeship.

Although my intention is to offer a comprehensive introduction to Morris, this book has two distinct emphases. First, because I believe most critical efforts to comprehend Morris's fiction have underplayed the impact of his photography, often dismissing the photographs as merely interesting adjuncts to his fictional practices, I examine in some detail the relationship between photography and fiction in Morris's imagination. What this often amounts to is a study of epistemological connections between images and language. Although this is a book on Morris as an *author,* much of Morris's writing, particularly his visual detail, can be better understood by examining the evidence of—and in—his photographs. This book accordingly includes a small portfolio of Morris's images. Analyses of the photographs *and* of the stylistic and substantive links between his writing and photography are found particularly in my chapters on Morris's apprenticeship and on the creative processes culminating in *The Works of Love* and *Plains Song.* I hope the reader will understand that my background is literary; I claim no special expertise in photography beyond profound appreciation and hundreds of hours of careful looking, often through lens and magnifying glass.

My second critical emphasis is on the importance of autobiography to Morris's career and, more important, on the relationship between autobiography, memory, and the imagination in Morris's virtual creation of self. For such a prolific writer, it is of some interest that Morris's first published work did not appear until he was 30. His apprenticeship, that is, was a long one, complicated by his seeming inability to decide which medium to employ—language or photography leading to much experimentation such that his first published work was a photo-text.

More important, however, was the subject matter of this extended autobiographical experimentation: Morris's attempt to find and define himself as a being in the world. It is crucial in understanding his work to make a distinction between *being* alive and *writing* about that life. In no other American writer, perhaps, is that distinction so formative. Morris protests—perhaps too much—that he lived his childhood with serene lack of self-awareness and that he came to self-understanding through self-invention. His mother's death when Morris was less than a week old and his father's benign neglect of him as a child—Morris's "orphaned condition"—loom as crucial factors, linked to both his cyclical obsessions and his creative practices. Morris's memoirs are central documents illuminating relationships among the artist's interest in patterns of light and dark, photography, and the ingredients of personal life, particularly as found on the Nebraska plains.

Wright Morris has had the advantage of a long life and the opportunity to bring his work to successful, orderly conclusion. From his childhood in Nebraska to his old age in Mill Valley, Morris consciously and critically shaped his work, and for this reason his career is an exemplary one for serious American writers and readers. Because of American needs—and Morris's concern—to examine the meanings of American culture and the idea of the American Dream, his work rewards careful study. I hope this book is instrumental in making Morris more widely known and in suggesting his importance for further critical contemplation.

Acknowledgments

Many thanks to a number of people over the years who have had a share of influence in getting this book written, beginning with Frank Sherman, who introduced me to Morris's work and got me thinking about photo-texts; Chester Eisinger, who nurtured my interest and held my feet to the fire; David D. Anderson, who invited me to the MLA; and Barbara Meldrum, who gave me a start in publishing on Morris. Very special thanks to Vernon Cheek for helping me think about photography, loaning me camera and dark room, and sharing ideas, visual and otherwise.

I am greatly indebted to David Madden for his kindness and support, his introductory study of Morris, and his reading of parts of this book in manuscript. I also owe a debt to Gail Crump, whose book on Morris was published just as I was completing my dissertation; Gail was magnanimous in welcoming me into the fold. Thanks to the following editors for printing my work and allowing me to borrow from it for this book: David D. Anderson at *MidAmerica*, Brian Bedard and the late John Milton at *South Dakota Review*, Victor J. Emmett Jr. of *The Midwest Quarterly*, Thomas J. Lyon of *Western American Literature*, R. K. Meiners of *The Centennial Review*, Neila C. Seshachari of *Weber Studies: An Interdisciplinary Humanities Journal*. Barbara Meldrum and Helen Winter Stauffer and Susan J. Rosowski graciously printed two of my essays as book chapters.

Many of the ideas expressed in this book had trial runs at conferences of the Western Literature Association, for which special thanks go to Carl Bredahl, Chris Coates, Fran Kaye, Diane Quantic, Rodney Rice, and many others. It was on the occasion of the Western Literature conference in Reno in 1992 that I enjoyed a splendid moment during my plane's descent into Reno. The flight from Salt Lake City detoured to Fresno before heading back to Reno, taking us at low altitude over Virginia City—where, suddenly through the window, perspective jolted, appeared the settings of two of Wright Morris's photographs, preserved, as Morris might say, in amber, and giving me a stunned moment of artistic intimacy.

For favors great and small, but mainly for discussing Morris in a variety of formats: Barb Allen-Langdon and Jerrine McCaffrey, Doug

Brown, Patty Cox, Katherine Howell, Nancy Johnson, Bette Klaphake, Robert Knoll, Clif Mason, John McKenna, Barbara Rippey, Phil Smith; Timothy Adams, Jack Cohn, and Stephen Longmire. Margaret Romweber welcomed me to Berkeley and showed me the right bridge to Mill Valley. Reg Dyke shared lots of good talk (and the occasional microbrew); Karen Schwartzbeck had a steady eye; Tony Jasnowski edited perspicaciously and sent life-enhancing e-mail Latinisms. Bellevue University paid much of my way and offered continuous professional support, including sabbatical time to visit Morris and plan my work.

My debt to Wright and Jo Morris is huge: they encouraged my intrusions, enjoyed my enthusiasms, and challenged my critical perceptions, always treating me with kindness. They gave ready permission to quote from the writings as I felt necessary and to reproduce the photographs appearing in the portfolio section of this book. I am grateful.

Finally, thanks to Alice for her patience, awesome textual tenacity, and abiding love.

Chronology

1910   January 6, Wright Morris born in Central City, Nebraska; mother dies within a week.

1910–1919   Lives in Central City and other towns along the Platte River.

1919–1924   Lives in Omaha; spends two weeks on Uncle Harry and Aunt Clara's farm.

1924–1927   Lives in Chicago, near Lincoln Park; works at Larrabee YMCA.

1927–1928   Travels to California with father, then back to Chicago; father takes job in drawbridge tower.

1930–1933   Meets Grandfather Osborn and mother's sisters, Winona and Violet, in Boise, Idaho; attends Union Pacific College in California (five weeks), then leaves to work on Uncle Dwight's farm in Texas. Attends Pomona College, Claremont, California.

1933   Begins European *Wanderjahr:* Vienna, Schloss Ranna near Spitz. Buys camera in Vienna.

1934   Bicycle tour of Italy; confined briefly in Grosseto Prison. Money stolen in Paris. Returns to Claremont and marries Mary Ellen Finfrock.

1935–1938   Writes novels and sketches; experiments with photo-texts. Buys Rolleiflex camera.

1938   Moves to Cape Cod. Works on *The Inhabitants*. Spends winter in cabin on Quassapaug Pond.

1940   First published photo-text, "The Inhabitants," in *New Directions*. First photo-text exhibition, New School for Social Research.

1940–1941   Extensive "photo-safari" around the United States. Meets and fails to impress Roy Stryker of the Farm Security Administration Photography Unit.

1941   Father's death. Lives in Columbia Heights, Brooklyn.

1942   *My Uncle Dudley*. Guggenheim fellowship. On return
       trip to Claremont, visits Uncle Harry and Aunt Clara
       and meets barber Eddie Cahow in Nebraska. Rejected
       for service first in the navy, then the army.

1944   Moves to suburban Philadelphia. Begins friendship with
       Loren Eiseley. Meets Maxwell Perkins at Scribner's.

1945   *The Man Who Was There*.

1946   Full photo-text of *The Inhabitants*. Awarded second
       Guggenheim Fellowship.

1947   Returns to Nebraska to make *The Home Place* pho-
       tographs, with a 4 × 5 view camera.

1948   *The Home Place*. Moves to Wayne, Pennsylvania.

1949   *The World in the Attic*.

1950   Participates in photography symposium at Museum of
       Modern Art, New York.

1951   *Man and Boy;* "Privacy as a Subject for Photography."

1952   *The Works of Love*. Writes *War Games* (withholds publi-
       cation until 1972).

1953   *The Deep Sleep*.

1954   *The Huge Season*. Receives third Guggenheim Fellow-
       ship. Summer, writer's conference in Salt Lake City;
       fall and winter in Mexico.

1956   *The Field of Vision;* National Book Award. Residence at
       Huntington Hartford Foundation.

1957   *Love Among the Cannibals*. "The Territory Ahead" in *The
       Living Novel* (editor Granville Hicks).

1958   *The Territory Ahead;* Summer, lectures at University of
       Southern California. September in Europe, including a
       return visit to Schloss Ranna; Amherst Lectures in
       October. Symposium at Columbia University with Saul
       Bellow, Leslie Fiedler, Dorothy Parker. Winter in Mex-
       ico, working on *Ceremony in Lone Tree*.

1959   Venice for seven months, where *Ceremony in Lone Tree* is
       completed. Travels to Greece and Mexico.

1960   *Ceremony in Lone Tree*. Takes one-year position at Los
       Angeles State College. National Institute of Arts and
       Letters Award.

1961   Divorced from Mary Ellen Finfrock. Marries Josephine
        Kantor.

1962   *What a Way to Go.* Venice for another seven-month
        stay; on return begins teaching at San Francisco State
        University. Edits *The Mississippi River Reader.* Special
        issue of *Critique* on Morris. Settles in Mill Valley, Cali-
        fornia.

1963   *Cause for Wonder.*

1965   *One Day.*

1966   "Arts and the Public" conference, University of Chicago.

1967   *In Orbit.*

1968   *A Bill of Rites, A Bill of Wrongs, A Bill of Goods. God's
        Country and My People.*

1970   *Wright Morris: A Reader* (editor Granville Hicks).

1971   *Fire Sermon.* Visiting professor, Princeton University.

1972   *Love Affair: A Venetian Journal. War Games* finally pub-
        lished.

1973   *A Life.*

1975   Retires from teaching at San Francisco State; writer in
        residence and subject of photography retrospective,
        Structures and Artifacts: Photographs 1933–1954, Uni-
        versity of Nebraska. *About Fiction.* Mari Sandoz Award.

1977   *The Fork River Space Project.*

1979   Six-week residency, photography department, Ben-
        nington College.

1980   *Plains Song for Female Voices* (American Book Award)

1981   *Will's Boy: A Memoir.* Photograph portfolio exhibition,
        Witkin Gallery.

1982   *Photographs and Words. Los Angeles Times* Robert Kirsch
        Award; Mark Twain Award (Society for the Study of
        Midwestern Literature); Commonwealth Award for
        Distinguished Service in Literature.

1983   *Solo: An American Dreamer in Europe: 1933–1934;* "Vic-
        trola" in *O'Henry Prize Stories 1983.* Photo-text exhibi-
        tion, *Time Pieces,* Corcoran Gallery, Washington, D.C.
        First recipient, Chair of Creative Writing, University of
        Alabama, Tuscaloosa.

1984   "Glimpse into Another Country" in *Best American Short Stories 1984* (in *O'Henry Prize Stories 1985*).

1985   *A Cloak of Light: Writing My Life*. "Fellow Creatures" in *Best American Short Stories 1985*.

1986   *Collected Stories: 1948–1986*. National Endowment for the Arts Life Achievement Award.

1988   Guest professor at Pomona College.

1989   *Time Pieces: Photographs, Writing, and Memory*. "How I Put In the Time" in *Growing Up Western* (editor Clarus Backes).

1991   *Paris Review* interview.

1992   *Wright Morris: Origin of a Species* photography retrospective, San Francisco Museum of Modern Art.

1993   Black Sparrow Press reissues three volumes of autobiography as *Writing My Life* and publishes *Three Easy Pieces* (*Fire Sermon, A Life,* and *The Fork River Space Project*). *Origin of a Species* show continues, Yale University and Boston.

1994   Black Sparrow Press publishes *Two for the Road* (*Man and Boy* and *In Orbit*).

1995   Black Sparrow Press publishes *The Loneliness of the Long Distance Writer,* reprinting *The Works of Love* and *The Huge Season*.

Chapter One
"No Place to Hide": Biographical and Critical Backgrounds

Throughout his active career, spanning the half century from 1942 to 1991 (when he stopped writing) and more than 30 books of fiction, commentary, and photo-text, Wright Morris remained resolutely independent, gradually establishing respectable reputations as both writer and photographer. He has resisted labeling as a realist or as a regionalist, and his experimentation has sometimes made his work difficult; he has insisted, particularly in his photo-texts and in his often extraordinarily visual prose, that readers be willing to cross generic borders, attend closely to detail, and draw conclusions from carefully crafted evidence.

Morris is less a storyteller than a brooder on stories he has already told. His work often has a cultivated ambiguity resulting from an understanding of reality as mysterious and complex, revealed through fragments and implications. This makes him, like the Henry James he admires, a novelist of consciousness. For Morris, it is the mind itself that is often at stake: In his photo-texts, Morris imposes a "third view" derived from photograph and written text; in his early fiction, he ponders the relation between memory and knowledge; and in his mature novels, he stresses the *making* of meaning and "meditative" motivations. G. B. Crump's statement that "the central focus of [Morris's] best prose is often on nuances of consciousness almost too elusive, too fine, to put into words"[1] is helpful in understanding Morris.

Consciousness for Morris means two things. It is first a condition of imaginative awareness in the individual human mind, making possible what he calls *transformation*, an expansion of consciousness. The second meaning of *consciousness* is pertinent to the condition of the national culture, the decline of which Morris mourns. It is the "diminishment of consciousness" that dismays him.[2] Against "unconsciousness" in the 1950s Morris pitted transformation, but he was increasingly alarmed, especially after the assassination of John F. Kennedy, by American cultural problems evidenced by the decline of reading, increasing puerility

1

in popular culture and the media, and a litany of other factors causing the trivialization of the American Dream.

Morris's most momentous writing is autobiographical, much of it evolving in counterpoint to his own experiences. From the beginning of Morris's experimentation with art, he was obsessed with *identity*, needing to comprehend and verify his past in order to anchor himself (and his characters) in space and time. Then, having explored and recreated the past, in the process coming to respect the powers of time, Morris turned to an artistic grappling with the problem of knowledge and *how* knowing takes place in the human organism.

This interest in epistemology is connected to his search for identity, for he recognized later that he had virtually created himself in his writing. The statement that Morris's work is autobiographical, then, must be tempered by a recognition that his conscious artistic purpose was to transform autobiographical facts into fictions. Over time Morris designed an elaborate theory of the relationships among memory, emotion, and the imagination in the creation of fiction. This theory—and its ramifications—is largely responsible for Morris's difficulty. He used his own life as a catalyst for investigations into identity and knowledge, but he was rarely satisfied that he had achieved closure. David Madden believes Morris never wholly solved his emotional problems in dealing with his Nebraska childhood, as evidenced by his need to seek new solutions to the same problems after writing "novels less personally concerned with the Nebraska past."[3]

Morris has often insisted that his novels cannot be fully understood in isolation from each other, conceptualizing his approach as "an up-and-downward spiraling of my preoccupations [that] would prove to lead me away and upward even as it led me back and downward."[4] This is essentially a way of visualizing the relations in his work among what he calls raw material, craftsmanship, and his need to repeat—even reshape—the past. Madden's view that "[i]t is as true of Morris as it is of Faulkner that full appreciation and understanding require a thorough reading of all the novels" (7–8) may be excessive, but it speaks to Morris's obsession to refigure the past. Attempting to explain Morris's autobiographical repetitions, Chester Eisinger suggests, "to use an overworked but precisely accurate term," that "Morris is haunted."[5] Repetition in writing is complicated, but in essence it is symptomatic of a need to *relive* original moments or events—summed up, perhaps, in Morris's perfect phrase "Home is where you hang your childhood."[6] Why relive seemingly insignificant events from the past? Because they were original, revelatory, pure, and often emotionally reducible to an idea—or even a photographic image.

By the time Morris realized his past might be important, it had already receded and could be recalled only with huge inaccuracies and gaping holes. Morris's recognition of this reality was essential. In mining his life, Morris discovered—long before this idea became the linchpin of autobiography study—that the passion for recollection consists as much of imagination as of memory. As he put it later, "If I attempt to distinguish between fiction and memory, and press my nose to memory's glass . . . , the remembered image grows more illusive. . . . Precisely where memory is frail and emotion is strong, imagination takes fire."[7]

As evidenced by such repetition, Morris was truly "haunted" by his Nebraska childhood. His adventures and vulnerabilities there are memorialized in his often repeated phrase "There is no place to hide," which becomes a metaphor for his career. Because on the Plains there is "no place to hide" from the elements, Morris often evokes means of physical and emotional shelter. The open spaces he emphasizes in his early works and the twisters that find their way into his work later are symptomatic of the need for shelter, and Morris's frequent placement of his characters hiding under porches or behind potted plants (as well as his own concealment as a photographer under the camera hood) suggests a desire for invisibility. This idea permeates Morris's work, suggesting both a psychological pattern for which hiding is a release and the basis for the creation of art as solace and solution. Hiding is a form of ritual preparation for the activity of perception.

Life and Career

Wright Morris was born in Central City, Nebraska, on January 6, 1910, the son of Will and Grace Osborn Morris. Six days later, one of the most important events in his life occurred: his mother died, leaving Morris "half an orphan."[8] Morris's father was a wanderer who frequently left his son behind in the care of neighbors, but he also took Morris on his first extended trips by car, at least once to California. Will Morris was not an ideal father; even as an adult, Morris was unable to be consistent about his feelings toward his father. Although Morris disapproved of his father's behavior with women, he admired Will Morris's manner of carrying himself as a successful man. Morris's sympathies for his father were mostly retrospective, for they drifted apart; Morris seems not to have known of his father's death until some time afterward. Nevertheless, the powers of attraction-repulsion were hard at work, and his father's life is imbedded in *The Works of Love* and *Will's Boy*.

Morris spent much of his childhood in various towns in Nebraska, perhaps inevitably in Omaha, where he moved in 1919 with his father and his new stepmother, Gertrude, a woman closer in age to Wright than to his father. Morris lived in Omaha from 1919 to 1924, part of the time with the Mulligan family, who saw the advantages of son Joey's having a "brother" who was like a twin to him.[9] During this time Morris acquired one of Babe Ruth's back pockets, an episode occurring when Morris, Joey Mulligan, and their fathers attended a barnstorming event. Mulligan Sr. caught Ruth's foul ball and sent Morris onto the field to have it autographed. By the time Morris got to the Babe, he was rounding third base and a number of other boys had decided to join him. Before Ruth escaped to the dugout, Morris had latched on to his pocket and torn it away.[10] This event shows up frequently in Morris's fiction (sometimes with Ty Cobb substituting for Babe Ruth).

Sometime during Morris's residence in Omaha, he spent part of a summer on his Uncle Harry and Aunt Clara's farm near Norfolk. This was an important place for Morris's imagination: first his summer there, then his visit in 1942, and later, in 1947, his return to take the photographs for *The Home Place*. Uncle Harry appears occasionally as a character in Morris's writing—usually with his own name—as does his Aunt Clara, appearing as Clara, Aunt Sarah, or Cora, usually with the real Aunt Clara's glass eye. Lacking a full-time father, Morris relished his relationships with uncles and aunts, often deliberately seeking them out. "In the family of American character I consider aunts and uncles my peculiar province—I take them in, like umbrellas, and after a few repairs put them back into service."[11]

Morris and his father moved to Chicago in 1924, perhaps arriving there with 14-year-old Morris at the wheel.[12] He lived in Chicago, sometimes with his father, from 1924 to 1927, with time out for a car trip to California that became the basis for his first novel. Life with his father was not easy, and he describes how he came upon the man having sex on the bed they both slept in. Morris "arrived on the scene too late; the machine would not stop. Coins dropped from the man's pockets to roll about on the floor. No, it was not a good scene. It considerably widened the widening gap." About his own proclivities, he added, "The boy was a great one for Sir Gawain, the Green Knight, and feared disease from stool seats and unclean thoughts."[13] Perhaps as a result, Morris spent a good deal of time at the Larrabee YMCA, a site of much significance to his fiction.

In 1930 Morris briefly attended the Adventist-run Pacific Union College in California, courtesy of his "God-fearing" grandfather; in relation to that experience he met the family, including two of his mother's sisters, Winona and Violet, an event providing him with "an image of human goodness that I had been lacking" (*WB*, 161). Morris was particularly impressed with Winona, making of her a belated mother surrogate, seeing in her physical presence "the time-stopped dazzle of Vermeer's paintings."[14]

Finding Pacific Union College stifling, and asked to leave because of his disruptive influence on other students (nothing personal, the dean assured him, he just "lacked an Adventist upbringing" [*WB*, 166]), Morris went to Texas to work for his Uncle Dwight. His time with Dwight epitomized futility, for it was necessary to plow the "dustbowl" around the clock and hope for the rain that never came. Though the experience was depressing, it was laden with images that penetrated Morris's imagination: Dwight showed up 40 years later in *Cause for Wonder* and as the source for Floyd Warner in *Fire Sermon* and *A Life*. Other events from Texas include Morris's responsibility for shooting a hog, getting in the pen with the animal and luring it with an ear of corn stuck in his fly, then shooting it between the eyes with a Winchester. This event haunts McKee's memory when he searches for parallels to the bullfight in *The Field of Vision*.

The following September, Morris entered Pomona College in California, a place he likened to the Garden of Eden. One of his professors there was Leon Howard, who became Morris's friend; later Howard wrote a monograph on Morris's work. Among Morris's readings was Spengler's *The Decline of the West*, which he underlined with a passion; this tome, read at a crucial period of his life, stuck in his mind, perhaps to influence his later pessimism about the decline of American culture. Morris wrote to Spengler "to question his assumption that the West had declined west of the Missouri River," adding that Spengler's failure to reply indicated "perhaps he needed time to think it over."[15]

Morris remained at Pomona until 1933, when he left, without completing his degree, for his *Wanderjahr* to Europe. This trip was momentous, its impact so great that he dedicated an entire volume of memoir and much of the novel *Cause for Wonder* to describing it. Morris is vague about what impelled him, at 23, to such a measure, but apparently he required of himself the European experiences of the generation of American writers preceding him.[16] For economic reasons, however, Morris found himself at first not in the expatriates' Paris but in Vienna, spending the winter in a castle, Schloss Ranna, contemplating the mysteries of time. "[I]t seemed to me that time, as I used to live it, had stopped. That what I saw before me was a snippet of time, cut from the moving reel, a specimen with more of a past than a future, a crack in time's door that I had my eye to, where no bird flew, no snow fell, no child played on the pond ice and no dog barked. To be out of this world was to be out of time. One day I liked it. The next day I thought I might go nuts" (*Solo*, 77–78). Occasionally he linked his own experiences to those depicted in old paintings, especially those of Breughel.

Other memories included a "blind Garten" in Vienna, where only blind people walked, providing for Morris "a visual metaphor that I found exciting. What I had seen from the window would prove—over the next fifty years—to be inexhaustible each time I looked" (*Solo*, 37). A bicycle tour of Italy included detainment "as a threat to Mussolini"[17] in a prison in Grossetto and his unlikely rescue by the native Italian grandfather of two boys Morris had befriended in Chicago. Finally, Morris managed to spend the summer in Paris, where he read French writers and "found time to ponder what I was up to, . . . to reflect on the separate lives I had lived as a boy" (*Cloak*, 10). One day he found his pocket picked and his money gone, and so his sojourn came to a close.

Morris returned from Europe in 1934, fully conscious of his stock of raw material and ready to begin his creative life. He married Mary Ellen Finfrock that same year and lived with her in Claremont, California. Morris has given several different accounts of this period, but apparently by the mid-1930s he was photographing seriously and experimenting with combinations of photographs and short prose passages. He had a part-time job with the Works Progress Administration and worked on drafts of several novels. In 1938, his wife took a teaching job in Middlebury, Connecticut, and she and Morris moved east.

During this time he was experimenting with a variety of cameras, among them a Zeiss Kolibri purchased in Austria, a Rolleiflex, a Japanese view camera, a $3^1/_4 \times 4^1/_4$—and later a 4×5—Graphic View camera with a wide-angle Schnieder Angulon lens (*Cloak*, 38),[18] and he set up a darkroom with an enlarger. That winter he spent a few months living in a cabin on Quassapaug Pond, writing a novel and reading Thoreau (*P&W*, 18). In 1940 his first photo-text essay was published as "The Inhabitants," and he had his first photo-text show, at the New School for Social Research, a review of which praised his writing and described him as "[o]ne of this country's distinctive camera artists."[19]

His successes led him to contemplate an expansive project on American cultural objects and structures. He intended a "photo-safari" through parts of the South, Midwest, and West, and a winter writing in California before returning east. This trip involved 15,000 miles by car—and an escape from domestic responsibilities. His artistic motives were, as usual, dual: on one hand, to photograph American icons; on the other, to preserve the past—as he put it later, "to celebrate the eloquence of structures so plainly dedicated to human use and to salvage those that were on the edge of dissolution" (*P&W*, 32). Thinking of attaching himself somehow to the Farm Security Administration photography unit, Morris looked up Roy Stryker in Washington, D.C., but Stryker was puzzled by the lack of people in Morris's photographs and unsympathetic to his motives.

The photo-safari went much as planned. It was the unplanned events that proved the most memorable—such as Morris's arrest in Greenville, South Carolina, "as a vagrant and . . . possible spy" (*P&W*, 26); in jail he met a "local desperado" named Furman, who would furnish the conclusion to *My Uncle Dudley*. While photographing in Alabama, Morris was warned off by a shotgun blast, an experience he used a decade later to begin an essay on the problematic relations between privacy and photography. In Mississippi he met Eudora Welty but hesitated to intrude on Faulkner. Instead he located Faulkner's friend Phil Stone, with whom he discussed Southern relationships between black and white (and who allowed Morris to spend the night in his driveway!). In Kansas he found the huge Gano grain elevator, the subject of perhaps his best-known photograph. Arriving in Los Angeles, Morris began work on what became his first published novel.

With the publication of *My Uncle Dudley* in 1942, Morris's career as a novelist began, but he still relished the photo-text medium and was determined to pursue it, most immediately through a Guggenheim Fellowship. With the money, he and his wife returned to California, stopping in Nebraska on the way. His father having died in 1941, Morris desired to revisit his childhood—including his first return to "the home place" of his Uncle Harry and Aunt Clara, where, "drugged by feelings that both moved and disturbed me," Morris took no photographs but resolved to return. He also met the barber Eddie Cahow—and took photos in Cahow's shop. This return to Nebraska was the key to Morris's "pact with the bygone": "By the time we left, . . . the setting sun burning on the windshield, I was committed to the recovery of a past I had only dimly sensed that I possessed" (*P&W*, 40–41).

In Claremont, Morris wearied of waiting to be drafted, so he tried to enlist in the navy and the army but was rejected by both because of a heart murmur. Morris was thus "home free," as he put it (*Cloak*, 108), to pursue his work. When Morris's wife got a job teaching piano in Bryn Mawr, Pennsylvania, they moved back east. In Haverford, the Morrises met Loren and Mabel Eiseley, and so began a long friendship, including book-hunting forays into Philadelphia and long conversations about the mysteries of nature and Darwin's theories. Morris playfully included Mabel Eiseley's name among Virgil Ormsby's newspaper staff in *Man and Boy*.

When *The Man Who Was There* was published in 1945, Morris's career was well on its way, though he still had not decided which artistic medium to give precedence. The following year Charles Scribner's Sons published the photo-text *The Inhabitants* after Morris convinced Max Perkins to take a chance on the book. In 1947, armed with his second Guggenheim, Morris was back at Uncle Harry and Aunt Clara's farm, taking the photographs that formed the basis for *The Home Place*. He also intended to incorporate photographs into the next novel, but the publisher demurred. This decision not to print photographs in *The World in the Attic* may have been a factor in precipitating Morris toward narrative, though he did not abandon his photographic practice entirely until the early 1950s.

Morris was a provocative participant at a 1950 symposium, "What is Modern Photography?" at the Museum of Modern Art in New York. According to John Szarkowski, Morris took on the talent in the room (all well-known photographers) by defending the idea of privacy from photographers who would snoop into people's personal lives. The argument "was offensive both to the Left, who felt that only the rich could afford privacy, and to the Right, who owned the magazines,"[20] but it was central to Morris's concerns as an American image maker.

Between 1948 and 1960, Morris wrote most of the major works that established his reputation, among them *Man and Boy*, *The Works of Love*, *The Deep Sleep*, *The Huge Season*, *The Field of Vision*, *Love among the Cannibals*, the impressionistic study of American writers *The Territory Ahead*, and *Ceremony in Lone Tree*. Popularity threatened briefly with a paperback reprint contract for *Love among the Cannibals*. Meanwhile, Morris's marriage had grown increasingly shaky, and he continued to make "welcome escapes" from domesticity, indulging what he called "my familiar flight pattern" (*Cloak*, 229). During a long stay in Mexico in 1954, armed with his third Guggenheim, he went to the bullfights, which focused his thinking for *The Field of Vision*; on another Mexico trip, he began *Ceremony in Lone Tree*. He took several trips to Europe, including one in 1959 when he "bolted" to Venice with Josephine Kantor, whom he had met the year before and married a year later, upon divorce from his first wife. In 1962 *Critique* published a special issue on Morris's work; in the same year he became professor of creative writing at California State in San Francisco, a position he retained until 1975.

For fully 20 years after *Ceremony in Lone Tree*, Morris turned away from writing about his Nebraska origins. *Cause for Wonder* and *What a Way to Go* are set in Europe, *One Day* in California, *In Orbit* in Indiana. In the 1970s *Fire Sermon*, *A Life*, and *The Fork River Space Project* are set once again in the American West, but these books are focused on other than regional concerns, such as the changes in perspective and perception experienced in old age. He collected his acerbic critical essays in *A Bill of Rites, A Bill of Wrongs, A Bill of Goods*.

In 1971 Morris's friendship with Granville Hicks led Hicks to edit *Wright Morris: A Reader*, perhaps thinking (erroneously) that its publication would lead to rediscovery of Morris as a major American talent. There were already signs that Morris was thinking about the end of his career. The books following the ambitious *One Day* tended to be short novels or collections—of snapshots taken in Venice, of short stories, or of essays, as in *About Fiction* and *Earthly Delights, Unearthly Adornments*. In 1975 he was novelist-in-residence at the University of Nebraska and the subject of the Montgomery Lectures (texts and interviews published as *Conversations with Wright Morris*); a retrospective of his photography was exhibited at the University's Sheldon Art Museum.

In 1980 Morris's final novel, *Plains Song for Female Voices*, returned him to the Nebraska Plains for his subject matter. *Plains Song* was an appropriate work with which to conclude his career as a novelist, for it allowed him to revisit the settings that had first nurtured him. The novel won the American Book Award. Morris must have known it was his final novel, for his activities in the decade that followed suggest a deliberate tidying up of his career. He composed three volumes of memoirs (the third, *A Cloak of Light*, carrying his life from the end of *Solo* to 1960), wrote short stories, and compiled retrospective collections of his photographs and critical essays on photography.

Morris's renewed attention to photography at this time was dramatic. *Photographs and Words* offers the best reproductions of Morris's photographs and his first extensive account of his adventures with photography. The editor, Jim Alinder, had been intimately involved in the

Morris *Structures and Artifacts* show, and he collaborated with Morris on *Picture America*, for which Morris wrote the words accompanying Alinder's photographs. Continued interest in Morris's photographs was evidenced by two shows of national prominence, the first at the Corcoran Gallery in Washington, D.C., in 1983, the second, perhaps the most significant Morris event in the 1990s—one Morris privately hailed as his "last hurrah"—a retrospective at the San Francisco Museum of Modern Art in 1992. Perhaps the most important Morris book of the decade was *Time Pieces: Photographs, Writing, and Memory*, including almost all the essays he wrote on photography and "photographic" perception throughout his career.

Among Morris's many awards are the Mari Sandoz Award, the Robert Kirsch Award, the Mark Twain Award, the Life Achievement Award from the National Endowment for the Arts, the Whiting Award, and the Commonwealth Award for Distinguished Service in Literature.

Patterns of Critical Response

Important criticism of Morris began in 1957 with an essay establishing the pattern for viewing Morris in terms of his dualities or polarities. Wayne Booth posited "a highly sophisticated dialectic that flows throughout Morris's works," a movement of transcendence of the everyday "phony" world through escape into the "real" world, through three methods: heroism, imaginative acts, and love. Booth asserted that Morris's subject was time itself; at the core of Morris's aesthetics is his view that "when you see something truly, and give it a name, it is taken out of time . . . and placed in a permanent world where time must have a stop."[21]

Subsequent criticism, however, has challenged this view of Morris as a Platonic idealist. Marcus Klein, for example, believes Morris's two worlds *cannot* be reconciled; rather, an "accommodation" must be reached between them. Booth's own student Carolyn Nelson rejected the Platonic thesis; she writes that Morris refuses "the brand of Platonism embraced by certain of his characters" because of its inherent escapism and suggests that Morris's quest "bears more resemblance to the 'creative evolution' of the process philosophers."[22] The best discussion of Morris's dualisms, however, is that of G. B. Crump, who isolates a series of contrasts in Morris's work and shows how Morris maneuvers between them. Crump rejects Booth's thesis because "the label *platonic* inevitably implies a preference for the timeless. It suggests that reaching for the transcendent world is somehow a higher and better course than trying to live in this world." Crump posits two kinds of structure in Morris's novels: the "still point" and the "open road." The first is characterized by focus on an object or event precipitating acts of consciousness, associated with James and transcendence; the second is more linear, involving greater lengths of time, emphasizing action, and associated with Lawrence and immanence.[23]

Other versions of Morris are broader in scope. The most important of these is David Madden's *Wright Morris*, the first book-length study of Morris and one of the first books for the Twayne United States Authors series. Madden was comprehensive in his desire to treat the whole of Morris, isolating many themes—including the relationship between the typical Morris hero and his witnesses—and emphasizing Morris's use of language and his examination of the cliché. Committed to no particular social issue, Madden's Morris "is *engaged* in the art of writing novels," his legacy an ability "to project upon the literary firmament a many-faceted, serio-comic view of the American Dream" (170–71). A shorter but useful attempt to view Morris comprehensively is Leon Howard's pamphlet for the Minnesota American Writers Series.

Another group of writers was interested in Morris primarily as a social critic, especially as a gauge of the nation's social health in the volatile 1960s. Irving Howe linked Morris to Salinger, Algren, Bellow, and others as "post-modern" writers dealing with their "distance from fixed social categories and their concern with the metaphysical implications of that distance."[24] Norman Leer studied Morris, Malamud, and Kerouac as searchers for social commitment in mass society. Chester Eisinger linked Morris to Anderson, Faulkner, and Bellow as writers committed to "love and the quest for America" (340). Marcus Klein studied Morris in tandem with Bellow, Ellison, Baldwin, and Malamud as writers rejecting alienation in favor of "accommodation" to "that tricky distance between the sense of one's . . . freedom and the sense of society out there."[25] Leslie Fiedler was enthusiastic about Morris but perhaps overstated his case by seeing Morris as "one with the great nay-sayers of our classical novel," a writer who "expresses a kind of hopelessly American anti-Americanism unparalleled since Mark Twain."[26]

Alan Trachtenberg focused for the first time on the relations between Morris's photography and fiction in the special Morris issue of *Critique*: "Morris's technique . . . owes a great deal to the art of photography. Morris was a photographer before he became a novelist and, in an original way, remains a photographer in his novels."[27] Literary critics were slow to follow Trachtenberg's lead; not until the 1980s did critics fully appreciate Morris's intertextuality and his incorporation of "photographic vision" into his fiction. Much critical attention has since focused on the problematic association between fictional narrative and factual photos in *The Home Place*. Carl Bredahl's statement that Morris "approaches language as though it were at the same time a visual and a verbal medium" is much to the point.[28]

To these works should be added the studies that see Morris's work as fundamentally problematic—particularly important works by Raymond Neinstein and Ralph Miller. Neinstein is troubled by Morris's pessimism and understands Morris's arguments for imaginative transformation as closed, "locked in a double bind." For him Morris offers no real solutions to the problems he uncovers; transformation is only available through the imagination, but "the very act of imaginative transformation can create and trap us in a metaphysical landscape."[29] Miller, surveying Morris's novels from *The Deep Sleep* through *A Life*, is dismayed by the "sense of ending" in Morris and by his focus on entropy and discontinuity; the novels conclude with neither proper endings nor hope, but emphasize instead "the slow dying of humanity."[30]

Finally there is that criticism—often understandably unappreciated by Morris himself—that attempts to comprehend Morris's work by reference to his childhood experience as "half an orphan." This line of questioning is hazardous because it often requires speculative probing of the author's psychology in relation to his work, but it is inevitable as Morris's future biographers come forward. Most critical studies have been devoted to the Nebraska works, especially *Plains Song*. Little attention has been paid to Morris's non-Nebraska works, though much remains to be said, especially about such novels as *Man and Boy* and *The Deep Sleep* that probe the postwar American family and relationships between the sexes and about those vitalistic novels, like *Love Among the Cannibals*, that have bearing on Morris's epistemology.

The Absent Mother: "She Died That He Might Live"

Because of the importance of the peculiarities of Morris's childhood and adolescence to his art, a few words are in order here to suggest the magnitude of his emotional involvement with his "missing" mother. It may be said that his father's frequent leaves of absence from Morris's life led to a classic pattern of a "search for a father," but perhaps even more important is the absence of Morris's *mother*. That absence, paradoxically, made for a rich presence in Morris's creative life. His career may be partially understood as a means of compensation for loss, especially losses long contemplated and replaced only inadequately with surrogates. G. B. Crump and Roy Bird have had useful things to say about this matter. Crump writes that "Morris's life-long search for 'imaginary gains,' often identified with timeless tableaux, scenes, objects, and suspended moments . . . expresses his need to recover the mother he never knew, and the memoirs link the loss of the mother to the loss of the past in all its manifestations."[31] Roy Bird asserts, "The absence of the mother helps to account for the darkness of the world view in Morris's novels, just as it helps to explain the yearning for completeness and connection."[32]

If patterns of flight are associated with travel as means of escape and are linked to the father, the absence of domestic happiness must be linked to the mother. Morris's novels focus often on domestic scenes and relations between people who seek—and often fail—to make connections with each other. Describing the dinner table on his first visit to his grandfather and Aunts Winona and Violet, he notes, "Seated around the table to which four leaves had been added were the parts of my life that had proved to be missing" (*WB*, 161). These table leaves are important, for Morris carries them into his fiction—most notably in the "Leaves of the Table" section of *Ceremony in Lone Tree*—where they signify both a domestic closeness *and* a comic inability of those at the table to communicate clearly with one another.

Morris's three memoirs make clear that the death of his mother, Grace (when Morris was less than a week old), marked one of the "real losses" in his life. It is revealing that when Morris told an interviewer he had retired from writing, she noted that "Morris sits in his easy chair a lot these days, thinking. Like everything in his past, the losses seem more acute now, especially the loss of his mother."[33] Morris's search for a *mother* took complex and convoluted forms, including a kind of fictional revenge for what Crump calls Morris's "primal loss" (Crump, 4), hence, the termagants and domestic tyrants who populate Morris's fiction, such as Violet Ames of *Man and Boy* and Mrs. Millicent Porter of *The Deep Sleep*, both founded on his mother-in-law, a woman who provided rich material to support Morris's obsession with loss.

Morris was forthright in acknowledging being "at once sorrowful, saddened and shamefaced" regarding his emotional tolerance for loss. When his father-in-law died he realized through the obvious sorrow of others how shallow his own emotions ran—and he felt an emotion "that filmed my eyes" at the recognition. "My family ties had been on the fringe of other families, from where I spied on them from pantries, or concealed by the cloak that draped the dining room table. . . . The losses I had experienced were real enough, but not of the sort that diminished my nature. No man was an island, but I was far from being washed into the sea" (*Cloak*, 142).

What Morris describes is the discovery of absence; the power of this discovery suggests a need to overrule absence through reiteration, often through *doubling of character*, in Morris's work. It helps to focus on the specific terms of Morris's relationship to his mother, for in several places in his work the relationship between mother and son is seen as a compensatory one. In *The Man Who Was There*, for example, readers find this inscription marking the grave of the protagonist's mother:

ETHEL GRACE WARD

1891–1910

She died so that he might live[34]

Readers learn that Ethel Grace Ward's maiden name was Osborn. Morris's mother's name was Ethel Grace Osborn, and she too lived from 1891 to 1910. The "he" in this tombstone inscription refers to Agee Ward, and his return to Nebraska to seek out his roots in *The Man Who Was There* reflects Morris's own need to uncover his ancestry. Agee Ward is obviously founded on Morris. The name Osborn is found often in Morris's novels: Dudley of *My Uncle Dudley*, for instance, is an Osborn, as is Howe's Uncle Fremont in *Cause for Wonder*. In *Will's Boy*, again, "I am born, and a few days later Grace Osborn Morris is dead, having given her life that I might live" (5). Obviously Ethel Grace Ward is a mother surrogate carried into a fictional role.

Morris exaggerates the absence of his own image in his childhood: "What my boyhood had been *like*—how I looked to those who looked at me—I had little idea. I had not been scooped to a lap to look at an album of pictures. No piano, dresser, or side table held objects framed for contemplation. No mirror captured for me my image."[35] This emphasis on absence appears to be a recipe for the concoction of fictional doubles. Morris's strange "gothic" novel *War Games* (written in the early 1950s but, on editorial advice, not published until 1972) appears both to offer an explanation for Morris's interest in dualisms and character doubling and to codify a pattern of ritual reconciliation with his mother's death.

Morris's observation that *War Games* "began with a scene and a character that had sprouted in the compost of *The Works of Love*"[36] is crucial, suggesting the novel was a byproduct of the long gestation and five years of intense writing that culminated in *The Works of Love*, the novel that ambiguously memorialized his father. Coming out of this period, then, *War Games* is a renewed attempt by Morris to deal with materials from his childhood. It may be that—consciously or unconsciously—Morris's artistic repetition had its origins in primal loss and in the art he deliberately created as a result. Although *War Games* is needlessly complicated and fragmented, largely unsuccessful as a novel, it is a revelatory book in its obsessiveness and ritual patterns.

When *War Games* opens, Colonel Foss has been struck by a truck and taken to a hospital, where "he hovered between life and death" (2). There he encounters Hyman Kopfman, "a small, rabbit-faced little man who belonged in the hopeless ward, but it had been overcrowded" (7); Kopfman suffers from a terminal blood disease, resulting in amputation of an arm and a leg. Morris places these two characters in distinct opposition to each other: Kopfman, an immigrant, is exuberant about the possibilities of American life; Colonel Foss, wearing military glasses, sees "a battlefield" wherever he looks and has little desire to live. This opposition is resolved in terms typical of tales of the double: as Kopfman's case worsens, Foss, who "had been failing . . . for no apparent reason . . . began to improve" (17); when Kopfman dies, the Colonel is well enough to be released.

The doubling of characters in *War Games* centers on Colonel Foss, the "first self" to whom several second selves adhere—most important, Hyman Kopfman. Curiously, Foss is "balanced" by Kopfman. Their relationship is one of a type that C. E. Keppler calls *counterbalance*, "the complementary oppositeness of the two halves of the being whom they together comprise."[37] In *War Games* this emphatic balance posits Hyman Kopfman's death as a necessary condition for Foss's return to the "battlefield" of the world. The blood disease afflicting Kopfman is another crucial connection to the Colonel, for at the conclusion of the novel, Foss feels kinship with Kopfman's "doomed condition—as if the blood that flowed in Hyman Kopfman's veins flowed in his own" (163). This organic simile supports the view that what doomed Kopfman makes possible the Colonel's newly developed sense of identity, his move from guilt and failure to freedom and responsibility.

Kopfman's function is primarily to make that transcendence possible. To effect the entry to the new experiences that open into Foss's future requires an elaborate counterbalancing of life and death, Foss and Kopf-man. At the center of this strategy, however, is a paradox not to be accounted for by the internal needs of the novel: Colonel Foss can only live to achieve transcendence *if* Hyman Kopfman dies. Because Kopf-man is given power to effect the future only through his death, he is a martyr.

One important ingredient in Morris's memoir *Will's Boy* has already been noted, that of primordial loss: the process by which Morris became "half an orphan." In Morris's strategy of counterbalance—"She died that he might live"—Morris very deliberately converted the death of his mother into myth. It may be speculated that the dualistic death-life for-mula accounts for the strategy of counterbalance informing the relation-ship between Hyman Kopfman and Colonel Foss (both "doubles" for Morris himself). The view that Morris's mother must die to make Wright's life possible—as implied in the inscription—is deliberately (if unconsciously) paralleled in the fiction. This apparent either-or fallacy (either the mother or the child must die) appears to support an elaborate ritualistic pattern in Morris's fiction. This pattern is curious, as it posits that rebirth may only occur through the death, not of the self, but of an other—or a mother.

This apotheosis of mother into martyr is echoed in Colonel Foss's rebirth through Hyman Kopfman's death, but also in Agee Ward of *The Man Who Was There*, who helps others live precisely through his absence; and in the character in *The Works of Love* who symbolically "feeds himself to the birds in a eucharistic parallel" (Eisinger, 339). It may also account in *The Deep Sleep* for Webb's outrage with his dead father-in-law's mother, who was "[g]etting stronger, bygod, right when he was getting worse," or his indignant comment to Parsons, "Everything I am or hope to be . . . I owe to my mother—I owe to the fact that she died when I was very young."[38]

The inscription on the tombstone—and what it implies about the relationship between dead mother and consequently surviving son—may be seen as a fictional device that came to serve a ritualistic purpose in Morris's artistic life. It served him well in coming to terms with his identity as an orphan, giving him a means to reclaim the past—or rather, to imagine a recreation of it in which the parts composing the whole have never been put asunder. This mythic denial of death allows Morris to reclaim his mother by means of a magical solution, one that always restores her to life when it is called upon. Morris in effect transformed his mother's death into the psychic energy that galvanized his career, transforming a profound primordial loss into life-enhancing "imaginary gains." If so, then the Kopfman-Foss relationship may be viewed as Morris's deliberate restoration of the golden past before time ruined it forever.[39]

Chapter Two

Style, Technique, and the "Raw Material Myth"

There are two contending portraits of Wright Morris. The first—derived from the subject matter of his Nebraska fiction and the patina of his photographs—is the simpler and more comfortable one, seeing Morris as a champion of rural virtues and pioneer values. This genteel view, however, always disappoints when closely examined, founded (and foundering) as it is on neighborly reader expectations. The other portrait of Morris pictures him as a writer who, far from romanticizing rural virtues, is wary of any conflation of *rural* and *virtue*—and as evidenced in *The Territory Ahead*, this Morris is ironic, sophisticated, and suspicious of nostalgia. The key to this more accurate understanding of Morris is polarity and Morris's poise between two worlds and two means (fiction and photography) of making statements about reality—making much of his work complex, reflexive, and intertextual.[1]

One of the major characteristics of Morris's thought is dualism or polarity, that habit of mind that sees reality in oppositional or dialectical terms, as many of his titles suggest: *Photographs and Words*; *Man and Boy*; *Real Losses, Imaginary Gains*; *Earthly Delights, Unearthly Adornments*. The subject of polarity is commonplace in Morris criticism, and Morris himself set polarity as one of his goals when in "The Inhabitants" he insisted on a "third view" between percept and concept: "The unexpected resonance and play between apparent contraries, and unrelated impressions, was precisely what delighted {my} imagination."[1] Later, discussing the virtues of American improvisation, he emphasized its inherent "destructive-constructive" qualities.[2]

The tension between opposing poles of thought often energizes Morris's work in ways that support his focus on consciousness. David Madden suggests this has something to do with his birth and childhood "astraddle the 98th Meridian, {where} polarities came spontaneously to mind,"[3] but there may also be more concrete causes, such as the psychology of his strange "half an orphan" childhood and Morris's reactions to the separate conditions of his parents. G. B. Crump thinks Morris's

18

repetition of "[t]he image of the hidden child . . . has two sets of connotations . . . , one clustering around the nature of the view seen from hiding and mixed up with his feelings about his mother, and the second clustering around the situation and character of the viewer and linked to his feelings about his father."[4] Attraction and aversion are characteristic ways that Morris approaches the world.

Polarities may serve two distinct purposes: On one hand they may express philosophical dualism, the two poles admitting of no unification; on the other hand, the polar terms may express a dialectic, with opposing terms unified through dynamic tension. Morris is clearly interested in the tension lying between poles and in the possibility of bridging the gap *between* them. He is interested in the conduits that might take him "out of this world," but he also seeks the still point at the heart of action—in *The Field of Vision*, the point of time in which the matador is indistinguishable from the bull, the two of them transformed into something more than mere substance. Morris often takes *intermediate* positions—*between* body and mind, nature and culture, perception and conception, the photographic distinctions between "essence" and documentary evidence, raw material and technique, and most important, fact and fiction—this last being Morris's most dynamic conceptual polarity. Not for nothing does Morris develop theories of *connection* and of relations *between* heroes and witnesses, write about the passing of knowledge from one generation to the next, and ponder the meanings of hotel lobbies and the photographer's shadow in his photographs.

Style and Method

Morris's style has received considerable notice from critics and readers, sometimes because it is thought to be too complicated to bear the weight of his "uncomplicated" subject matter. Morris's "difficulty" is that he is deceptively simple, merging modernist interest in language with vernacular Midwestern usage. His style is founded on the language of everyday experience, but it is seldom straightforward; rather, he calls it "a modified vernacular style to permit the intrusion of tones, moods, and qualities that ordinarily would be excluded from the vernacular."[5] His quarrel with *pure* vernacular is revealing. Everyday language "reflect[s] the mind at its conscious level," and as such it is immediately accessible. The problem is that it is *too* accessible and has "the effect of depressing the imagination."[6] Because the vernacular is not equipped to deal with complexity, it oversimplifies experience and causes "vernacularitis" in its users—"what," Morris says, "I'm attempting to cure them of" (CWM, 110).

Two other American prose stylists come to mind in describing Morris's style. The first is Hemingway, largely because of his sometimes enigmatic minimalism. Morris admits that his own early prose employed "an economy that occasionally defied comprehension" (CWM, 105), and many of the novels contain passages requiring ingenuity to decipher. (Hiram Haydn once described Morris as "terrified, beyond all else, of the possibility of being obvious.")[7] The other stylist, very different from Hemingway, is Henry James, whom Morris called the "master of consciousness . . . by whom we measure our fall from grace."[8] For Morris, "The mind of James, opening like a flower at the virus of suggestion, gives off and receives a series of vibrations that find their resolution in parenthesis. Nothing is closed. Closure means a loss of consciousness."[9]

Perhaps the two most characteristic qualities of Morris's style are its self-conscious, reflexive character and its extraordinary visual detail. For David Madden, Morris's style involves a "rhetoric of meditation" (CWM, 102), through which Morris slows down his narrative in order to interrogate his material and leaves narrative gaps for the engaged reader to fill. Morris has said, "My concern is not to have these things in my novels brought to a conclusion, but to indicate that they represent states of American sensibility, of the American soul; and just as I am brooding over the alternatives, I want the reader to brood, too. I do not want to present anybody with a settled conclusion" (CWM, 33). Granville Hicks linked Morris's style to the sounds of vernacular speech: it "calls for response" and "constantly challenges the reader" to use "creative imagination."[10]

As part of this "meditative" approach, Morris's novels are often extraordinarily visual. His narrations include carefully described still lifes and subtly suggestive images saturated with conceptual meaning. His close attention to objects derives both from Morris's need to anchor himself to things "about to disappear" and from the aesthetic framing required of his photographic practices. His most complex work is richly pictorial—to the point, as discussed later in regard to The Works of Love and Plains Song, that some chapters seem similar in intent to photographic sequences. Charles Baxter says, "The effect [of Morris's style] is to reduce to nothing the dynamics of the action and to increase to absolute proportions the attention to things at rest."[11]

Morris, often described as a novelist of character, even dwells on his characters as if they are still lifes, emphasis on their characteristics often taking precedence over their actions. His apprentice prose was primarily concerned with characters in relation to objects. His photographs from that period rarely picture nature, but rather artifacts made by humans and imbedded in the cultural settings they "inhabit." In his novels with large casts, such as *Ceremony in Lone Tree* and *One Day*, Morris spends much time examining each character's particular understanding and "place" in the universe, as if character itself precipitates actions and defines meaning. In *One Day*, for example, Morris examines a group of ordinary citizens in Escondido, California, on November 22, 1963, rather than the key historical event of that day, the Kennedy assassination.

These characters, though sometimes coolly appraised, are dear to Morris's heart, a point that is obvious from the humor the writer expends on them. As George Garrett says, "Morris has great compassion for his characters . . . without permitting himself or the reader one faint whiff of sentimentality."[12] Though Morris maintains a "fictive distance," his empathy is always a factor, even if not always immediately obvious. This distance may be one reason he has a limited audience, for many readers want fiction to reflect themselves. "These readers do not want fictive distance," says Morris. "In fact, they want this 'distance' eliminated. . . . It is not the *other*, the fictive character they want, but the discovery or the confirmation of themselves" (*CWM*, 18). A similar dynamic is at work in Morris's view of objects in his photographs: Viewers are encouraged to examine the pictured *thing* itself.

Morris's world is full of characters drawn from everyday life—characters described with the mundane motives and flaws of people everywhere—even the readers'. Readers able to acknowledge their own flawed humanity are likely to enjoy Morris most and to appreciate his humor. He has always taken great delight in describing octogenarian curmudgeons and other characters with traits and habits peculiarly subject to vernacular exaggeration. His observations of the characters in *Fire Sermon* help readers empathize, as when we learn that Floyd Warner in his role as school crossing guard "gleams in the sun like a stop sign," that Warner's sister "had faith enough to save half the people in hell," and that Warner's acquaintance Mr. Yawkey "is actually part of the mindless forces that are taking over the country."[13]

Even in a book full of the pathos of inarticulate desire, *The Works of Love*, humor lurks everywhere, as in Brady's letter to his son (versions of which show up in other Morris works):

Dear Son—

Have moved. Have nice little place of our own now, two-plate gas. Warm sun in windows every morning, nice view of park. Plan to get new Console radio soon now, let you pick it out. Plan to pick up car so we can drive out in country, get out in air. Turning over in my mind plan to send you to Harvard, send you to Yale. Saw robin in park this morning. Saw him catch worm.[14]

Then there is Brady's desire to hire a "new mother" for Willy. In the hotel lobby where he conducts his interviews he meets a series of "matronly" women with inappropriate behaviors—such as Miss Schumann, who "seemed to be digesting, and enjoying it very much"; Miriam Ross, who "lay in the lobby chair," making "little cries, like a puppy, while dusting her cigarette"; and another, "her tongue wagging in her mouth, like a piece of live bait" (*WL*, 176–82). Morris's humor controls the tone; readers are held in this tension between pathos and humor.

Morris is fond of Charlie Chaplin and Buster Keaton, and so as might be expected, slapstick occasionally sneaks into his books, even in serious moments, as when Uncle Dudley, in the police car on his way to jail, thrusts his arm out the window to signal the turn; or when, in the farcical activity at the center of *Ceremony in Lone Tree*, Calvin and the mules careen past Scanlon, Scanlon cries out in memory of the past, and Lois McKee shoots the gun that frightens the old man to death. This is a serious moment, but the slapstick renders it comic as well. In the same book the absurd Bud Momeyer kills Colonel Ewing's prize bulldog with his bow and arrow, and the colonel's wife cries, "My God, Clyde, the insurance cover something like that?"[15]

In conversation with John Aldridge, who was pursuing Morris's "dark strain," Morris made the exactly appropriate response: "Conceivably I would be the blackest black humorist—if I were not a son of the Middle Border" (*CWM*, 33)—that is, his vision of life is somber, but as Mark Twain's countryman, he views the world with wit and a rich comic sensibility. Despite the seriousness of much of Morris's fiction, it is almost always leavened with humor, sometimes wicked, sometimes droll and dry. That humor, in conjunction with his expansive cast of characters and his "meditative" still life depictions, distinguishes Morris's style from start to finish of his career.

Morris's Major Themes

David Madden has made an exhaustive list of Morris's themes: "the conflict of the phony and the real; the conflict of the habitual and the natural; improvisation; the acting out of the American Nightmare in the context of the American Dream; audacity; the transformation of the cliché; the cross-fertilization of fact and fiction; the impersonality of love; the life of objects; the transforming effects of travel."[16] In looking for Morris's principal overriding themes, however, the canvas may be more limited. What most interests Morris at the core is *consciousness* and the costs of lack of consciousness both to personal life and to American culture at large.

One place to begin looking into Morris's interest in consciousness is at that point in his career when he needed to assess his progress—in *The Territory Ahead*, his attempt to evaluate his work by juxtaposing it broadly to American literature. The importance of *The Territory Ahead* to all of Morris's work—even the fiction and photography preceding it— can hardly be overemphasized. In *The Territory Ahead,* Morris examined his own consciousness, as well as that of the nation at large, and boldly asserted himself as a writer to be reckoned with, along with the likes of Melville, Thoreau, James, and his immediate predecessors Fitzgerald and Hemingway. He did so by focusing on important distinctions between *technique* and *raw material*. Raw material—experience—is captivating because it points to the past; technique is the conscious transformation of raw material to provide meaning in the present and the future.

American writers, Morris argued, were overwhelmed from the outset by the sheer continental mass in which American experience was set. These writers, he charged, succumbed to the "raw material myth" of the inviolability of Nature and the impossibility of encompassing it intellectually, leading ultimately to a celebration of acceptable failure in which Nature, the past, and the "raw material myth" reigned supreme; most American writers have simply done homage to them. There is, however, an exception—Henry James, "the most fully conscious mind and talent of the century," the only American writer who did not depreciate intelligence (*TA*, 189, xvi). James and D. H. Lawrence are the heroes of *The Territory Ahead*, James because he provides a model of consciousness to emulate, Lawrence because he shows how to make one's way into the future through "the immediate present."

In clarifying *consciousness* Morris moves explicitly from cultural "consciousness" to a more dynamic use, in which the mind having consciousness is described. In so directly confronting consciousness Morris employs concepts that are usually the domain of psychology rather than fiction: imagination, "transformation," conception, distinctions between percepts and concepts, relations between mind and body. All these concepts are crucial to Morris as he unriddles experience. "My feelings and my thoughts do not lend themselves to recommended practices of simplification," he has said. "Since I find nothing simple, why should I simplify? The releases I need, and sometimes get, are at the heart of the maze, not at its exit."[17]

Morris's critiques in *The Territory Ahead* occasionally make clear that there is an implicit model of consciousness at work. For instance, the problem with Whitman, "the man who returned the body to the transcendental soul" (*TA*, 71–72), is that there is *only* the body, with its enormous appetite for sensations. As a result, Whitman is ultimately solipsistic: "When the poet is his own object, his own subject, the open road of the imagination is closed. Without the stars, the real stars, to chart its course by, the mind wanders in the labyrinth of self-awareness, its only raw material the sweet or bitter fat on its bones" (*TA*, 61). Again, Morris is critical of Thomas Wolfe, who suffered from too much raw material and lacked a synthesizing imagination.

One of Morris's purposes in *The Territory Ahead* is to support his claim for the performance of art as the most integral activity of consciousness. For Morris the essential value of art is not its existence as a *product* but its qualities as *process*: art is consciousness in action. As Morris says, questioning "one of the sentiments most congenial to our nature," "Art is indeed unique and inviolable—but its uniqueness may lie where we do not choose to look: in the creative response it generates in the participant; in the need he feels to repossess it in his own terms" (*TA*, xv).

Morris's concerns in dealing with questions of consciousness are primarily of two types. The first is *ontological* (exploring questions of being and identity); the second is *epistemological* (inquiring into functions of the mind and the origins of creativity). These two types sometimes run together, but they are obvious in their purest forms. Morris's ontological interest is neatly encapsulated by *The Home Place* narrator Clyde Muncy's reflections upon his return to the settings of his rural childhood. Contemplating a grain elevator, one of "these great Plains monoliths" visible for miles, Muncy philosophically regards the purposes of "the perpendicular": "Anyone who was born and raised on the Plains knows that the high false front on the Feed Store, and the white water tower, are not a question of vanity. It's a problem of being. Of knowing you are there."[18] Connected to ontology is the problem of identity and one's relation to the social world, precipitating three recurring themes in Morris's work: the discovery and formation of the self, the quality of relations between men and women, and the nature and meaning of the American Dream.

In Morris's world, the self is tenuous and tentative, in constant need of verification—a condition derived from his childhood. Morris's obsession with genealogy is one piece of evidence for this. Another is Morris's interest in what David Madden calls "the hero-witness relationship" (Madden, 32–48), in which the witness certifies the existence of the hero. Yet another is Morris's photography, especially in *The Home Place*—where photographs of real Nebraska objects and structures anchor the fictional narrative and simultaneously support and undermine the identification of Muncy, the narrator, with the author. This ambiguity makes for a dazzling postmodern intertextual tension.

The creation of the self by means of art is found in its purest form in *The Man Who Was There*, Morris's second novel. The protagonist is a missing man, Agee Ward, and some of Ward's experiences are clearly Morris's own. Like his creator, Agee Ward travels to Europe and undergoes self-discovery. Ward misses America and attempts to bring home closer by making sketches of artifacts he remembers; he discovers, however, that some details elude him; he realizes that his desires to call up the past require *invention* to fill the gaps left by memory.

In *A Cloak of Light*, Morris recounts the next step: "Something about being an exile, traveling around alone, had aroused in me a curiosity about who I was, and where I was from. Yet my reflections did not reach a conscious level until I found myself seated with pen and paper, my mind a blank until I began to write." Here is how the texts for the photo-texts came into existence: "The [described] scene had the characteristics of a still life. The writer sought a distillation, a decisive moment, that was both visual and verbal. The narration itself introduced a movement he seemed at pains to minimize."[19] It is telling that Morris describes the content of the text as a "decisive moment," photographer Cartier-Bresson's term for the perfectly appropriate instant to shoot a photograph. All these texts are autobiographical, essentially about the discovery of self.

Morris's second ontological theme has to do with personal relations between men and women. As one might expect, given Morris's childhood and adolescence (and even his first marriage, from which he frequently fled to the open road), relations between the sexes in his fiction are frequently conflictual. One has only to think of the marriages in *The Home Place*, *Man and Boy*, *The Deep Sleep*, *The Field of Vision*, and *Ceremony in Lone Tree*—all marked at best by extraordinary querulousness, at worst by failures of reciprocity and communication. The male usually has the worst of this bargain, for the female is often an avenging angel recouping her losses from the midst of the male's failure to provide *her* life—as well as his own—with meaning.

Given the impact of his mother's absence from his life, it may be appropriate to think of Morris's view of women as his psychic revenge on them. This view might account for the remarkable overdetermination occasionally to be found, especially in *Man and Boy* and *The Deep Sleep*. In *Man and Boy* Mother gets her revenge on Virgil by outlawing Christmas and Santa Claus—a significant occurrence in Morris's moral universe, given the importance of Brady's final role as Santa Claus in *The Works of Love*. In some later novels, perhaps with passion subdued, Morris attenuates this attitude toward women. In Eva Baum of *Love Among the Cannibals* and Cynthia Pomeroy in *What a Way to Go*, for example, Morris deals with Woman as archetypal embodiment of nature. In *One Day*, the female protagonist is most important for her audacity. In 1975 Morris noted his "shifting over to the female some of the audacity that seemed to be wasted on the males" (*CWM*, 100).

After *The Deep Sleep*, almost all of Morris's male protagonists are bachelors, some of whom, like Cowie in *One Day*, have deliberately fled from women and marriage. These bachelors are often withdrawn observers who study life from afar and are characterized by captivity to the past and inability to act in the present. One explanation for this enforced bachelorhood is easy to conceive: relations between the sexes were for a time an important theme for Morris, but as a theme it distracted from other facets of American culture that he wanted to explore. By positing protagonists as bachelors, Morris could avoid probing into the conflict derived from sexuality, resulting in a sometimes curious blend of passivity and meditative ability. That Morris sees them as misfits may be part of the price he pays for their celibacy; he often appears to mock their ineffectuality.

A third ontological theme Morris explores—at length and with increasing ferocity—is the nature of American culture. Morris is most optimistic in "Made in U.S.A.," a cautious celebration of American improvisation. In part, improvisation matches Morris's own development: the improviser, who "creatively produces something new out of something that was old," supports his explanation of his own method of writing by spiraling repetitiously back, then forward into the new. But following Henry James, who spoke of a "*creation* of arrears," Morris suggests that American culture is a "culture of arrears." A key passage shows his aesthetic discomfort with American *cultural* success: "However repellent it seems to the mind, however inadmissible it is as an aspect of culture, we are obliged to admit that a principle of waste can generate and sustain a great civilization." He adds, "Perhaps not forever, but no principle has met this test" ("USA," 491–93).

But Morris is most characteristically a critic of what American culture has made of itself, particularly in the name of nostalgia. For David Madden, the first to focus on Morris's representation of the American Dream, Morris's "books compose a kind of *Crack-Up* for America" (Madden, 27). While focused on the "inhabitants" who haunted the structures pictured in his photographs, Morris was able to celebrate the American Dream, but almost as soon as he turned to narrative, his novels probed American failures. Morris wanted to believe in the American Dream, but having seen it elude his father, he was suspicious of it. He often generalizes American culture through images of hell and hellfire, flames and burning flares. As Brady, for example, takes leave of his American scene, he looks at fires beyond the freight yards, and imagines that "All of the juices of the city were there on the fire, and brought to a boil. All the damp air of the chill rooms that were empty, the warm soiled air of the rooms that were lived in, blown to him, so it seemed, by the bellows of hell. An acrid stench, an odor so bad that it discolored paint, corroded metal, and shortened the life of every living thing that breathed it in" (*WL*, 268).

In *A Bill of Rites, A Bill of Wrongs, A Bill of Goods*, a later book of satirical essays, Morris appears to despair of American culture; his final essay echoes James Baldwin on the horrors of continued racism, despite the efforts of President Johnson's Great Society. "It is not the intent of the white American to destroy the black American, but that is what he is doing," Morris writes. "We are preparing for the fire next time by preparing for fires. Everything has been said, everything has been heard, and nothing has changed."[20] In the same year, in *God's Country and My People*, across from a photograph of a fire hydrant and huge liquid storage containers, Morris writes, " 'Boys and girls, when you pass a fire hydrant I want you to think of your beloved country. There's no place that has such a fine erection, so little seminal flow.' "[21]

In addition to Morris's ontological themes, there are other themes that focus on *how* one comes to know anything and on how to use that knowledge as a basis for action. These *epistemological* themes are among Morris's more mature, acquired through self-consciousness regarding the methods he had used earlier. There are two such fundamental themes in Morris's work. The first is the result of his need to recover his past through autobiographical fictions. Having recovered his self, Morris found that he had in effect created a persona named Wright Morris and that this persona was as much an imaginative construction as a product of memory: Because memory is fallible, its *re*constructions are also *con*-structions. Morris pursued this puzzle in "Origins: Reflections on Emotion, Memory, and Imagination," in which he speaks of the "ceaseless, commonplace, bewildering commingling of memory, emotion, and imagination," implying that the mind is a dynamic flux as it grapples with the past. Morris says the remembering mind perceives neither a "whole" nor a "general impression" but rather an "overlapping of many 'snapshots,' in the manner of a cubistic painting. . . . The mind is an archive of these sensations" (*CWM*, 167, 156–57).

The second epistemological theme, for which he was perhaps indebted to his friend Loren Eiseley, derived from an imaginative view of nature that Morris incorporated into his fiction, especially following *The Territory Ahead*. This is the theme of *transformation*, which he used to explore the possibilities of the human capability to change one's "nature"; he may have borrowed the term from Darwin, who had so named the process by which species evolved. This theme derived its epistemological cast from Sir Charles Sherrington's inquiries into "the wisdom of the body"—a wisdom gained prior to the mind's reflections upon it.

Transformation is connected intimately to consciousness in Morris's work. An important way by which readers may realize that a Morris character is moving toward transformation is through a kind of mythic *ritual of entry*. Morris knows the human animal is recalcitrant to change, its imagination blocked by fear, conformity, and the clichés of daily life. Because change does not occur without some impetus, human beings require two kinds of experiences. First is what in *The Field of Vision* Morris calls the "thrust from behind"—a term signifying some impetus by which one is *impelled* into change. Second is a tangible preparation of consciousness. In the early novels this process is primitive, as when the characters in *My Uncle Dudley* find the road to Phoenix closed and are forced onto difficult mountain roads—leading them to O'Toole, who appears to understand the secrets of the universe. Morris perfected this device by the time of *A Life*, in which the atheistic old man, Floyd Warner, is drawn into a prayer circle that "left his mind fuzzy, like a blow on the head." This experience leads him to wonder, "Was it common to people made dizzy by twirling, or by prayer, to inwardly smile? For a brief moment did they feel free of this world, like children tossed in a blanket?"[22] In this way Warner is prepared for his meeting with Blackbird. In *Plains Song* Sharon becomes "[a]s if drowsy with ether," making her aware of a "lower level of feeling" she is beginning to associate with human fulfillment.[23]

This ritual of entry is linked to the imagination and to Morris's theme of getting "out of this world." It is tempting to believe this ritual originated for Morris in his experiences at Schloss Ranna. Morris has noted how his "captivity" in this medieval castle haunted him, evading final resolution in words. Of his entry to Ranna, he provides great detail: first the invitation, then the approach by local train (leaving time for careful descriptions of the terrain) and on foot. He notes how copiously strangers greeted him ("only here did it occur to me how remarkable it was") and emphasizes the brightness of the snow and the winter sky. He focuses on perception: repeated references to *acts* of seeing and hearing, including the preparatory note, "the shiny film on my eyes made everything I looked at glitter like tinsel." After this elaborate entry, Morris describes his stay in the castle over the winter, the memory of which blurred dimensions of time and raised crucial questions about the reality of the world and his appropriate stance in coming to terms with it.[24]

Wright Morris's Photography: A Small Portfolio

Because much of this book is concerned with the impact of photography on Morris's fiction, it is essential to look briefly at samples of Morris's photographs. There has been a tendency by literary critics to downplay the importance of the photographs, and until the 1980s there was little commentary on Morris's photography that went beyond the appreciative. The growth of interest in postmodern intertextuality, however, has made room for Morris, but there has still not been much interdisciplinary criticism that supports Jane Rabb's unequivocal judgment of Morris as "the most significant American writer-photographer of our century."[25]

One of my central purposes in this book is to support the view that the same sensibility that went into the making of Morris's photographs is responsible also for the creation of his fiction, an argument first made by Alan Trachtenberg in 1962, though for 20 years virtually no one followed his lead. The argument is that something of the same themes and aesthetic motives are found in the fiction and the photographs. Colin Westerbeck put it precisely: Morris's "photographs and writing are inextricable. Neither could have developed as it did without the other."[26]

FIGURE 1. Gano Grain Elevator, Western Kansas, 1940. *Photograph by Wright Morris.*

FIGURE 2. Reflection in Oval Mirror, Home Place, 1947. *Photograph by Wright Morris.*

FIGURE 3. [Ohio Family]. *Photograph by Wright Morris.*

FIGURE 4. Straightback Chair, Home Place, 1947. *Photograph by Wright Morris.*

FIGURE 5. Rocker, Home Place, 1947. *Photograph by Wright Morris.*

FIGURE 6. Uncle Harry, Home Place, Norfolk, Nebraska, 1947.
Photograph by Wright Morris.

FIGURE 7. Through the Lace Curtain, Home Place, 1947. *Photograph by Wright Morris.*

FIGURE 8. Model-T with California Top, Ed's Place, 1947. *Photograph by Wright Morris.*

FIGURE 9. Near Pocatello, Idaho, Wooden Log Out Buildings. *Photograph by Wright Morris.*

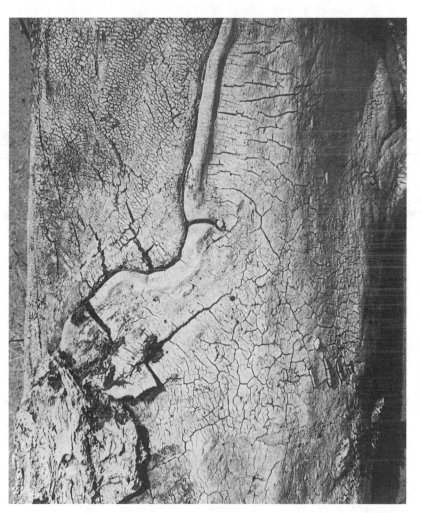

FIGURE 10. [Metaphysical Landscape]. *Photograph by Wright Morris.*

Although Morris practiced photography for only two decades (creating an "archive . . . of only 1,700 images" [Westerbeck, 278]), his interest in it never abated. His early experiments with photo-texts culminated in *The Inhabitants* and the photo-text novel *The Home Place*. Even after Morris withdrew from active photography, he carried elements of the visual contextually and stylistically into his novels. He did not return specifically to photo-texts until *God's Country and My People* in 1968 (with recycled photographs and new texts) and *Love Affair: A Venetian Journal* in 1972 (with color snapshots not initially intended for publication). Finally, in the wake of Susan Sontag's controversial *On Photography*, Morris contributed several cautionary essays on the cultural meaning of photographs, and collected all his writings on photography and visual epistemology in *Time Pieces*.

Morris has often said that one of his motives in photography is *salvage*, expressed cogently in his epigraph from Samuel Beckett for *God's Country and My People*: "Let me try and explain. From things about to disappear I turn away in time. To watch them out of sight, no, I can't do it." His photographs "are not documents of social relevance: they are portraits of what still persists after social relevance is forgotten. Having escaped obliteration by time and progress, some artifacts are in fear of becoming antiques. This might be described as their death after life."[27] But there is another important motive for Morris's photographs, one that might be called a *ritualization of desire*, using the camera to provide evidence of deliberate polarity between this world and another more mysterious and potentially rewarding one. Morris's photographs ask viewers simultaneously *to verify* the existence of the pictured object and to *interrogate* it—to witness the object's presence in the world of experience and, in its peculiar pictured form, its attempt to escape "out of this world." This is one reason Morris appears indifferent to reversed negatives.

Even as Morris almost always employed a frontal stance, his photographs show a reaching out for connection. This idea of connection is implicit in critical attempts to discover patterns in Morris's photographs. Colin Westerbeck, for example, finds in the sequencing of photographs in *The Home Place* a strategy of relating "absence to presence," seeing Morris's use of *Through the Lace Curtain* (figure 7) as leading the eye deliberately from the empty chair in the foreground to the occupied chair within the room (Westerbeck, 291). This is the kind of effect Sandra Phillips implies when she writes that Morris's *The Home Place* "is filled with passageways; it is a collection of entrances and exits, visually represented: doorways, windows, parted curtains, and thresholds." She briefly discusses a photograph entitled *Tool Shed with Scythe*, noting how Morris "illuminates the threshold and the scythe that leans near the door, but clouds the interior in mysterious darkness."[28] But she does not remark that the photograph also shows a doorway *beyond* the interior darkness—as if the viewer is invited to enter the shed precisely in order to emerge once more into the light. The photograph appears to emphasize movement from foreground to background, from foreground light to middle darkness and back again into the light, from the interior self to the world beyond.

This visual passageway is a telescopic focal device, paralleled in Morris's fiction by his idea of the hotel lobby as an emblematic passageway from one world to another, expressed most concisely in *The Works of Love*, when Morris says "the purpose of every lobby is the same. To be both in, that is, and out of this world" (*WL*, 172). Just as his fiction is often about movement from one world to another, Morris's photographs are frequently visual counterparts to the ritual of entry found so often in the fiction. The same photograph may show both reality and the means of transcendence—or at least of negotiation between them. Many of Morris's photographs are *centripetal* in effect, emphasizing entrance into a scene and drawing the eye toward its center. This is particularly true when Morris points his lens toward mirrors and cultural objects from a frontal position.

Morris's insistence on perception in such photographs as *Reflection in Oval Mirror* has its prose counterparts in those scenes in which Morris has characters peer out from under or behind something, or when he describes the making of a window *in* a window—where the emphasis is clearly on the *process* of seeing, the real subject perception, clarity of consciousness. The flawed glass in Scanlon's Lone Tree Hotel window comes immediately to mind, as do the many windows in Morris's fiction that require preparatory ritual acts of clearing in order to make perception possible. That so many of these acts are effected by people on trains suggest their relation to *movement* from one world to another, one way of thinking to another.

In *The Deep Sleep*, for example, Webb travels to his father-in-law's funeral; he observes an "old man who . . . wiped a hole in the window so he could gaze upon [the world he loved], and through this hole Webb could see flares burning along the tracks," reminding him "of Bosch and Brueghel, or any nightmare world rather than the actual scene itself."[29] In *The Works of Love* Brady looks through the window of his train car *into* the window of the station from where he fears he is being spied upon. In *Plains Song*, Sharon Rose watches a young man who wants to see the town he is leaving behind as he rubs "a clear spot on the glass with the heel of his hand" (*PS*, 137). Sharon remembers not the view out the window but the boy's reflection—a scene similar to one in *The Huge Season* when Foley, seeing flares on the track from a cleared spot in the window, also sees his own reflection in the glass, reminding him of the devil.[30] Such events, in trains or not, are everywhere in Morris's writing, emphasizing the eye's passage—or its blocked passage—in relation to shifts in consciousness.

Morris's photographs often emphasize the mystery of time, as when he speaks of the "séance" in which photographic images emerge mysteriously in the chemical bath and of the photographic blur indicating time's actual passage. He occasionally refers to blurred snapshots in his novels—as in *The Huge Season*, when Foley ponders the relationship between blurred human figures in photographs and the solidity of the objects surrounding them: "Curious feeling, therefore, that these people *existed*, that they were really *there*, but by now . . . they would be gone." In one photo "the delicate trees cast their permanent shadows, but the feet of this woman—like the wings of time—were blurred. Flushed with life, with impermanence, that is" (*HS*, 161–62).

Figure 1. Gano Grain Elevator, Western Kansas, 1940

There is something almost surreal about this view of the gigantic grain elevator. The photograph is a good example of Morris's frontal stance— but because he stood *so* deliberately frontal when focusing his camera, the object appears to have no sides, as if it is cut from a huge strip of the rippled metal and stuck flat against the sky. The elevator's size can be deduced from the dwarfed train at its base. The elevator points inexorably toward heaven, the black shadows under the split eaves emphasizing its "religious" purpose. As an object, framed and centered, the elevator exists as both ontological guide and imaginative icon—simultaneously in and out of this world. Morris's feelings, expressed through Muncy, are clear: The elevator is "the monument":

> That's the way these elevators, these great Plains monoliths, strike me. There's a simple reason for grain elevators, as there is for everything, but the force behind the reason, the reason for the reason, is the land and the sky. There's too much sky out here, for one thing, too much horizontal, too

many lines without stops, so that the exclamation, the perpendicular, had to come. Anyone who was born and raised on the Plains knows that the high false front on the Feed Store, and the white water tower, are not a question of vanity. It's a problem of being. Of knowing you are there. (*HP*, 76)

Figure 2. Reflection in Oval Mirror, Home Place, 1947

This metaphotograph expresses the history of mortality and mortality's captivity in time. As in many of Morris's photographs—but considerably more than in most—this image allures through a centripetal principle: viewers are drawn from their own world into the layered past. Looking into this mirror, viewers are led to considerations of time similar to those to which photography has historically addressed itself; viewers are left with the paradox that they are *at this moment* involved in times already long past. The photographs on the wall and table reinforce this view. The watery door, its attachment ambiguous, is as unstable as memory itself.[31] Of interest is the wall, framed flatly as a rectangle, against which the mirror rests, yet another step back into the past. In this way time is rendered spatial, reminiscent of Howe's meditation in *Cause for Wonder*: "Due to certain accidents of my boyhood I feel that time exists in space, not unlike the graphic charts that hang on the walls of up-to-date schoolrooms. On the charts the past lies below, in marble-like stratifications."[32]

Like the camera, the mirror functions as a lens, this one focused on and reflecting back objects of past experience. Viewers feel the photographer's presence precisely because they are led to look for him: he *must* be there, just beyond the mirror's frame. The mirror, like a lens, becomes a deliberate instrument for the attainment of knowledge and clarity of thought.

Figure 3. [Ohio Family]

Like the reflecting mirror, this image is thoroughly centripetal, drawing the eye from the rectangular frame to the door set in the symmetrical face of the house. The snapshot of "the Morris family, taken in Ohio in the late 1880s" (*P&W*, 47) is pinned to the clapboards to create a further ritual occasion: such framing induces reflection on the photograph as an act of memory. The family members are lined up before the house to have their picture taken. In *The Home Place*, where this photograph is spread across two pages, Morris makes much of the ritual in which present family members add commentary. The snapshot, they remark, has faded: "Most of us dead and gone, think it would be fadin'! . . . Same as me an' you are fadin' " (*HP*, 154–55).

Again time is visually layered: the time *within* the snapshot when it was taken, the time when the snapshot was pinned to the background clapboards, then the moment when the photographer took the back-grounded image—and finally, the time of the viewer's present percep-tual act. How can viewers *not* draw personal conclusions from the visual evidence of the lives assigned these fourteen people standing in the snow? Or not wince at the significance of the act by which this snapshot was taken in hand and tacked to the clapboards, then rephotographed for fresh contemplation?

Figure 4. Straightback Chair, Home Place, 1947

This is a tightly composed photograph, the chair a *character* in a drama involving, in Walker Evans's words, "Some of the shoddiness and all the heartbreak of the century." Evans admired this work as "a perfect exam-ple of photography's habit, when guided by a master, of *picking up* sear-ing little spots of realism and of underlining them, quietly, proportion-ately." He remarks the "hideous designs on the chair back, . . . the peeling plywood of the chair seat, the stains on the floor linoleum, . . . that cheap door hardware," and suspects "there is fly-paper somewhere in the room, just out of sight." The photograph shows the constrictions of farm life, but Evans nevertheless concludes that "Morris's detailed comment is a waft of rather pleasant melancholia."[33]

Despite his appreciation of Evans, Morris found his perceptions of this photograph questionable—and perhaps his "rather pleasant melan-cholia" too detached. He thought Evans an "acute social historian," but his cool objectivity, which saw "the cruelty of rural environment, its stark shearing off to what is minimally human," missed Morris's own sense of "the poignancy of that deprivation [as] moving and appealing. I *love* the chair. Other and more expressive forms lacking, I would accept it as an icon" (*S&A*, 118). Morris is obviously unwilling to be detached.

What may strike some viewers as even more moving is not the rural minimalism, but the hint of another world beyond this stolid one. As an object in a formal field, the chair takes its place amidst the structured verticals, horizontals, and diagonals of the cultural world. But how can one account for the mysterious force of the fluid, watery shadow cast by the chair? Against the swirled texture of the wallpaper, this shadow has a separate existence, vaguely related to the world it reflects, but also impalpable, mysterious, off on its own—and for these reasons, expressive of imaginative freedom.

Figure 5. Rocker, Home Place, 1947

This image seems designed to illustrate Morris's meaning when he wrote that he photographed "anything that appeared to have served its purpose. Except people. Only in their absence will the observer intuit, in full measure, their presence in the object."[34] Is that oval on the left a reflecting mirror, or a window through which objects may be seen, interpreted, and transformed? Does the light come from inside or outside, from the "presence" in the chair or from outside the window? The ambiguity is easily solved, of course, by noting that the bar across the window does not reflect the chair arm—but by the time viewers recognize this they have already grasped the essential ambiguity Morris appears to count on. No matter how the photograph is interpreted, the ambiguity of the light, the chair, and the "presence" in the chair suggests the viewer's simultaneous presence in both of Morris's two worlds. That chair might once have held Scanlon at his flawed window in *Ceremony in Lone Tree*—and from the visual evidence it might hold him still. Flooded with light, the chair is a ritual place to imagine and to dream.

Figure 6. Uncle Harry, Home Place, Norfolk, Nebraska, 1947

This is the well-known photograph that concludes *The Home Place*, and it marks one of the rare occasions in which human beings are found in Morris's photography. Viewers get no glimpse of the man's face, individuality reduced for the sake of more general comment. The old man *represents* something; his particular identity is not at issue. (Westerbeck even suggests Morris *deliberately* effaced another Uncle Harry photograph [288].) Here Harry enters the darkness of the barn through an archetypal doorway. The message need not be belabored; the quotation across the page in *The Home Place* is sufficient:

> Out here you wear out, men and women wear out, the sheds and the houses, the machines wear out, and every ten years you put a new seat in the cane-bottomed chair. Every day it wears out, the nap wears off the top of the Axminster. The carpet wears out, but the life of the carpet, the

Figure, wears in. The holy thing, that is, comes naturally. Under the carpet, out here, is the floor. After you have lived your own life, worn it out, you will die your own death and it won't matter. It will be all right. It will be ripe, like the old man. (*HP*, 176)

Figure 7. Through the Lace Curtain, Home Place, 1947

This eerie photograph is about the act of spying—of which Morris had much to say in his fiction, in which characters "peer out" from concealment under tables or behind potted plants in hotel lobbies. More important, the photograph is emblematic of Muncy's queasiness about his violations of privacy in *The Home Place*. Ironically, this view provides another meaning to Morris's "no place to hide" on the Plains. What he usually means is the existential effect of horizontal extensions of the landscape, but this metaphotograph encapsulates Morris's views about the twentieth-century war between photography and privacy.

Knowing fully what he is doing, Morris captures his subject, Uncle Harry, without the subject's knowledge. This is carrying what Linda Hutcheon calls "complicitous critique"[35] to the nth degree: the photographer has created a deliberate self-portrait of premeditated self-incrimination as an intruder upon privacy. The photograph is, finally, a warning about the destruction of privacy when the camera is in the wrong hands—as it increasingly seems to be in late-modern times. Such intimate knowledge of the potential for human interference led Morris to write that as a photographer, "It seems to me that there are places where I do not belong."[36]

Figure 8. Model-T with California Top, Ed's Place, 1947

This is another classic example of metaphotography—a self-conscious use of the camera to comment *on* photography—a photograph Morris initially rejected as inappropriate to his intentions. Later he learned to appreciate it, perhaps seeing in it visual evidence for the two world dualisms in his fiction. Peter Bunnell refers to the photographer's shadow as Morris's "self-portrait presence" (*CWM*, 149). John Szarkowski says the photograph shows an object having its picture taken, and he notes "a quality of ceremony and ritual . . . heightened by the inclusion of the photographer's shadow."[37] The inclusion of the photographer within the frame adds a ceremonial significance: *Now* the photograph is one of an interaction between automobile and photographer, and the Ford appears posed and proper as an object with a personality of its own. The photographer's shadow adds a vivid epistemological comment, drawing attention to the camera as a means of knowledge.

Figure 9. Near Pocatello, Idaho, Wooden Log Out Buildings

This is an example of the kind of photograph in which Morris seems to have deliberately pointed his camera *into* and *through* structures, from light and detail into darkness, then through the darkness once again into light and visibility. Variants of this strategy are the photographs in which Morris photographs an object or a person on the threshold between light and dark—Uncle Harry entering the barn—or from darkness into light and back into darkness, as in the view of Uncle Harry through the lace-curtained window. This brings to mind Sandra Phillips's passageway aesthetic discussed earlier, and so draws attention once again to movement back and forth between Morris's two worlds: the world of "reality" represented by his photographed objects and the world of the "image" found in the deliberate ambiguity imposed by his method.

Plains Song contains an exceptional prose corollary to the visual cue given in this photograph. Sharon Rose, sitting at one of those ubiquitous dinner tables to which leaves have been added, observes Blanche's bird hovering above the table, and she is led into thought about windows and frames, light and dark:

> She felt withdrawn from the scene, as if she saw it through a window, or within the frame of a painting. In something she had read, so long ago it seemed a memory, a bird had flown into a hall crowded with warriors, in a window at one end and out at the other, leading one of them to observe that its brief flight, out of darkness and back into darkness, was like life itself. (*PS*, 213)

Both Sharon's remembered image and the photograph under discussion come from the mind of Morris, together revealing something of his intentions.

Figure 10. [Metaphysical Landscape]

Once again viewers find themselves in transition between Morris's two worlds. This is one of a number of Morris's "map" photographs. This one shows a detail of a log with various patterns etched into it by the weather. The cracks in the wood give the appearance of rivers and tributaries—precisely what one might see in an aerial view of sun-bleached geography. In this case Morris provides the key, in the accompanying text from *God's Country and My People*:

> Some time before this landscape became a state, it was a state of mind. The land itself was tipped so the waters flowed eastward, and where it flowed underground they called it Nebraska. There were few records. There was no history. Time was reckoned according to the plagues and blizzards. The territory itself was not yet part of the Union and only the hand of God had shaped it. . . . Many things would come to pass, but the nature of the place would remain a matter of opinion—a log drying in the sun or the dry bed of a river seen from space.

Rarely is Morris so explicit in linking photo to text, but this text supports an assumption that Morris made the photograph in the first place because of the similarity he saw between nature writ large and nature writ small—a metaphysical correspondence his practiced eye was quick to see.

Chapter Three
"The Third View": Photographs and Texts, 1933–1948

Morris returned from his *Wanderjahr* to Europe in 1934, determined to be a writer. His own accounts differ as to the timing of his apprenticeship and his dual relationship to typewriter and camera, but it is apparent that the impetus to his creative life was curiosity regarding his personal past. As subsequently proved, the array of characters and events from his childhood and adolescence offered an extraordinarily rich field to till. No doubt he exaggerated the degree of his naïveté as a young man, but it is clear from later accounts that he felt a need to magnify this ostensible lack of self-knowledge in his youth. This emphasis is found often in explicit references to memories he lacked and to the image he did *not* see reflected in mirrors.

About his intellectual development Morris was explicit. Realizing he had lived through an emotionally rich but relatively shapeless childhood, Morris explained,

> In an effort to come to terms with the experience, I processed it in fragments, collecting pieces of the puzzle. In time, a certain over-all pattern *appeared* to be there. But this appearance was essentially a process—an imaginative act of apprehension—rather than a research into the artifacts of my life. The realization that I had to create coherence, conjure up my synthesis, rather than find it, came to me, as it does to most Americans, disturbingly late. Having sawed out the pieces of my jigsaw puzzle, I was faced with the problem of fitting them together.[1]

This quest for coherence was the central focus of his apprenticeship, as it was the galvanizing motivation for all his work.

Morris's apprenticeship was long and hesitant, involving considerable experimentation. Six years passed between his return to the United States and his first publication, "The Inhabitants," published when Morris was 30. Because of the peculiar circumstances of his trial and error development, however, it is appropriate to extend his apprenticeship through the publication of his first four books, two of which were photo-texts. Between the shorter version in 1940 and the publication of *The Inhabitants* as a complete book in 1946, Morris also established himself as a novelist. After various false starts, *My Uncle Dudley* appeared in 1942, then *The Man Who Was There* in 1945. Both these novels, although of interest as guides to Morris's desire to make sense of his past, were baggy, fragmented curiosities. The culmination of his apprenticeship was *The Home Place* in 1948, Morris's only photo-text novel, the book in which he exhibited full understanding of the philosophical complexities of his material.

One of the most important elements in the development of Morris's aesthetics is his parallel and simultaneous experimentation with photography and fiction. His accounts of his creative development are often at variance. For example, just when did he buy his first camera—in Vienna in 1933 (as reported in *Structures and Artifacts*),[2] or in 1935 (as Morris implies in his preface to *The Inhabitants*)? It is important to see that almost from the start Morris seems not to have been able to make up his mind which of the two—photographs or prose epiphanies—would take precedence. From this indecision originated the causal chain that constitutes much of his early career: he opted for intertextuality.

"The Inhabitants" appeared in *New Directions in Prose and Poetry 1940*, edited by James Laughlin. Morris's contribution appeared in a section entitled *The American Scene*, accompanied by the "Colon" section of the soon-to-be-published *Let Us Now Praise Famous Men* by James Agee and Walker Evans. Agee's text was accompanied by Evans's now-famous portraits of Annie Mae and George Gudger and two interiors of their house. Despite differences in method and presentation, the two "experiments" were strikingly similar both in their use of photographs and prose and in their tone of reverence. It is interesting that Morris was linked so early to these two men, for his photographic intentions would later be confused with those of Walker Evans and the name Agee, as will be seen, showed up soon as the name of a Morris protagonist.

The subtitle of "The Inhabitants" was "An Aspect of American Folkways," suggesting that Morris was searching for characteristic patterns in American life. In his preface Morris spoke of the prose as representing "the composite man. His task is to remain in character with himself. He concerns a Folk individuality, rather than one man's eccentricity—he speaks not so much as one man has, but as many men might."[3] Most interesting is the theory Morris brought to the photo-texts, as explained in his prefatory note, and Laughlin's introductory comment that Morris echoed Archibald MacLeish's "fusion of photograph and soundtrack (words) for poetry"; Laughlin quoted MacLeish's statement that "there is possible a play between words heard in the ear and images seen in the eye which is . . . capable of creating a third experience between the two" (145). Morris echoed Laughlin, then implied a new responsibility for the reader-viewer: "Two separate mediums are employed for two distinct views. Only when refocussed in the mind's eye will the third view result. The burden of *technique* is the reader's alone. His willingness to participate—rather than spectate—will determine his range. It makes no demand beyond a suspension of old formula" (147).

Morris never explained the dynamics of the "third view"—or how it might be attained—but his intentions were clearly both verbal and visual. Later he told James Alinder, "This very American blending of facts and artifacts is at the core of my mingling of words and pictures" (*S&A*, 119). Alan Trachtenberg suggests that Morris's texts do "not so much reconstruct the image as lend the image a voice, an imagined utterance from within, as if the picture were the occasion of a memory rather than the fact of that memory."[4]

"The Inhabitants" consists of 15 photo-texts, each pairing one of Morris's photographs (on the left page) with a distinctive prose passage (on the right), titled with the name of the subject or the "speaker" of the passage. The photographs appear without framed borders, "bleeding" off the page, the better to suggest the relationship of the photographic content to the "real world" beyond. The prose passages—sketches, memories, character portraits—are intended to evoke some unspecified response from the reader. There is no "proper" attitude to take toward the prose; the response develops as readers allow themselves to accept the experience. For example, the first, "Kirby Lee," offers the subject's reflections, in vernacular "folkway" language, on the vagaries of memory: "Sittin here I'll just be lookin at the cars when somethin turns my mind to somethin past. A street somewhere or bright lights in a store, or music comin from a phonograph. An I'll be there an not there, funny like . . ." (151). The juxtaposed photograph pictures an abandoned, weathered church with a missing door and window, beside a winter tree.

Readers may recognize in several instances the germs of ideas Morris later developed into narrative strands or character portraits in his novels. Perhaps the best-known example is "Uncle Harry," across from a photograph showing a detailed close-up of a grainy wooden door attached to a weathered structure with a simple hook and eye latch. The prose reads:

She put the loose pennies in the sugar bowl. She wiped the table with the dish rag then leaned there, propped on her spread arms. A few leaves rattled in the yard. The dusty leghorns waited at the screen. She left the rag on the table and emptied the pan toward a soggy spot of leaky shade. She stood there awhile watching them scratch. Turning, she looked down the trail bright now with copper leaves at an old man's knees, white in the sun. She watched his hand lift Monkey Wards, tear out a page. She watched him read both sides, then tip his head. Rising, his overalls came up with a sigh and one strap hung between his knees. She watched him step into the sun and button up. Then he found a match somewhere in the rear and turned to strike it on the door. (153)

The two characters in this passage are the Aunt Clara and Uncle Harry who appear later in *The Home Place*. Other photo-texts in "The Inhabitants" look forward to *The Works of Love*—for example, the passage entitled "Dear Son," an early version of the letter Brady writes, but never sends, to his son—and even to *The Field of Vision*.

Morris's experimentation in "The Inhabitants" constituted an important milestone in his development, helping to make his creative agenda concrete. First, Laughlin's enthusiasm must have given Morris confidence that what he was doing was fundamentally sound. Second, the piece made credible Morris's intention to refine photo-text as a new form (perhaps comparable in some ways to William Blake's fusion of poetry and design as a "composite art" in the eighteenth century). The "third view," whatever it was, combined percept and concept and became for Morris, even after he abandoned the camera, an important ingredient of his fiction. Third, "The Inhabitants" established Morris as a "meditative" writer who required his readers to slow the processes of comprehension. Laughlin pointed to this when he wrote, "But do not confuse [Morris] with the cinema. . . . He is attempting to fix things in immobility, in the way that a great lyric can fix an ephemeral mood for all time" (146). Morris suggested that the results of this meditative approach were open to individual interpretation (rather than *having* a meaning). Finally, "The Inhabitants" established Morris as quintessentially American, following in the footsteps of Whitman and Thoreau in their emphasis on the creative process as an organic activity.

My Uncle Dudley

Between the early photo-text and its fuller development as *The Inhabitants* six years later, Morris turned to fiction. *My Uncle Dudley*, the culmination of many false starts, is a slight novel, interesting now mostly as a signpost to Morris's future creativity. Its open road form is perfect for a man who had been writing photo-text fragments, but it is clearly a novel built from parts. It has a tripartite structure, the third related only adventitiously to the first two. In the first part, "The Roundup," the Kid—the only name the narrator is given—and his Uncle Dudley, having decided to return to Chicago from Los Angeles, concoct a scheme to buy a car and finance it with fares from other back-trailing riders. They assemble a "carful of picaresque loafers and idlers,"[5] whose names alone express American diversity: Olie Hansen, Natchez, Red Ahearn, Demetrios and Pop, Mr. Liszt, and Jeeves.

In the second section, Dudley and company make their passage, highlighted by a variety of mechanical breakdowns and dialogues among the characters. At the center of this section the car, seemingly guided by its own volition, ends up in the mountains outside Tucson—where its passengers are welcomed pointedly to "Valhalla" by Jerry O'Toole, a character Morris clearly intends as a kind of rude American sage. Given a year to live, he had come to the mountains to die, and when he remained alive, he decided not to return to a civilization toward which he was increasingly skeptical. O'Toole is opposed to sentimentality ("This soul stuff is a lot of gook spread on a man before he's learned to wash himself"), but he has all the right instincts.[6]

Morris deliberately figures O'Toole as a double for Uncle Dudley—the two men at one point wear each other's clothes—and O'Toole provides the essential "thrust from behind" motivating Dudley later to seek action against evil. The Kid notes that Dudley's unusual silence is explained by his absorption in O'Toole: "It was like hearing himself talk without troubling to. Being able to sit and enjoy it at the same time" (97). In O'Toole's hearing, Dudley describes himself as "the horseless knight. . . . I got all the armor but I can't get on a horse" (104), meaning he has a social philosophy but lacks the courage of his convictions.

The third part, "Two Men on a Horse," takes place almost entirely in jail; inspired by Morris's own arrest in South Carolina,[7] as a conclusion it seems tacked on in order to supply an appropriate rationale for the novel. Dudley and the Kid are arrested, apparently for hitchhiking, and they are locked in a large cell with other prisoners: Dewey, Kirby, Hal, and Peanut. Another prisoner, Furman (also from Morris's own stint in jail), is locked more securely inside a small inner cell because of his defiance of the law, literally spitting in the eyes of the police. Furman is in jail because, like Walt Whitman, he believes "his place come to be wherever such basterds [*sic*] is" (188). But Furman has not had the courage to spit in the eye of a despicable sheriff named Cupid. This deed is left to Dudley, who upon his release from jail deliberately spits "full flush" in Cupid's eye. The last the Kid sees of Dudley is the back of his head in the police car and his hand defiantly signaling the turn.

The essential theme of *My Uncle Dudley* is the nature of courage and the ability to employ it in the service of humanity, no matter how puerile the action might appear to others. But that theme appears more or less arbitrary, and Morris's motives divided: part of him wants to memorialize his road trips with his father; the other wants to complete a novel acceptable to publishers. Lack of motivational clarity may also account for the novel's haphazard politics. At times the novel contains vague echoes of Depression-era protest à la Steinbeck's recent American road novel, *The Grapes of Wrath*. Morris occasionally gives his characters the correct social attitudes, but in episodes that often do not relate to the point of the novel. When Dudley puts a twist on the war fought "to make the world safe for democracy" by telling another character "they'd both live to go to jail for democracy again" (44), the irony is clever but it is relevant only if democracy is defined broadly. It is not democracy Dudley goes to jail for, but some conception of courage and protest against petty tyranny. Much the same is true when Dewey implies that jails exist "to show we got law in our town" (168).

Until Cupid makes his appearance late in the novel, Morris's major subject is the cross-country trip and the attitudes of the male passengers, especially toward sex. Sexuality is seen as a gauge of manhood and value. Morris carefully reveals the Kid's sexual innocence—he is on the cusp of puberty at the outset and so is positioned to learn throughout the novel. Yet Morris—not surprising given what he reveals about his responses to adult sexuality in his memoirs—is unclear about the significance of attitudes toward sex. Apparently it is permissible, even manly, to ogle women, but not to talk "dirty" about them.

The overriding evil in the book is invasion of sexual privacy, particularly the sin of voyeurism. Morris equates voyeurism with social evil, and when he mentions it, it is intended to enforce the readers' disapproval of the offenders. When the Kid is first in jail he watches three policemen; one of them "had a grin that looked friendly until I grinned at him and then it was like I'd caught him peeking somewhere" (162). Readers are told that Cupid is evil but there is little actual evidence of evil; it seems sufficient for Morris's character to suggest that Cupid is the "kinda man like to 'vestigate lady crappers all the time" (171).

My Uncle Dudley has its flaws, but it is an interesting first effort, and it may be seen as a Morris primer, adumbrating later developments. For one thing, its language is condensed, demanding close attention and cautious extrapolation. Remembering reviews complaining of the subtlety of his language in the novel, Morris said, "It was my first exposure to the problems of a writer addicted to compactness, and economy of statement" (*Cloak*, 85). Much of this economy is due, perhaps, to the language experiments Morris had been conducting in his photo-texts; many passages in *My Uncle Dudley* have the clipped visual and aural qualities found in *The Inhabitants*.

Some of the language is reminiscent of Hemingway and Sherwood Anderson, particularly the latter's use of naive youthful narration. A throwaway line like "We had relatives in Little Rock so we didn't go there" (143) may catch careless readers flat-footed. Some of the subtlety seems borrowed from Hemingway, with humor added by Morris, as in this exchange between Dudley and the one-legged Demetrios as they discuss the fare for him and Pop:

> "For two—" said Uncle Dudley, "Kid and I might make it forty-five."
> "He's no bigger than the Kid," said the man, "and hell—I'm only half here!"
> "Thought of that—" said Uncle Dudley.
> "We're actors—we're in the Miracle Play."
> "It didn't work?"
> "How can I work?"
> "Maybe forty-two fifty," Uncle Dudley said. (20)

The apparent non sequitur actually links the Miracle Play to its failure to work miracles, a connection clear to the reader, but assuredly not to Demetrios. The pronoun confusion is deliberate.

In addition, Morris introduces other characteristic ingredients: he employs real people without change of name, such as his childhood friend Mulligan, the prisoner Furman, and even Uncle Harry; and he refers to places and objects of importance to his personal life, such as hotel lobbies with potted plants, the Larabee YMCA, and the six-sided stones that constitute potential evidence for God's existence. He employs also what David Madden calls "the hero-witness relationship" and the process whereby "the real thing" is stripped to its essentials. Finally, Morris incorporates the myth of ritual entry. Readers may be sure in a Morris work that when characters lose their way or experience a condition akin to dizziness, the author is signaling the advent of a transformative event—as when Dudley and his picaresque cargo make a forced detour leading them to O'Toole's "Valhalla" and to the philosophical support for Dudley's final foolhardy act of courage.

The Man Who Was There

Morris's second novel, *The Man Who Was There*, is more impressive than *My Uncle Dudley*, and although it is fragmented and composed of mismatched parts, it evinces Morris's desire to come to grips with his past. It is a catalog of Morrisiana, including early versions of characters, particularly the middle-aged and older characters that Morris appears to cherish: an array of uncles, aunts, and grandmothers—even cats and dogs (including the dog who provided the title for "Victrola" 35 years later). There are also the archetypal family mealtime gatherings, another ritual Morris resolutely describes. As with *My Uncle Dudley*, however, Morris needed considerable trial and error, prodding from editors, and the addition of extra material to round out the work. He finally managed to achieve a loose unity by cobbling together three novellas with a common mythic theme.

It is in *The Man Who Was There* that Morris introduces inquiry into rebirth and mythic identity. Whereas *My Uncle Dudley* had dealt with exteriors and landscapes, the new novel is marked by its *interiors*, its focus on domestic scenes and character portraits, and Morris's desire to explore possibilities of rebirth and regeneration, the ground for his later theme of life-enhancing transformation. In one sense this book seems a natural development from the photo-text experiments: from a conviction that people may be inferred from their intimate artifacts to the view that people may be actively influential upon others *because* of their absence—including Morris's first fictional use of his mother as a redemptive figure.

The Man Who Was There is dedicated to the memory of Geddes Mumford, the son of Lewis Mumford, reported first as "missing in action" in Italy, then as killed, on September 13, 1944,[8] so its theme of presence-in-absence receives poignant transcendent purpose. The dedication from Job ("For there is hope of a tree, if it be cut down, that it will sprout again") sets the theme of regeneration, and the book's epigraph supports Morris's archetypal approach, an alternative to the realism he had used in *My Uncle Dudley*:

> *Water seeps downward, fire flickers upward, wood can bend and stretch, metal follows a mould, the earth creates the seedtime and the harvest. By means of that*

which seeps downward a salty taste is engendered; by means of that which flickers upward, a bitter taste is engendered; through the bending and stretching, a sour taste is engendered; through that which follows a mould, a sharp taste is engendered; through seedtime and harvest, a sweet taste is engendered.

The three sections of the novel are "The Vision of Private Reagan," "The Three Agee Wards," and "The Ordeal of Gussie Newcomb." The title character is Fayette Agee Ward. The choice of Agee is surely a mark of debt to James Agee, Fayette is the name of Morris's short-lived brother,[9] and Ward suggests the condition of orphanhood that the character shares with Morris. Agee is "there" precisely because he is missing (in action). It is his latent influence on other characters that is Morris's primary subject. Like Morris, Agee is shown to be a returned native, and in many other ways he shares his creator's own experiences.

Morris began with a story "concerned with the ritual of burials in Southern California," and as it developed, he remained "blithely unaware that he was engaged in what would prove to be black humor" (*Cloak*, 106). In the first section, the theme of rebirth is imaginatively, although weakly, developed. At age 92, Grandmother Herkimer had been persuaded by her daughter to move in with her, and Private Christian Reagan had agreed to accompany her on her train trip to California. She had known both Reagan and Agee Ward when they were children, and on the third day of the trip west she permanently confuses Reagan with Agee.

When she dies, her survivors—Miss Elsie, Roy and Adelaide (and daughter Annie Mae), Aunt Agnes and Uncle Ben—request Reagan's presence at a funeral presided over obsequiously by Mr. Lakeside and Reverend Horde. In effect, Reagan comes as Agee Ward's double. In the ensuing satire, Reagan manages to fascinate Annie Mae and to interrupt Rev. Horde's "born again" sermon with the announcement "He has come again"; when he rescues Annie Mae from her fall into the grave he announces, "She has come again." Presumably Reagan and Annie Mae will henceforth carry on the lives of Agee and Grandmother Herkimer, suggesting in a comic manner that personal influence may constitute "rebirth."

The final section, "The Ordeal of Gussie Newcomb," is a domestic comedy in which Gussie changes because of the missing Agee Ward, whose influence as an artist is the key to this section. Gussie had been Agee's landlady, but now that he is missing, the newspapers report her as his "next of kin." Because she is associated with his belongings—books, clothes, paints, and album of memories—Gussie is led to a new and fulfilling life, always with the understanding that Agee's life—more than her own conscious decision making—is what propels her to action. She moves into Agee's room over the garage, rents her old quarters to the parents of Agee's friend, and makes new friends of others who want to rent her property. Recognizing Agee's influence over her, she accepts that she is indeed "kin" to him: she dresses in his beret, shoes, and jacket and comes to read and even enjoy his books. Most important, she meets the strange Mr. Bloom and, after leading him to water, decides to marry him, with the understanding that any future child might be named Agee.

But it is the middle section, "The Three Agee Wards," that is of most interest, because it constitutes Morris's first fictionalized autobiography. This intention is revealed in the album section, which offers descriptions of photographs that are identifiably Morris's own, including the Ohio Family photograph (see figure 3) and one of a child standing by an empty bird cage that Morris used later as the frontispiece to *Will's Boy*. The Agee Ward who makes his personal appearance in this section is obviously a surrogate for Morris, and Agee relays Morris's own "journey back" to find his origins. This section also includes Eddie Cahow, the Larrabee YMCA, the Texas Panhandle, Morris's schooling in California and trip to Europe, and most important, his return to his Uncle Harry and Aunt Sarah's Nebraska farm. Many incidents in this section later found their way into *The Inhabitants* and *The Home Place*—even the beets pickled by the glass-eyed Aunt Sarah (Clara).

Like Morris himself, Agee Ward slowly comes to understand his overwhelming need for identity by describing objects pertinent to his past. Agee leaves one of his sketches unfinished, for instance, because he can't remember the correct disposition of the objects:

> One of the hardest pieces to fit has been the pump. It has twice been in—and once erased out—for either the barn is much too close or the pump is much too far away. This problem may have more to do with the weight of a full pail of water—*fetched* water—than it has with the actual location of the pump. The only solution to this was to draw both pumps in, reconsider the matter, and then take one pump out. This he did, but the pump that he left was where no sensible pump would be. And the one he took out was the pump in which he couldn't believe. (82)

Memory confuses the felt pump with the one that makes visual sense, a dilemma Morris explores in his memoirs.

In one of the middle chapters of this section, Morris makes his first narrative use of the real Eddie Cahow, who greets Agee Ward with "You

be quiet a minute and I'll tell you who you are" (125). Although Agee
has been clearly identified as belonging to the "Ward line," Cahow recognizes him because he distinctly has the "Osborn Look." As noted
earlier, Agee Ward and Wright Morris have the same mother, sharing
first and middle names (Ethel Grace) and birth and death dates
(1891–1910). In this way Morris bridges the narrative gap between fiction and reality and sets the tone for his inquiry into "real losses, imaginary gains."

That *The Man Who Was There* is autobiographical is not surprising;
rather, it is the degree of Morris's apparent need to work so assiduously
the borders between fiction and memoir that is remarkable. The book
appears to have split intentions, on one hand about a search for identity,
on the other about the powers of "influence"—hinting that one might
achieve *identity* by becoming *influential*. But to be influential through
absence is a problematic concept and suggests the depth of Morris's passion for identity. It is Morris himself and his personal need for a surrogate identity that make this work of fiction important and interesting.
This search for identity and Morris's desire to make the search mythic
are monumental—if troublesome—efforts.

The Inhabitants

After Morris convinced Max Perkins to publish his book of photo-texts,
The Inhabitants appeared in 1946, dedicated to

THE INHABITANTS
Who know what it is to be an American

Partially indebted to Depression aesthetics and ideology, *The Inhabitants*
appears to continue the documentary mode of the Farm Security
Administration photographers, depicting American scenes and objects.
But Morris eschews any documentary motive whatsoever. For one thing,
Morris almost never photographed people, wanting to avoid at all costs
the invasion of personal privacy. His interest was in "anything that
appeared to have served its purpose. Except people"—who were
excluded from his photographs because "people, as I knew them, were
the subject of my fiction."[10]

Morris's Americanism takes immediate form in *The Inhabitants* as a
running response to Henry David Thoreau, from whom he borrowed
the book's major epigraph:

What of architectural beauty I now see, I know has gradually grown from within outward, out of the necessities and character of the indweller, who is the only builder—out of some unconscious truthfulness, and nobleness, without ever a thought for the appearance and whatever additional beauty of this kind is destined to be produced will be preceded by a like unconscious beauty of life . . . it is the life of the inhabitants whose shells they are . . .

Morris's response begins, "Thoreau, a look is what a man gets when he tries to inhabit something—something like America." In the pages following, Morris divides his text (on the left page) into two sections. At the top, in boldface, he continues his response to Thoreau; underneath is the text specifically accompanying the photograph. The photo-texts, then, are in three parts: the photograph, the linking text, and Morris's response to Thoreau, the last providing a sequential continuity lacking from the shorter 1940 version.

Morris's interests in American culture are thus already recorded; his idea of culture is founded less on material factors than on some mystical affinity with the objects he chose to record. "In the matter of selection of such objects," Morris wrote in his preface, "I relied entirely on my feelings about them: They spoke to me or they did not speak. Behind my eyes, in the complex of my nature, I had a reliable Geiger counter. When exposed to radiant raw material, it ticked." His phrasing, "in the complex of my nature," is characteristic and revealing. He appears to assume that the patterns and truths he was seeking had to be discovered, then revealed, through induction, through an accumulation of photographs and accompanying texts.

Morris's preoccupations are visible in the themes and patterns of *The Inhabitants*. As he admitted in his preface, elements of aesthetic design often entered into his choices. But just as interesting are Morris's depictions of ontological conditions, his sense of the being of the "inhabitants." If his photographs often incidentally depict poverty, it is not poverty itself he explores, but a quality of *use*: older things are understood to have life organically imbedded in them. This quality of use is one of many evidences of culture. Another is Morris's manner sometimes of pointing his camera *through* structures (see figure 9), a visual metaphor emphasizing both inner and outer and the relations between them.

This visual quality is reinforced throughout *The Inhabitants* by Morris's self-conscious allusions to instruments and acts of seeing as a human activity. One text begins, for example, with a view of Bickel's

General Store "[t]hrough the vines" (text 32); another begins by show-ing what the narrator describes as being seen "[i]n the mirror" (text 50). As discussed later in relation to *The Works of Love*, this intense awareness and conveyance of what is available to the eye is a characteristic of Mor-ris's most concentrated and most autobiographical work.

In his elaborate response to Thoreau, most of the photographs Morris includes are of buildings, architectural ornaments, and textures. In most cases, he shot frontally, from ground level, emphasizing his sense of equality with the objects and structures. His stance is relational, giving poignancy to his second epigraph, from Rilke: "Love consists in this, / that two solitudes protect, / and touch, and greet each other." Morris adds his own solitude to the cultural things he depicts, linking his pres-ent to the human history imbedded in these objects. Joined to his Amer-icanism and his ontological concerns is Morris's ubiquitous interest in connection—the "love" he borrows from Rilke, that protects, touches, and greets.

Connections and failures of connection—social, sexual, metaphysical ("What is there between the branch and the apple when it falls?" [text 7])—are among the major themes in *The Inhabitants*. One poignant first-person autobiographical example recounts a birthday party given by the narrator's father for an undisclosed "she," whose cake has "eight more candles . . . than there'd been on mine." She asks the narrator "if I thought I was old enough to kiss her good night. I said it wasn't me that wasn't old enough, but that it was her." His father calls for her, but she does not go to him (text 16). As a text in *The Inhabitants* this passage seems an odd fragment, especially for readers of the time, who could not know "she" is Gertrude, Morris's young new "mother," later probed in considerable detail in *The Works of Love* and *Will's Boy*. In both novel and memoir Morris uses her real name.

Finally, *The Inhabitants* employs a recurring theme of relevance to Morris's view that there is "no place to hide" on the Plains, expressed through the language of *cover*. Morris reiterates throughout his work two available strategies for cover: One is to hide one's own body from others and then peer out at them from shelter; the other is to cover peo-ple metaphorically. In one text this latter approach is central, the idea of cover being used as a conceptual unifier of opposites, a means to har-mony: "I guess what there was of Mordecai was mostly in God. Willie liked his right to be left alone and Mordecai liked his right to come and butt in—sounds contrary, but it's the same man, top and bottom side. Willie used to say that anything that would cover him and Mordecai would cover everything—and where there was room for the likes of them there was room for us all." (text 5). Again, "What he saw wasn't the people so much as something over the people, like the smell of leaves burning or the dust that hangs over the square" (text 3).

That the element of "cover" is crucial to Morris is indicated by its recurrence in the final text of the book—as earlier it had been spoken by O'Toole in *My Uncle Dudley* (103). The bold print response to Thoreau at the top of the page reads, "What it is to be an American," followed by the text: "There's no one thing to cover the people, no one sky. There's no one dream to sleep with the people, no one prayer. There's no one hope to rise with the people, no one way or one word for the people, no one sun or one moon for the people, and no one star. For these people are the people and this is their land. And there's no need to cover such people—they cover themselves." Morris hints that it is their existence as "American" that unifies them despite their diversity and occasional opposition. The text simultaneously attempts to allow for difference and to argue for a unifying transcendence—echoing the optimism of Crève-coeur's "What Is an American?" Perhaps this optimism is Morris's response to the ravages of the Depression, coupled with a faith that in rational thought it was possible to find adequate protection for transcendent human meaning. Morris was not to remain so optimistic for long.

The Home Place

By the time he made his visit to Uncle Harry and Aunt Clara's to take the photographs for *The Home Place*, Morris had come to understand the ramifications of the epistemological fault separating photo from text. He seems to have accepted the virtues of the "the third view" as *always* problematical and unresolvable, just as he learned to appreciate the significance of the photographer's shadow in the model-T photograph (figure 8). In the impossibility of reconciliation between photograph and text lies the epistemological significance. The result is that *The Home Place* is willfully postmodern: ironic, metafictional, and intertextual. *The Home Place* is Morris's first important book, marking the end of his apprenticeship and the culmination of his photo-text experimentations.

As a photo-text, *The Home Place* has tended to elude traditional critical approaches, especially formalism, the primary method of modernist literary aesthetics. Madden, for example, sees little connection between words and photographs in *The Home Place*: "Although the photographs are excellent, their relation to the text is more literal and less interesting than in *The Inhabitants*."[11] Crump is even less interested in the photographs, and his commentary conventional: After suggesting that for *The Home Place* to work, "the reader must be able to associate the objects depicted in the photos with some significance gleaned . . . from Morris's text," he dismisses the novel "because the narrative is weak as fiction and tends to reduce the photos to the status of illustrations."[12] Jefferson Hunter, in a book devoted wholly to photo-texts, considers *The Home Place* "an intelligible and stylistically consistent work of illustrated fiction,"[13] a point of view that wholly dismisses the dynamics of Morris's polar imagination and border aesthetics.

Raymond Neinstein is more to the point when he writes, "Few critics seem to know what to make of the combination . . . of words and pictures" in Morris's photo-texts. "What is seldom discussed . . . is the tension between text and photographs." In *The Home Place*, "Each casts doubt on the status of the other; the tension is mutually subversive."[14] The fact that in *The Home Place* "factual" photographs and fictional text come together for the first time is emblematic of the many polar tensions Morris incorporates into the book (with Clyde Muncy representing Morris as the troubled arbiter): rural vs. urban, male vs. female, rights of privacy vs. desires for public knowledge, past vs present—and to add Peter Halter's appropriate terms, "distance and desire, separation and identification."[15] *The Home Place* is an incomparable introduction to Morris's complexity, a guide to problems of consciousness in late-modernist American culture.

It is not narrative that interested Morris in composing *The Home Place*; its weakness as a novel is beside the point. Rather, Morris wanted to do homage to the rural past, but also to position a protagonist within a narrative collision between past and present. The major task of the prose is less to carry a story than to probe Muncy's divided mind and to explore the reasons for his very American ambivalence. The photographs affirm the existential realities of the rural environment that confound him, relating as they do both to his past and his possible future. The plot is a skeleton on which to hang ideas, the vehicle a more or less rudimentary return-of-the-native formula. The story has gaps and seems rather to stop than to close.

Clyde Muncy, a Nebraska native, returns to the farm of his Aunt Clara and Uncle Harry (with city-wife, Peg, and two children) after years in New York; the purpose for their visit is given as a search for housing. What passes for a plot is fundamentally in four parts, all occurring within one day. In the first part the return has already occurred, and Morris spells out Muncy's ambivalence, expressed through observations of the irony in Muncy's uncomfortable but obligatory defense of opposing positions. On one hand is his Aunt Clara, who is simple-mindedly bemused by these city folks; on the other is the citified sophistication of Muncy's wife, Peg, and her acerbic observations about country narrowness. In addition, the text reveals a continuing tension between Muncy and Peg, for reasons undisclosed. The two children are hardly differentiated; they are simply city kids who know embarrassingly little about croquet and chickens. Muncy explores the farm and his memories of it and, with Aunt Clara and others, discusses the family tree.

In the second part, Muncy and the children accompany Uncle Harry on a trip into Lone Tree, where Clyde visits Eddie Cahow's barbershop and is identified as "Grace Osborn's boy"[16]—in another violation of the border between reality and fiction, directly conflating Muncy and Morris. When the two children encounter flypaper for the first time, it is Cahow who cuts it out of their hair for them. (Muncy's reflection regarding Peg's potential reaction upon seeing her now nearly bald daughter is of interest: "Her mother would drop dead, we would bury her, and that would be that" [111]. The text, however, fails to record Peg's response.)

In the third part, Muncy and Peg make their way to Ed's place, a potential house for the Muncy family to live in because Ed is ill and living elsewhere. As they explore the house, the chief obstacle to their taking it is removed when one of the children brings the news: "We can have it Mummy—he's dead." But by this time Peg and Clyde have made their decision to retreat to their city lives. The principal issue is one of privacy: having entered Ed's place to examine its fitness for them, they find his presence haunting the premises. There Muncy does obeisance to "abstinence, frugality, and independence—the home-grown, made-on-the-farm trinity. Not the land of plenty, the old age pension, or the full dinner pail. Independence, not abundance, is the heart of their America" (143).

In the final part, Morris returns to genealogy and the persistence of the past in the present. Here the focus is on a faded photograph of the Muncy family said to have been taken in 1892. The photograph under discussion—or one very like it—appears spread across two pages of the book, the only photograph in the book so disposed (see figure 3). At the end, Clyde and Peg prepare to depart, but Muncy has final reflections on rural life. Following a pattern developed throughout the novel, Morris writes: "The carpet wears out, but the life of the carpet, the Figure, wears in. The holy thing, that is, comes naturally. Under the carpet out here, is the floor. After you have lived your own life, worn it out, you will die your own death and it won't matter. It will be all right. It will be ripe, like the old man." Across the page is a photograph of Uncle Harry crossing the threshold into the dark barn (figure 6). (The first photograph in the book had shown him facing the camera, although his head is down and his face obscured.) The final line reads: "The figure on the front of the carpet had worn through to the back" (176), a comment both on the photographic evidence and Morris's theory regarding the philosophical "figure in the carpet" of rural life.

The opening paragraph of the novel establishes the tone: " 'What's the old man doing?' I said, and I looked down the trail, beyond the ragged box elder, where the old man stood in the door of the barn, fooling with an inner tube. In town I used to take the old man's hand and lead him across the tracks where horses and men, little girls, and sometimes little boys were killed. Why was that? They didn't stop, look, and listen. We did" (1). Subtle ambiguity of tone is established immediately. How are readers to take this ironic voice? By inserting the idea of death by train into the narrative so early—perhaps echoing Anderson's *Winesburg, Ohio*[17]—readers are led to expect that the material may be less than sunny. Moreover, at times Muncy directly addresses the audience and occasionally makes direct reference to the photographs on facing pages. Introducing cousin Ivy, for example, Muncy says, "That's my fauntleroy he's wearing on the wall" (20), and across the page is a wall bearing a photograph of a boy clothed in a fauntleroy outfit. What this procedure amounts to is an ontological puzzle—one Morris seems to want because it appears to mirror the reality of everyday life.

The Home Place is obviously a "meditative" book in which narrative is secondary to the kind of reflective thought Morris wishes the photographs to suggest and support. The meditative quality is enhanced by Muncy's conflicted consciousness. The tone of *The Home Place* is one of the keys to its importance, having a great deal to do with Clyde's precarious position as interpreter and reconciler of two ways of life. Defending his seven-year-old son for not knowing what "cro-kay" is, Muncy realizes his voice is rising, but he is also critical of the boy's statement that the weather-beaten croquet ball smells like the subway. Muncy is caught between his Uncle Harry's sarcasm and his son's recognition that the sarcasm is taking its emotional toll; later he is caught between Peg's critique of rural life and defense of the city and his own apparent need to valorize the rural past. Pointing out two swallows, Muncy tells Peg they live in the barn, to which Peg responds, "Not a bad idea"—a rejoinder, Muncy wryly notes, that "could be taken several ways" (11). Muncy's cautions to his wife to "control" herself are also aimed at himself. In acting as arbiter, Muncy gives himself the defensive solace of irony, allowing him to appease both sides while indulging his own critical sense.

Obviously, narrative in *The Home Place* is less important than the problematic rivalries between past and present, country and city, rural values and urban values. This importance seems to be announced at the outset, with the epigraph Morris chose from Henry James's *The American Scene*:

> To be at all critically, or as we have been fond of calling it, analytically, minded—over and beyond an inherent love of the general many-colored picture of things—is to be subject to the superstition that objects and places, coherently grouped, disposed for human use and addressed to it, must have a sense of their own, a mystic meaning proper to themselves to give out: to give out, that is, to the participant at once so interested and so detached as to be moved to a report of the matter.

That Morris returns so often to this passage throughout his career suggests its importance to his aesthetics as a whole; here, as epigraph, it influences the readers' entrance to the text. It is crucial that it does so by emphasizing ambiguity, as if Morris wishes readers to focus on the mysteries of things in the environment without necessarily reaching corollary conclusions from the narrative.

The passage from James appears to ask readers to accept three contradictory propositions: first, that objects, arranged for human use, have an inherent "mystic meaning"; second, that that mystic meaning may be merely a superstition; and third, that the superstitious acceptance of that mystic meaning is a valid part of the analytical enterprise. This kind of richly suggestive paradoxical statement may have more significance for a photographer than for a writer, because the photographer must deduce and intuit meaning from purely visual phenomena, relying on an educated eye for which meaning must often appear "mystical." Clearly James's statement supports Morris's ambiguous intertextual purposes.

The James quotation is pertinent to the book's ambivalence, for it allows Morris to exploit James's notion of "superstition" in relation to Muncy's skepticism while making it possible for Muncy to continue to *want* to believe that the home place is "holy." Pertinent to his forced identity as both rational sophisticate and emotional rememberer, Muncy cannot quite make up his mind, and so he weaves and dodges throughout the text. Nor is he wise enough to keep quiet! Early on he says, "I managed to keep control of myself by picking up the pail. I put it down again" and launches into a defense of his motives (6). His position as arbiter even puts his identity at stake, as when he has an "odd feeling" and thinks, "For a moment I wondered who I was" (20).

Because Morris eschews the protective coloration of fictive identity, there is a further blurring of distinctions: he makes Morris over into Muncy but refuses to rename his own Aunt Clara and Uncle Harry—or the ubiquitous Eddie Cahow, the barber who recognizes Muncy as an Osborn. This unsettling conflation of factual and fictional identity in itself might have little significance but for the presence of photographs in the book—because photographs, thanks in part to the inherent nature of the medium and in part to the documentary tradition off which Morris plays, have always been confused with reality, offered as evidence *of* reality. Morris appears purposefully to manipulate and obfuscate the boundaries between fact and fiction, photographic evidence and "truth." This manipulation is thoroughly metafictional—that is, *The Home Place* is a fictional work that deliberately questions the ontological status of fictional meaning.

It may help at this point to return to the photographs and their relationship to the text in *The Home Place*. Where do the photographs come from, and how did they make their way into this text? David Nye writes, "By releasing these photographs from definition through language and from closure through framing, [Morris] makes them problematic, without a fixed meaning or stabilized relation to the text."[18] What Nye writes is true, but it is indeed only part of a much larger problem, for the narrator is himself a destabilizing factor. According to the convention of first person narration, Muncy—who is a writer—is unquestionably the writer of his story. Does this mean that he is the maker of the photographs as well? How does Muncy get access to the photographs to which he occasionally refers?[19] Readers naturally assume the photographs are evidence of the "real world," so here is the problem of a fictional character referring to pictured photographs as evidence of (fictional? real?) existence. Nye says, "The combined frameworks of language and photography do not refer to each other." Rather, "text and image offer the reader/viewer the chance to infer the reality of *The Home Place* by triangulation" (Nye, 166). Through this blurring of crucial lines of demarcation, Morris incorporates a demand for reader involvement— in many ways similar to Faulkner's insistent use of oxymoron.

Of utmost importance is Morris's simultaneous collusion with and authorial distance from his narrator. It is primarily on the grounds of such collusion—added to the ontological indeterminacy of the photographs—that *The Home Place* is most intriguing. This mixed-mind collusion may be accounted for by Linda Hutcheon's "complicitous critique," a term Hutcheon considers essential to any definition of postmodernism, signifying a paradoxical, necessarily ironic, condition in which an author offers a social critique while being implicated in the very problem criticized. Hutcheon's view that "postmodern photographic practice interrogates and problematizes, leaving the viewer no comfortable viewing position"[20] is thoroughly applicable to Morris, for his disquietude toward photography is well documented.[21] In reality, the ethics of photographic practice constitute a vital subtext in *The Home Place*, where Clyde Muncy is critical of invasions of privacy while involved in an act of invasion. Further complicity in *The Home Place* consists of Morris's use of sometimes "intrusive" photographs to make his case for privacy. That the camera is an intruder is frequently noted in the narrative text.

Morris's "complicitous critique" may be seen to advantage by a comparison of *The Home Place* with Evans and Agee's *Let Us Now Praise Famous Men*, a work Morris was surely attentive to, particularly because his first publication had been so intimately linked to Evans and Agee. Both *The Home Place* and *Let Us Now Praise Famous Men* rely a great deal on photographic "verification" and on textual undermining of this verification; both deliberately challenge visual assumptions through probing of the very evidence the books provide. The chief irony is that in both cases the camera was taken into the sphere of rural privacy precisely in order to attempt to preserve—at least to defend—the values of that private world. Both parties took their cameras with them, knowing that they were spying, and both needed to come to terms with ensuing guilt.

In the "Shelter" section of *Let Us Now Praise Famous Men*, for example, Agee deliberately violates the privacy of the Gudger house; he feels he must do so if he is to know these people as he desires and to explain them as whole human beings. In the house he attempts to understand their lives by descriptive analysis of rooms and objects. He describes in close and careful detail the rooms themselves, the objects within sight, and finally the private and personal objects secreted in drawers. He concludes with warnings of the family's return: "But now . . . I hear her voice and the voices of her children, and in knowledge of those hidden places I have opened, those griefs, beauties, those garments whom [*sic*] I took out, held to my lips, took odor of, and folded and restored so orderly, so reverently as cerements, or priest the blesséd cloths, I receive a strong shock at my heart, and I move silently, and quickly." He concludes, "It is not going to be easy to look into their eyes."[22]

Something very similar occurs in *The Home Place*. It must be remembered that unlike *Let Us Now Praise Famous Men*, Morris's novel incorporates photographs directly into the text, where they are meant to testify to the "inhabited" qualities of the rural environment. The crucial scene is Muncy and Peg's entrance into Ed's place in order to consider the house as a potential residence for their family. It is important that though Ed is dying, he is still alive when Clyde and Peg enter his house; their guilt, based on their intrusiveness into Ed's personal possessions, resonates in the prose. Muncy's first entrance to Ed's bedroom is narrated in a passage across the page from a photograph of a sagging bed, a carpet, and upon the carpet, a worn pair of shoes. The relevant passage reads: "There are hotel beds that give you the feeling of a negative exposed several thousand times, with the blurred image of every human being that had slept in them. Then there are beds with a single image, over-exposed. There's an etched clarity about them, like a clean daguerreotype, and you know in your heart that was how the man really looked. There's a question in your mind if any other man, any other human being, could lie in that bed and belong in it" (135).

At one point they glance through Ed's album of newspaper clippings, connecting Ed's selection of clippings to his personal life. Suddenly—like Agee in the sharecropper house—Muncy understands:

> I felt more and more like some sly Peeping Tom. I put my hand up to my face, as it occurred to me, suddenly, how people look in a *Daily News* photograph. A smiling face at the scene of a bloody accident. A quartet of gay waitresses near the body slumped over the bar. God only knows why I thought of that, but I put up my hands, covering my face, as if I were there, on the spot, and didn't want to be seen. I didn't want to be violated, that is. The camera eye knows no privacy, the really private is its business, and in our time business is good. But what, in God's name, did that have to do with me? At the moment, I guess, I was that kind of camera. (138)

When Muncy prepares to leave the house, certain now that this privacy is "holy," he feels "like a man whose job it was to close up a church. In this passion, that was the word for a man's house. The citadel, the chapel, of his character" (145).

It is instructive that, while Agee calls himself a "spy" and Walker Evans a "counter-spy" (Agee and Evans, xx), Muncy thinks of himself as "some sly Peeping Tom." Agee writes early in *Let Us Now Praise Famous Men* that "the camera seems to me, next to unassisted and weaponless consciousness, the central instrument of our time; and is why in turn I feel such rage at its misuse" (Agee and Evans, 11). For Morris, as quoted, "The camera eye knows no privacy, the really private is its business, and in our time business is good."

This conception of privacy in *The Home Place*, beginning with the camera lens, is poignantly applied as well to the human lens and so also to the complexities of the intersubjective gaze. After one of the many disconcerting city-country verbal exchanges in the book, Muncy sits across from Aunt Clara: "She rocked, her right eye covered, and looked at me. I did not look at her with my camera eye. I looked at the floor and the hole she had worn in the patch of linoleum, and the hole beneath the patch, by rocking and dragging her heel" (43). Clara is blind in one eye and may wear a patch, but she nevertheless looks at Muncy, and Muncy refuses to meet her gaze, instead recognizing her in her "presence" in the linoleum. Morris/Muncy chooses the metaphor of the "camera eye," showing that there are lessons for human communication to be inferred from the camera's objectivity.[23]

In these ways, *The Home Place* appears to employ some of the devices associated with postmodern artistic attitudes and methods. Some of these devices Morris carried into future works, though never again with such direct challenge to readers. Having completed *The Home Place*, having combined his photographs and prose into a tenuous narrative, Morris completed his apprenticeship. The refusal of Charles Scribner's Sons to publish his next book as a photo-text may have in the end been fortunate, for Morris had realized the potential for narrative to move among ideas. He had in two books explored—and in a fashion discovered—his identity. So much for his need to recover the past and to locate himself within it. Having done this, he now needed to use this research into identity to discover the world beyond himself. Morris returned to his childhood again and again, but henceforth he was able as well to pursue larger and broader themes, having to do with the meaning of conscious existence and his central theme, the shaping of comprehension to make the most of experience.

Chapter Four

Morris's Discovery of a Literary Voice, 1949–1954

With the publication of *The Home Place*, Morris's importance as an American artist was assured. He had discovered something about literary voice and the significance of ambiguity between photograph and prose that he was about to employ in the formation of an ever more flexible prose style. His next book, from which Charles Scribner's Sons banished photographs, benefited from the conceptual complexities only narrative could provide. In *The World in the Attic* Morris, confronting his own temptations toward nostalgia, faced what Marcus Klein called "the crisis . . . of his career"[1] and transformed the American penchant for nostalgia into his subject; with this book, he completed his conversion from an incipient pastoral regionalist to an inquiring modernist. That shift made it possible for Morris in the next five years to produce such "American" books as *Man and Boy* and its more refined companion, *The Deep Sleep*; the intensely personal *The Works of Love* (and its quirky offshoot, *War Games*); and his only "political" novel, *The Huge Season*.

The World in the Attic

In *The World in the Attic* Morris brilliantly succeeded both in escaping his "captivity" to the past and in holding up his "favorite disease," nostalgia, to critical examination (Klein, 226). Although Morris says he "thought long and hard" before concurring with the publisher's desire to publish the new novel without photographs,[2] he might privately have had another opinion: Photographs were perfect for *The Home Place*, but perhaps less appropriate to the tone of the new novel, in which conceptual interrogation was the key. At this point Morris needed to probe Clyde Muncy's—and his own—guarded skepticism about the emotionally constricted character of rural life.

Morris had misgivings about the sentimentality of *The Home Place*, questioning his early affirmation of "abstinence, frugality, and independence." Even though *The World in the Attic* is a "continuation" of *The*

Home Place, the new novel supplied "Clyde Muncy, and the author, with deep mind-clearing draughts of small-town nausea. This I very much needed, after *The Home Place*, but more important, in the character of Tom Scanlon I acquired a key to my future as a novelist, a freshet of emotion, memory, and imagination that would prove to be inexhaustible."[3] Morris makes it sound as if everything followed from the unexpected appearance of Tom Scanlon, but it might be argued instead that Morris's progress as a novelist made Scanlon inevitable, emerging from the underbrush Morris had been beating since 1934. Scanlon gave symbolic focus to Morris's ambivalence toward rural virtues and provided, from his residence in the New Western Hotel, the perfect means of probing the pioneer American Dream.

Death pervades *The World in the Attic*, not the quiet death of *The Home Place*, in which ultimately it is the final stage in a fulfilling natural process, but death as a resolution, at its worst a subconsciously desired end to despair. As Muncy puts it, "For reasons of their own all kinds of men, with a bottle in their hand and one in their stomach, figured there was no finer place in the world to walk than the {railroad} ties. Right down the center, right down the middle, to Kingdom Come. Men who didn't seem to give—as my father said—a good goddam."[4] If Scanlon is an urgent presence, so is Emil Bickel, his watch stopped at 11:17, the exact time a train had struck and thrown him "on the telephone wires," where "he swung, like a sack of grain, his arms dangling like the sleeves of a scarecrow, and every last button gone from his vest" (45). The railroads—always symbolic—produce the grid supporting the plot: The C.B. & Q. cuts the novel's space into east and west (48), the Union Pacific into north and south.

The World in the Attic is in two parts. "The World" moves Muncy and his family down the road, some days after the events in *The Home Place*, to Junction, where Clyde was "born and raised," and where he reestablishes acquaintance with a boyhood friend, Bud Hibbard, and recalls the social conflict that energized the town in his youth—personified by Bud's aunt, Miss Caddy, and grandmother, Aunt Angie Hibbard. This section continues the ironic pastoralism of *The Home Place*, though with a sharper edge, and introduces the concept of nostalgia surfeited. The second part, "The Attic," probes small-town consciousness, expanding the cast and setting up a central revelatory scene, Miss Caddy's death and Aunt Angie's triumph in outliving her. Muncy, an ironic observer in the earlier novel, here becomes an active participant for whom the meaning, not of the past, but of the *future*, is at stake.

First entering Junction with his family, Muncy stops in Mabel's Lunch, where he feels—and vividly describes—the sudden effect of an overdose of nostalgia:

> I can get it in a lunch room like this, or at the bend of a road, any country road, where a telephone pole tips out of a clutter of dust-heavy weeds. Or a track crossing, where you lean out to peer into nowhere, in both directions, the rails a long blur with the hot air, like smoke, flowing up. At such times it's hard to tell where the nostalgia stops, the nausea begins. While you're in the grip of one, the other one sets in. Before you know it you're whipped, you're down and out, you're sick with small-town-Sunday-afternoon. This sickness is in your blood, like a latent fever, a compound of all those summer afternoons, all those fly-cluttered screens, and all those Sunday papers scattered on the floor. The idle curtains at the open windows, the heat over the road like a band of light, and the man on the davenport, with his pants unbuttoned, the comics over his face. The dog who wants in, the cat who wants out, the smothered sound of dishes under soapy water, and the smell of chicken gravy when you lift your fingers to your nose. Everything is there in the hot afternoon, there in the room and at the open window, everything is there, in abundance, to make life possible. But very little is there to make it tolerable. Any one of these things, at a time, is nostalgia—but taken together, in a single lump, it is home-town nausea—you are sicker than you think. You had better sit down. (26)

With this acute diagnosis, Morris begins his attack on American cultural nostalgia, one of the central themes of his career.

With queasy stomach, Muncy takes a sentimental journey through the town—the barber shop, the railroad, the station ticket office where his father had worked. Remembering his father, Muncy launches into "Tom Scanlon's story": Scanlon had turned his back on the future to face the impossible past; when he died, he showed his disdain by pouring a nightpot of cigar butts on his head. While alive he looked West—where there was little to see but the railroad, and what he seemed to see most were men driving their teams into the east-bound train. It was Scanlon who told the authorities where to find Emil Bickel, hanging from the wires. Pondering Scanlon, Muncy links his own queasiness to his father and the men who "walked right down the middle of the tracks." Muncy's recognition that nausea is a corollary to nostalgia is set in deliberate contrast to Scanlon's entombment in the nostalgic mythic West.

Clinton Hibbard, Bud's uncle, had married a woman from "the South" (in truth, Southern Indiana [84]), Miss Caddy, building her a mansion in the town. When no children issued from the marriage, Clinton's mother, Angeline, and Uncle Billie Hibbard also moved in. The mansion is reminiscent of Gatsby's house in West Egg; Muncy remembers the extravagant parties held there—with tinkling music, women in frilly dresses, and romantic light from Japanese lanterns. Muncy says, "The great Gatsby, don't forget, was born and raised out here" (76). He links Miss Caddy's parties to Bud Hibbard's guilt in merely remembering the blonde Swenson girls of his youth. Muncy recalls, "We both had been tempted, incurably. Nothing had happened—but the skin of that apple, the dream of that love had been so delicious that twenty years later Gatsby Hibbard knew he had sinned. He had gazed upon loveliness and desired her." These memories, equated by Bud to betrayal of his marriage, must be carefully repressed. To Gatsby's resolutions, beginning "No wasting time at [S]hafters," Muncy adds, "Be true to the finest creature on God's Green earth" (77).

The Junction of the second half of *The World in the Attic* emphasizes polarity. The mansion remains, but now it is at the edge of town, not its center ("The town went the other way," Bud's wife, Nellie, explains [88]), and directly across from it is the smoking town dump, lit by a street light. The mansion, now inhabited only by the two widows, symbolizes opposition: Miss Caddy, "a primrose among the flowering corn" (132), represents the life of parties and pleasure; Aunt Angie, duty and suppression of desire. In the America Morris critiques, pleasure and responsibility may not live together. Inside the house, in fact, the two women live separate lives: Miss Caddy has most of the house, Aunt Angie only the kitchen. While still alive, Uncle Billie had resolved the conflict by predicting Aunt Angie would outlive Miss Caddy by one week. When Muncy visits Aunt Angie he is witness to her vision of "the Dead Wagon"—coming not for her, but for Caddy.

The novel details Muncy's accidental involvement following Miss Caddy's death and Aunt Angie's triumph. Muncy must supply the larger meaning of Angie's triumph, because the people who live in Junction are void of objectivity: to Nellie, for example, Caddy's death means only that her family can now move into the mansion. After the body is prepared for burial (giving Morris another opportunity to satirize the funeral industry), the townspeople come to see an era ended. Muncy understands that this occasion represents a crisis. "Here in the [casket], at least, one could really look at her. As you would look at your childhood, or the best impression you had of yourself. I knew this as well as any man, and if I did not come for a look at Caddy it was because I knew it, because it privately scared me to death. For I knew that more had died, upstairs, than I had reckoned with. I had also died, and the gist of my life was to be born again" (147). Muncy too must reconstruct a way to live, although he recognizes, as the townspeople do not, that life is a compromise between desire and reality. "A great current had once passed through this town," Muncy observes, "with one pole in Miss Caddy, one pole in Aunt Angie, and one could string up a wire in this force and be alive" (174). With Caddy's death, it is likely that Junction will lose its bearings, and Aunt Angie's constricted view of the world will triumph.

When Muncy prepares to leave town, driving his family past the mansion, he finds it aglow with light "like a house burning" (180), and he sees that "Aunt Angie had come to the viewing"; she stands "framed in the wide, arched doors . . . her legs wide spread" (186). But then an odd thing happens. Approached by someone intent on aiding her, she wards him off, asserting her independence. Then she turns to the others: "Facing them, her apron blowing in the draft down the stair well, she felt again what she had known all the time. The folly of it. They were witless. And now they were dead" (188). Aunt Angie's judgment is based on her understanding that the real issue between herself and Miss Caddy is largely incomprehensible to the town.

The World in the Attic is not a perfect book, but it advances Morris's critical skepticism about the possibilities of "the good life" when that life is based on myth and nostalgia. In opposition to his tone of reverent inquiry in *The Home Place*, a chastened Muncy now queries:

> On other frontiers, right now, were the young men who entered Nebraska, with the same dream, just eighty years ago. That dream was young. Was ours growing old? Had we found replacements for these parts of our life? Or had we been victimized by the fact that abstinence, frugality, independence were not the seeds of heroes, but the roots of the great soft life. Out of frugality—in this rich land—what could come but abundance, and out of abundance different notions of a brave new world. For every man—as we now say—a full dinner pail. Another way to say that—the one I heard from my father, and perhaps you heard it from your father—"I don't want my son to have to go through what I went through." What was that? What made men of them? What made *that* kind of man, anyhow, and perhaps there was more than a casual connection between that kind of man and what we call our way of life. It was his. He had earned it. Can you give such a life to anyone? (66)

Exploration of the rhetorical questions Morris raises here became his future literary agenda.

Man and Boy and The Deep Sleep

In his next book, *Man and Boy*—and its thematic reconsideration two years later in *The Deep Sleep*—Morris took on directly as subject matter what had only been subtextual before: relations between the sexes. Tension between man and woman, questionably comic in the relations between Clyde and Peg Muncy, now became an important characteristic of Morris's work. Because this theme is so central to both novels, these works are discussed together, delaying consideration of the important novel published between them, *The Works of Love*, until later in the chapter.

Perhaps the best opening into the question of Morris's portrayal of relationships between the sexes is provided by Morris's response to David Madden's question: "[H]ow do you regard women in our society?" Morris began by saying that Henry James, in *The American Scene*, had preceded him; he continued: "Betrayed by man (deprived of him, that is), woman is taking her abiding revenge on him—unconscious in such figures as Mrs. Ormsby [in *Man and Boy*] and Mrs. Porter [in *The Deep Sleep*], where she inherits, by default, the world man should be running. Since only Man will deeply gratify her, the Vote and the Station Wagon leave something to be desired."[5] Once readers accept the mid-century assumption that men "should be running" the world, this passage holds considerable interest, suggesting that both men and women are trapped in false consciousness, playing out debilitating, culturally assigned roles.

Women, according to this view, have exchanged vital relations with men for material possessions and the civic rights once considered the male's dominion. In addition, because men have defaulted on their "responsibilities," women have "inherited" the responsibilities while attaining privileges of questionable value. Many of Morris's women respond by practicing stratagems of revenge; their spouses, in turn, grow even more distant. Given time, this way of life becomes a habit; valorized by consumerism, it becomes institutionalized—and men and women are driven ever further from satisfactory lives together.

Morris has sometimes been narrowly criticized for his views of women, but if this analysis of his understanding of American sexual politics is sound, he might be credited instead with considerable insight.

No doubt Morris's satirical edginess gets in the way. He accepts his diagnosis as a given American condition, and then—without explanation or apology—shows his men and women locked into the very debilitations he is examining. His women appear often to be termagants and tyrants. That his male characters are often passive and socially inept may not appear acceptably to balance the equation.

But there is more to the question than this. The peculiar qualities of *Man and Boy* and *The Deep Sleep*—beyond the querulousness of the Muncy books—suggest that behind his intellectual convictions, Morris had personal reasons for his apparent acidity toward his female antagonists. Leon Howard suggests that Morris suspects "every woman is an Eve . . . a potential instrument of his destruction."[6] Webb's sarcasm about women in *The Deep Sleep*—"No man can do enough for his mother, but he can always die," and "Everything I am or hope to be . . . I owe to my mother—I owe to the fact that she died when I was very young"[7]—is so excessive that readers may suspect Morris, as Webb's creator, of reacting to a threat to his own identity. No doubt this quality may be understood in relation to the absence of a nurturing mother in his childhood, as discussed earlier. The conflict as found in these novels, however, is displaced onto "Mother" in *Man and Boy* and mother-in-law in *The Deep Sleep*, both founded on the mother of Morris's first wife. Morris recalls the moment when "I had been brought face to face with my subject. . . . Mother was a mystery only a novelist might solve" (*Cloak*, 157).

The title *Man and Boy* is something of a misnomer, for it leaves out a crucial member of the odd American triangle, the figure of Mother, named Violet Ames Ormsby. She is a woman who knows the Latin names for objects in nature, particularly birds, and who, almost abstractedly, has designs (aims/Ames) that empower her as a force not only in her home, but in the nation at large. She has Washington connections that she exploits to have her projects forwarded—her husband's phrase is "to push through the House [of Representatives]." His discomfort with the term stems not only from his perception that it implied "the opposition was being pushed around,"[8] but that it ironically applies to his own domestic situation.

The novel, an expansion of a story called "The Ram in the Thicket," centers on Mother as a woman whose domination of males is abided both by the males who admire her and by public "male" institutions. The action is precipitated by Mother's selection by the United States Navy to dedicate a battleship, the Ormsby, after her son Virgil. The boy is once again a "missing" person (occasionally described as "missing" even while he lived at home), later revealed to have been killed in action. On this momentous day, Mother and Warren Ormsby make their way from Philadelphia to Brooklyn. On the train, Mr. Ormsby runs into a soldier named Lipido, to whom he is drawn. The Ormsbys are met by Commander Sudcliffe, whom Mother convinces to drive into the city to pick up her friend Mrs. Dinardo, "an armored Amazon" (197). When they arrive at the ship, Mother insists that Mrs. Dinardo be allowed to accompany her on deck. Against the navy's protests that such an action would violate protocol, Mother is insistent. " 'Am I to understand,' said Mother, 'that my son Virgil fought and died so you silly men could keep a lady off a boat?" To which Private Lipido shouts, "VIVA MRS. ORMSBY! . . . NUTS TO THE NAVY!" (202–3). The navy is forced to relax its protocols and Mother triumphs.

Although Morris said later that the tone of *Man and Boy* "wavered between pathos and farce, a mix that seemed appropriate to the subject" (*Cloak* 122), the comedy has a sharper edge. Even though Mother blames Warren for first arming Virgil with a Daisy BB gun, taking him (in her view) on the first step toward the violence that ultimately kills him, Mother is presented as a more likely cause for Virgil's going off to war—by vengefully depriving him of a *home*. Even as a baby, Virgil felt aversion to Mother, refusing to nurse from her, requiring the milk of Mrs. Dinardo. And because Ormsby had bought the gun, Mother responded by refusing to bake pies "for people like that" (17–18) and by banishing Christmas: "no tree, no Yuletide season, no Christmas in the Santa Claus sense of the word" (69).

The home is *hers*: she covers the linoleum and furniture with newspapers, driving man and boy to the remote consolations of the basement or the out-of-doors, where Virgil uses his Daisy rifle to hunt the birds Mother knows only distantly from their Latin names. When she rises from sleep and proclaims, "*Fiat lux*" (37), she demonstrates her belief in her power to control, as she does with her use of the silent treatment. In these practices she is aided and abetted by American culture. As Ormsby points out to Lipido, citing the importance of Mother's Day as a national event, "Would the United States Government, the Secretary of the Navy, the commander of the boat . . . write letters [regarding the naming of the ship] just to *her* if that wasn't the way everybody felt?" (139).

One way Mother gets her way is by dominating her home as a kind of emotional terrorist (Violet suggesting both *flower* and *violence*);

another is by challenging the navy itself. Further, she turns the males' sense of noblesse oblige against them, opening them to emotional blackmail. It is characteristic of Morris that he leaves considerable ambiguity regarding the placing of blame for this default, beginning with his choice of epigraph, from John Donne: "If man had beene left *alone* in this *world*, at first, shall I thinke that he would not have *fallen*? If there had beene no *Woman*, would not man have served, to have beene his own *Tempter*?" One inference is that man *needs* a tempter and therefore grasps at the opportunity Eve presents. This inference suggests a darker, Freudian theme, that there is something in man that can only be satisfied negatively. A creature with a devious mind, he acknowledges his loss of power and authority with simultaneous regret and relief.

Part of Morris's point in *Man and Boy* is that in his inability to assert his manhood, Ormsby enables Mother in her destruction of the family. Unable to stand up to her, he inevitably supports her in her role as overbearing woman. Where Ormsby's passivity comes from is difficult to say, but it has something to do with his compassion "for all those things that were *nipped in the bud*. For young men, taken in their youth, for lovers, taken in their blossom, and for old men in the sere and yellow leaf" (133). Ormsby's knowledge of himself as a failure is brought closely home through Virgil's double, Lipido. Warren tells him "stuff he hadn't thought of, even dreamed of, for more than forty years" (91); the scene in which he and Lipido exchange stories about candling eggs is one of those rituals by which Morris signals that important revelations are to follow. As in Ormsby's most intimate moment with Virgil, Lipido calls him "Pop," and he is outraged with Warren's references to Mrs. Ormsby as "Mother." At one point, trying to quiet Lipido's criticism of him, Warren pushes Lipido to the floor, knowing, "even as he pushed, that he owed this strange power to Mother who had once disciplined the boy with the same strategy." But when Lipido cries at the treatment, Ormsby comforts him, saying, " '[E]asy, easy now—easy boy,' which was what his father had said to horses, but which Mr. Ormsby, until this moment, had said to no one" (124).

Much of the meaning of *Man and Boy* is delivered through birds and bird imagery, beginning with Ormsby's dream in which Virgil wears a "crown of bright, exotic plumage," his arm extended toward "a procession of birds, an endless coming and going of all the birds he had ever seen" (3–4). That in the dream the birds turn against Ormsby follows from the fact he "had once fed the birds himself, but he had given it up when the pigeons became so friendly they were more or less menacing"

(84). Later, however, Morris returns to Ormsby's reasons for ceasing to feed the birds, and here his motive is more complex. Ormsby had never understood the *meaning* of feeding birds until he had seen an old woman adding her spittle to the bread and "realized that it was a religious ceremony, this spittle she added was her flesh and the birds gave it wings." Henceforth, with "this knowledge he spent one summer feeding the birds, all of the birds, and every Sunday there would be this Eucharist." It was during such activity that Mother "had her eye on him," and thus, it is suggested, they married (168–69). From this explanation it may be understood that Mother found him at his most "religious" and captured him, thereafter to deprive him of this sacred, life-enhancing activity. The birds, now associated with Mother, had become too "menacing."

Man and Boy is a quirky novel, its exaggerations rendering it perhaps even more grotesquely comic than Morris intended, as well as masking his deeper psychological attitudes toward women. At the same time that Morris was writing *Man and Boy*, he was revising *The Works of Love*, which is based on his father's life. Obviously the *idea* of family and the significance of genealogical origins were much on his mind. So it should come as little surprise that Morris wanted to reconsider the question of Woman, this time in *The Deep Sleep*, striving both for realism and psychological complexity.

The Deep Sleep, though it begins with the same basic concern as *Man and Boy*, is much more ambitious, its subject the American family and the *causes* of strained relations between the sexes in American culture. Leon Howard's observation that *The Deep Sleep* might become a "classic study of American family life" (17) is apt, but the novel seems no longer even to be remembered—despite its pertinence to the American "family values" jeremiad in the 1990s. The title is from Genesis: "And the Lord God caused a deep sleep to fall upon Adam, and he slept; and he took one of his ribs, . . . and the rib, which the Lord God had taken from man, made he a woman, and brought her unto the man." The Adam is Judge Howard Porter, his Eve, Mrs. Millicent Porter.

Much of the craft of this novel has to do with Morris's use of photographic vision as an aid to comprehension of the Porter family and, more broadly, of American culture. More strongly than in *The Home Place*, Morris links the *idea* of the lens to epistemology and the "superstition" that cultural meanings might be derived from sharp enough focus. He suggests that if one could understand certain habits of "as big a man as the Judge . . . you could understand something about America" (142). As an artist, Paul Webb's task is to get "the whole picture" of American life, presumably by studying its effects in the microcosm of a "typical" American home. That he achieves the whole picture is doubtful; more important is that by the end of the novel he has changed his mind and is willing to give credit where credit is due.

Morris employs the epistemology of vision from the outset, when Webb recalls his stay in the guest room of the Judge's house 15 years before, upon his return from Europe. His return then had led him to think—with copious references to lenses and mirrors—about "discovering" America:

> So he had looked at the bed, then he had turned and faced the mirror on the dresser, where everything in the room seemed to be gathered, as if seen through a lens. . . . Gathered around him, as in a composition, were the photographs on the walls of the room . . . .
>
> It was all there in the mirror, but Webb could not describe the impression it had made on him. He had been led through the house, room by room, so that this room had come as a symbolic climax, as if the house had gathered itself together in the lens of the mirror. Beginning at the back, beginning with the kitchen, each room seemed to open on a wider vista, a deeper, more ambitious prospect of American life. . . .
>
> It had seemed to Webb, right at that moment, that he had gone abroad not to find himself, or other such prattle, but in order to return to this room and rediscover America. To find in this house the spaciousness of American life. There in the mirror, as neatly ordered as a painting, were the sentiments that painting had failed to grasp, and it seemed to Webb that the heart of this secret was the house. It was the house, the house itself, set in its miniature suburban [*sic*] forest, that brought the conflicting forces together and gave them shape. It added up to more than the sum of the separate lives. (6–7)

Later, when Webb says, "It's the goddam house" (143), Morris seems to suggest that the riddle of the Porter family centers on the management of the house; but he also means that the Porter family—including the Grandmother—is an *American* family—and to grasp it is to understand America.

The precipitating event in *The Deep Sleep* is once again a funeral, this time of Judge Porter. When the novel opens, the Judge's daughter, Katherine, and her artist-husband, Paul Webb, have arrived and are staying in the house in which Katherine grew up. The novel details the day following their arrival, predominantly from Webb's point of view: his observations when rising from sleep, the making of funeral preparations (with Webb in charge of the judge's suit), the gathering of mourners, and Webb's discoveries in basement and attic. The Judge's 99-year-old mother and Mrs. Porter are the antagonists.

The novel documents Webb's increasing outrage when faced with the Grandmother's self-centered longevity and evidence of Mrs. Porter's icy prepossession (Katherine describes her mother as "a hermetically sealed unit" [149]). From Webb's point of view these two women, especially Mrs. Porter, have made his father-in-law's life miserable. What he discovers is that Mrs. Porter has ruled the house as she desired, setting rules and standards fitting her own interests, while her husband's boxed-up law books were "hiding under the basement stairs" (141). Parsons, the handyman, tells Webb, "Around the house [the Judge] left it up to the Missus. . . . Said it was her bailiwick. . . . Said he'd run the country if the Missus would run the home" (85). When the Judge "got out of the house, he sneaked off an' . . . had the cream, and the sugar, an' just about everything she wouldn't let him have" (87), including the hidden banana candy Katherine finds and the evidence of smoked cigars Webb finds in the attic.

The key symbol in *The Deep Sleep* is the Judge's expensive watch, which he had bought in Italy to commemorate the occasion of his daughter's conception, when "things," as the Judge said, "came to a head" (270). The Judge had lost the watch (deliberately?), then his wife had found it; now, however, it has disappeared, though the Judge had "put it in a safe place" (96). Toward the end of the novel, Webb finds the watch in the attic near the basin holding the floating cigar butts. Webb sees the watch as a symbol of womanly power—power capable of driving a man into his own basement or attic. From the attic he spies Mrs. Porter's gigantic shadow, which "made the hair on Webb's neck rise, and if there had been blood left in his veins it would have run cold" (307). Later, in homage to the woman's power over the man—more correctly, her power to have the male accede to his own exile—Webb puts the watch where Mrs. Porter will be able easily to find and repossess it as a symbol of her life with the Judge.

What gives Webb's restoration of the watch its peculiar significance is Webb's observation midway through the novel of the behaviors of a woman and her young son. The woman grasps the boy's hand; the more he struggles to free himself, the more she resists. Sitting down, the mother still holds on to the boy while she examines his face.

> [S]he couldn't seem to get enough of it, her eyes clung to his lips, peered into his mouth, studied first one side, then the other, and passed like a

damp, lightly soaped rag over all of it. They were, it seemed to Webb, not two people at all but one joined person, and the child was a mirror in which the mother saw herself. . . . They were not, for the moment, two people but one, the child straddling the leg was still part of the mother, as if the hydra-headed monster had learned to spawn and admire itself. Nothing, it seemed to Webb, would ever tear them apart. Through the clasped hands a current seemed to pass, the same force that drew the salmon up the river, leaping, and drove the lemmings on their suicidal movement to the sea. *Thy will be done*, Webb said aloud, *on earth as it is in heaven*, and wondered if the nature of the day had made him soft in the head. (182–83)

Obviously, Webb sees in this tableau something of greater import: "The woman and the child, the hook-up of nature that was both public and private, seemed to sum up all the problems that he was powerless to resolve" (183). Several pages later, Webb sees the dead Judge's photograph in the newspaper, a photograph that "made him look strangely distracted, as if the Judge . . . had just turned his gaze from the mythic, hydra-headed mother and child. The pair of them drawn together by the same force that drew the salmon, leaping, up the river, and men, as well as lemmings, to some fatal rendezvous with the sea" (186).

The repetition of the "hydra-headed monster" and the forces of nature it represents is not gratuitous. If Webb had earlier returned to America to grasp the key to American culture, he now finds that at the basis of that culture, in the relationships between men and women, is a hydra-headed monster representing the demands of nature itself. Webb's efforts to get "the whole picture" of American life are stymied by the simple fact that the relationships between American men and women are conditioned by a natural determinism admitting of no final *cultural* explanation. The entrapment of the male by the female is "natural," linked to "the only bond that mattered, the only cord that bled," that "had been cut many years before" (184). No doubt some such conviction explains Webb's sarcasm regarding women in his conversation with Parsons.

The novel as a whole seems a commentary on *Civilization and Its Discontents*, in which Freud writes:

[W]omen soon come into opposition to civilization and display their retarding and restraining influence—those very women who, in the beginning, laid the foundations of civilization by the claims of their love. Women represent the interests of the family and of sexual life. The work of civilization has become increasingly the business of men, it confronts them with ever more difficult tasks and compels them to carry out instinctual sublimations of which women are little capable. . . . His constant association with men, and his dependence on his relations with them, even estrange him from his duties as a husband and father. Thus the woman finds herself forced into the background by the claims of civilization and she adopts a hostile attitude towards it.[9]

In *The American Scene*, James had made much the same point—as quoted by Morris in *The Territory Ahead*. James wrote of the male default in American civilization, "his default having made, all around him, the unexampled opportunity of the woman—which she would have been an incredible fool not to pounce upon. It needs little contact with American life to see how she *has* pounced, and how, outside business, she has made it over in her image."[10]

The Deep Sleep points to a deliberately unresolved conflict between natural and cultural explanations in Morris's work. Morris's American civilization may work *against* the "natural" reciprocity of the sexes, but in truth, the male is *always* tied to his mother (and to all women) by the umbilical cord. Webb strikes out against what he considers Mrs. Porter's inhumanity, but by the end he accepts her as a fact of nature and nurture, his response to her influenced by "natural law." This recognition lies behind his act of homage in placing the watch where she will find it.

The Works of Love

The Works of Love has given readers considerable difficulty, although some readers have deeply appreciated its craft and Morris's distanced compassion for his protagonist. David Madden's observation that *The Works of Love* is like a tone poem is apt,[11] but so is Charles Baxter's description of it as a "terribly eerie novel about a specific kind of American emptiness."[12] That Morris called this work "the linchpin in my novels concerned with the Plains" is appropriate,[13] not only because *The Works of Love* encapsulated his themes, but because the novel further developed the groundwork for his project of probing the American psyche.

Dedicated in part to Sherwood Anderson, *The Works of Love* continues Anderson's analysis of men and women subject to peculiarly Midwestern failures of communication. But whereas Anderson often dealt with psychological trauma, Morris develops his protagonist, Will Brady, as a person moved paradoxically by an *absence* of motivation. Brady seems to exist as little more than a receptor of sensual stimuli, unable to convert perception into conception in the interests of fuller consciousness. The chief irony of *The Works of Love* is how little knowledge Brady achieves from so many detailed acts of perception. Unable to cope with the hostilities of environment, Brady retreats from the world, transcending it only within his imagination.

The novel follows Will Brady from his birth in Indian Bow, Nebraska, to his death in Chicago, where, dressed in a Montgomery Ward Santa Claus suit, he plunges to his death in a sewage canal. The novel follows Brady's moves eastward, recounting his passive acceptance, as his "son," of a child dropped off the freight train and tagged simply "My name is Willy Brady" and the pathos of his two marriages. In the country he builds a huge city-house but "forgets" to put into it either a furnace or a stove. His chicken empire (5,000 laying hens) collapses, his relationship to his son is strained, his second wife runs off with a "Hawayan." Unable to connect with wives or child, Brady makes his way to Chicago, where he ages and once a year receives a dutiful letter from Willy. When Brady dies, readers cannot be certain if his death is accidental or deliberate.

What is crucial to *The Works of Love* is not plot, however, but style, Morris's use of language to show the processes of thought—or what passes for thought, carried primarily through the senses. Just as Brady is "a man with so much of his life left out" (4), the authorial voice is extraordinarily selective in the knowledge it provides. No wonder some readers complain that Brady is incomprehensible. Criticism of *The Works of Love* is often divided between those who find Brady excessively passive and those who believe he achieves some kind of mystical fulfillment. Another alternative, however, is to suggest that Morris deliberately created a style allowing him to *empathize with both* passivity and desires for transcendence.

This alternative argues that Morris shaped the narrative method of *The Works of Love* through an imaginative fusion of his dual preoccupations as novelist and photographer. That Morris had photography much on his mind throughout the writing of *The Works of Love* is obvious from the chronology of his creativity at that time. *The Works of Love* went through seven drafts between 1946 and 1951, when it was finally published in severely shortened form. The first draft was composed in 1946, the same year *The Inhabitants* appeared. About the time of the second and third drafts, Morris paused to write and take the photographs for *The Home Place*.[14] The year before *The Works of Love* was published, Morris published "Privacy as a Subject for Photography."

The method of *The Works of Love*, proceeding by anecdote, vignette, epiphany—fragments of Brady's reality with few transitions—has called forth many explanations. G. B. Crump, acknowledging the source of Brady in Morris's father, suggests that "Morris's tone is sometimes out of control in the book; his sympathy for Brady threatens to become sentimental and his commentary, condescending."[15] Wayne Booth observes that the novel's narrative technique is "simply one version of . . . *style indirect libre*" that "enables modern authors to convey a counterpoint of two or more voices at once."[16] Roy Bird believes Morris is himself "[u]nable to unravel the enigma of Will Brady's personality," and thus "forces the reader to draw his own conclusions—or admit his own uncertainty—about the meaning of [Brady's] life."[17]

What the criticism emphasizes are fragmentation and narrative gaps—suggesting that Brady's story is *intended* to be ambiguous. The method through which Morris maintains this ambiguity in *The Works of Love* is conceptually similar to the evidence found in family photograph albums—incorporating gaps in chronology, unexplained gestures and expressions, and silence about meaning. What Morris employs subtly in *The Works of Love* he used explicitly in *The Man Who Was There*—an album (described in detailed prose) from which his narrator deduces information and from which both narrator and audience extrapolate possible meanings.

Comprehending the ambiguities of *The Works of Love* might be facilitated by an inquiry into Morris's need to come to terms with his father, who had died a few years before. Morris says, "I was pondering [my father's] life, and how little I knew him. This led me to think about origins. In point of fact I knew very little." These reflections led to the creation of "a mythic past of my own, gratifying to my own needs and imaginings."[18] Morris had to *imagine* his father's life, but as he writes of Brady, "What is there left to say of a man with so much of his life left out?" At the core of the book was a dilemma: How to make public through art—and so to commemorate—the essential human bond between father and son *against* the evidence in his own case that there was hardly a bond at all? Morris accomplished this by creating a style allowing him to temper the cruelty of social judgments with the mercies of irony; to rationalize failures of will by calling on psychic, social, and geographical determinisms; and to balance his father's failures with veiled suggestions of timeless mystical fulfillment. In these terms, *The Works of Love* is a work motivated by Morris's sympathetic desire for his father's mutual regard.

Artistic necessity in *The Works of Love* led Morris to a strategy of deliberate ambivalence, to the invention of a style that not only justifies ambivalence, but in fact *exploits* it to make the novel artistically coherent. This style paradoxically allows Morris to approach his subject intimately and yet to remain distant; it provides a means for Morris to hint that Brady's very helplessness is the essential condition for his transcendence. Morris derived this method in large part from his involvement with photography, exploiting the reality that although the camera is a crucial instrument for revealing the world, it fails to explain what events *mean*. Morris turns the camera's inability to explain to advantage. What he presents in *The Works of Love* is a series of pictures of Brady "posed" in his world; the "explanations" of meaning are the responsibility of the carefully crafted narrative voice. This method allows the narrator continuously to question Brady's consciousness, mock its limitations, and defend its pathos. The narrative shifts rapidly back and forth between these various modes of presentation, sometimes sympathetically, sometimes critically—although Morris's irony ensures that the audience will not always agree with the narrator. Occasionally, when the narrator seems too hard on the protagonist, the reader is encouraged to Brady's defense.

Whereas Morris had used the practice of photography as direct referential support in some early drafts of the novel (Cohn, 244–45), there are no explicit epistemological references to cameras or lenses in *The Works of Love*, possibly because they would be too self-conscious and conceptual for the narrative voice. Nevertheless, in order to support his deliberately fragmented method, Morris introduced photographic strategies into the final version of *The Works of Love*. Three of these strategies are of particular significance: first, Morris's emphasis on photographic detail; second, his frequent use of windows and mirrors as framing devices; third, his use of mirrors as epistemological indicators.

Regarding the first strategy, in *The Works of Love* Morris frequently employs closely detailed prose descriptions: Objects in Brady's world are "photographically" observed. One example must suffice, although the text contains many. This description details Brady's final room in Chicago:

> To get from the stove to the sink it was better to drop the leaf on the table and then lean backward over the back of the rocking-chair. On the shelf over the sink were four plates, three cups and one saucer, a glass sugarbowl, two metal forks, and one bone-handled spoon. On the mantel-

piece was a shaving mug with the word SWEETHEART in silver, blue, chipped red, and gold. In the mug were three buttons, a roller-skate key, a needle with a burned point for opening pimples, an Omaha street-car token, and a medal for buying Buster Brown shoes. At the back of the room were the folding doors that would not quite close. (216–17)

The room is obviously closely observed, and Morris suggests its cramped size and the pathetic nature of the objects. He provides more information than a camera lens would provide. Readers would not be likely to see in an actual photograph (from the perspective provided) the contents of the cup, and they would have to infer necessary body movements "from the stove to the sink."

Photographic detail, however, is hardly unique to Morris (although he refined the practice and frequently relies on it). More important to *The Works of Love* is his use of framing techniques. One typical example is the window in the tower room where Brady works in Chicago: "On one side of the room was a large bay window that faced the east. A man standing at this window—like the man on the canal who let the draw-bridge up and down—felt himself in charge of the flow of traffic, of the city itself. All that he saw seemed to be in his province, under his control." Even more emphatically, "The bay window in the tower room was a frame around this picture" (237–38), an obvious reference to artistic vision as well as a suggestion that the life outside, framed by borders, is of particular significance. The window becomes a lens; the frame around the resulting picture both emphasizes the importance of perception and portrays that subject as open to viewer-readers.

Another example is more complex. Here Brady is about to make his way to Chicago, having decided to ride the train to the end of the line rather than to get off at his proper destination, Omaha. Morris deliber-ately writes that Brady "wiped a small hole in the frosted glass" in order to see out. The scene appears through Brady's eyes: "He could see the winter dawn, a clear ice color, and far out on the desolate plain, like the roof of the world, were two or three swinging lights. He could make out the dry bed of the river, and as the train was stopping for water, he could hear, down the tracks, the beat of the crossing-bell." When the train slows, "he could see the frame of the cattle loader, and then, sud-denly, the station along the tracks" (211–12).

Peering through the hole he has made, Brady sees the telegraph oper-ator in the station, and Morris provides a detailed description of the man; then, however, he takes readers into Brady's perceptual imagination. Like Brady, the telegraph operator perceives in turn, and Brady sees him staring absently into the windows of the passing cars.

> Will Brady saw all of this as if it were a picture on a calendar. Nothing moved, every detail was clear. He could smell the odor of stale tobacco, and the man's coat, wet with snow, gave off the stench of a wet gunny sack. . . . [A]nd as Will Brady gazed at his face he raised his head, suddenly, as if a voice had spoken to him. He gazed into the darkness where Will Brady lay on the berth. And Will Brady fell back, he held his breath, and as his hands gripped the side of the berth, he heard again the mechanical throbbing of the crossing-bell. He seemed to see, out there on the horizon, the snout-like mound of the buried soddy [his birthplace], where he had been, even then, the last man in the world. (213)

This descriptive narration warrants closer examination.

First, the passage is typical in its emphasis on perception. Morris focuses on three senses—hearing, smell, and, vision—and he does so by emphasizing a passive use of the senses: "he could see," "he could make out," "he could hear," and so on. Such repeated phrasing gives the impression that Brady is a waiting receptacle for stimuli—or a camera without a motivated operator. Without human volition, the camera can only record the scene "objectively." Brady responds to what he perceives, but only rarely does he conceptualize patterns that might allow him to shape his environment.

The second point is that Morris is extremely deliberate in the use of framing devices. First, readers observe Brady wiping a hole allowing him to see through the frosted glass. It would be sufficient for Morris simply to show Brady looking through the window, but he obviously wants to emphasize this device. To have Brady clear a peephole is to suggest that the hole is an aid to vision clearly limited by its frame. This hole allows Brady to focus and to look through yet another framing device—for the telegraph operator is himself framed by the station window. Brady believes that the telegraph operator, with his own "lens" of consciousness, is gazing at him.

The carefully structured frames that Morris places around these two men emphasize the intersubjectivity of Morris's approach to his characters. Through these frames, Morris shows Brady in dread of *being seen and "exposed"*; believing himself under examination, he experiences a self-conscious distortion of self, and he feels dehumanized. Although Morris eschewed the photographic portrait in practice, he capitalizes on the problematics of the pose in his fiction. Discussions of "the pose" in photography often stress the exchange between subject and object as a struggle for equilibrium: Harold Rosenberg, for example, writes of "a silent wrestle of imaginations" between sitter and photographer.[19]

In the exchange of gazes imagined between Brady and the telegraph operator, Brady appears to be involved precisely in "a silent wrestle of imaginations." When he perceives he is being perceived, Brady panics, as if in fear of psychic violation. He falls backwards, holds his breath, and grips the berth—actions resulting from his perception that the telegraph operator's eyes have penetrated him. This psychic penetration informs Brady that he is visible to others—that others can "see *through* him." Morris uses this double framing device to intimate Brady's guilt: what Brady feels when he remembers his birthplace is that he has made little human progress. This response is appropriate for a man whose second marriage has dramatically failed and who is now in flight to "the end of the line," Chicago.

One more observation might be made about imaginative framing. After Brady wipes the frosted glass to see through the train window, readers find him "peering through" the hole he has created. This action of "peering"—linked to "no place to hide" on the Plains, as discussed earlier—recurs frequently in this novel, usually to show characters looking *through* something at something else. For example, in hotel lobbies, Brady "would peer through the palm trees" (200); Manny Plinski is often found "peering in" Brady's room through the door frame (223); Brady's son is more interested in being able to "peer out through" a catcher's mask than in the game of baseball itself (141). When Brady has his last view of Mickey Ahearn (the girl who refuses to marry him but gives him a "son"), she is standing on a caboose platform: "Mickey Ahearn looked straight down the tracks toward the sawmill until the caboose passed the hotel, when she turned her head sharply as if she had thought of him. But the sun was on the window, and besides he was behind a potted plant" (32).

In addition to the use of deliberate framing, Morris uses another intersubjective device borrowed from photography: the mirror as epistemological reflector and lens. One example occurs when Brady first begins to take notice of Ethel Bassett, who works in the Hotel Cafe. They exchange looks frequently through the reflecting glass doors of the pie case, and the looks become gradually more pointed—as in the following instance: "On the wall behind her was a mirror, so that Will Brady saw her both front and back, in the round so to speak, while she looked him straight in the face. Which was odd, as she never seemed to see anything" (24). Later in the "relationship," Brady catches Ethel, "her eyes wide," observing him in the reflecting glass: "He saw that this blank expression, this look she gave him, was meant to be an open one. He was meant to look in, and he tried, but he didn't see anything" (46). Morris uses the reflectors as indicators of consciousness, used ironically to heighten both intersubjective failure and Brady's inability to comprehend Ethel's motives. As their eyes meet only indirectly, their subjective isolation is intensified.

Perhaps Morris's most complex example of the mirror as an ironic guide to reality occurs in the store in which Brady buys his clothes: "In Fred Conlen's private fitting-room he would see himself in the three-way mirror, and it was there that he saw the new expression on his face. While he was talking—at no other time. While he talked this man in the mirror had a strange smile on his lips. This smile on his lips and a sly, knowing look about the eyes. Something shrewd he had said?" (148). It is the three-way mirror, showing Brady in perspectives not otherwise available to him, that gives him an "objective" identity, an exaggerated sense of himself that renders him heroic to his own eyes. This point is emphasized later in the novel, when Brady seeks self-assurance in hotel lobbies. Brady muses that in the hotel lobby a man is transformed, taking on "the air of a man who was being fitted for a new suit. A little bigger, wider, taller, and better-looking than he really was. And on his face the look of a man who sees himself in a three-way glass. In the three-way mirror he sees the smile on his face, he sees himself, you might say, both coming and going—a man, that is, who was from someplace and was going somewhere. Not the man you saw, just a moment before, out there in the street" (171–72). This mirror is an agent of (false) self-discovery—comparable to discoveries people make when they study photographs of themselves, generally biased by what they want to see. Brady is exceptional only in the vastness of his need for identity and value, allowing the visual evidence to show him what he needs to see. So he drifts, attuned to experience but not to reflective assessment, unable to use the past in shaping a future and consequently forced to use his imagination to serve his needs.

This analysis might be extended to include other examples of Morris's method, such as his use of light (that necessary photographic medium) in his frequent references to venetian blinds deliberately drawn to keep light out and in the final irony of Brady's near-blindness from overexposure to a NU-VITA sunlamp. Such evidence for a "photographic reading" is found in abundance.[20] In developing a method founded in the possibilities of photography, Morris found a way to fragment Brady's existence artistically and so to view his protagonist in many of the contradictory poses that make up his reality—and that are available to an ironic narrator and a participating audience. Morris devised this method in order to come to grips with conflicting emotions toward his father, creating a strategy that harmonized his emotional and aesthetic needs and preserved both his own and his father's right to privacy.[21]

The Huge Season

In *The Deep Sleep*, Morris had linked the social arrangements inside the Porter house to American public life. Whether he had thereby uncovered national American sentiments or merely some local example, Morris's desire to comprehend America and the American Dream was clear. His next novel, *The Huge Season*, forwarded Morris's exploration by focusing on the potential betrayal of American promise in the 1950s. *The Huge Season* can hardly be considered a political novel, but it is the closest thing to it in Morris's work—an outraged response to the tone of repression set by Senator Joseph McCarthy.

The Huge Season is largely about the nature and significance of evil in the world of the early 1950s and the "decline" of American cultural values since the 1920s. Morris works these concerns out through two different conceptions of time. The first is a contrast of the McCarthy era with the "huge season" of the 1920s in which protagonist Peter Foley's generation was educated. Much of the novel takes place in relation to the California campus of what Morris calls Colton College. Morris's enthrallment by the "huge season" is clear: echoes of Hemingway and Fitzgerald occur throughout.

The second understanding of time, operating on a symbolic level, contrasts Foley's conception of time with that of his father—represented by his father's watch, inscribed "*Incipit Vita Nova*" and keeping a time radically different from his own: "Time, for my father, seemed to be contained in the watch. It did not skip a beat, fly away, or merely vanish, as it does for me." Foley finds his own times to be "out of joint."[22] The novel concludes with Foley glancing at his father's watch and seeing the "time—the captive time" stopped "[a]t two o'clock in the morning, the first day of [Foley's] escape from captivity" (306).

The Huge Season has two alternating levels of narration. The first, "The Captivity," is Foley's first-person manuscript recounting his relationships with Lawrence, Proctor, Lundgren, Lou Baker, and others with whom he had shared the 1920s. Opening with Foley's matriculation at Colton, the manuscript deals with the magnetic attraction Foley and others felt emanating from Charles Lawrence, a tennis star who had had to overcome physical handicaps to achieve his "habit of perfection." This manuscript concludes with Lawrence's suicide in 1929. The importance of the manuscript is that it lies, throughout the second level of narration, in Foley's fireplace, evidence that he wants to annihilate it. He cannot seem to finish it, even though publishers have been anticipating it for 20 years. Much of the novel has to do with the reasons why the man uscript defies completion.

The problem, as the second narrative level makes clear, is a profound ambivalence founded on the contradiction between Lawrence's promise and his suicide. If the outcome of Lawrence's "habit of perfection" is suicide, then it makes suspect the magnetism that so attracted the others: Are their *own* lives similarly devoid of meaning? Foley has deeply pondered this question; his problem now is to reconcile not only Lawrence's life and death, but more important, the private aspirations of the 1920s with McCarthy's very public attack on privacy.

Foley finds, however, that little reconciliation is possible. McCarthy is stirring the embers of American communism that came to flame in the 1930s but were first lit in the Romantic despair of the 1920s. McCarthy forces men and women to repudiate their youthful intellectual attachments—thus revising history and simplistically dismissing the relevance of personal motivations. When Foley opens his newspaper on May 5, 1952, he finds a picture of his old friend, J. Lasky Proctor, and news of his defiance when asked if he had ever been a member of the Communist Party:

> Well, in a sense—
> What did he mean, "in a sense"?
> Back at that time, he replied, he had been a very good American. A good American had to believe in something good. The Party had been it. It had been something in which a man could believe.
> Did he mean to say he was no longer a good American?
> If he was, he answered, he wouldn't be here.
> In Russia, perhaps?
> No, just in jail, he had replied. (12)

The day Proctor so confronts McCarthy is the 23rd anniversary of Lawrence's suicide, and both Proctor and Foley know that it is Lawrence who provides the impetus for Proctor's foolhardy courage.

Since Lawrence's death, Proctor has been, in his own word, "disinherited" (52).

In his manuscript Foley had written: "Young men are a corn dance, a rite of spring, and every generation must write its own music, and if these notes have a sequence the age has a style" (104). He attempted to comprehend the age by examining its style: "The great style, the habit of perfection, united George Herman Ruth and Charles A. Lindbergh, Albie Booth and Jack Dempsey, Juan Belmonte and Jay Gatsby, and every man, anywhere, who stood alone with his own symbolic bull" (105). The "style" of the 1920s, he concludes, was private, composed of one's personal resources in a time when personal gestures still counted. The indictment of this generation is simply recognition of its failure to see that the rules have changed. The Depression demanded a conversion of personal gesture into social action, but these men and women continued to indulge in idealisms. Foley's manuscript is unfinished because its idealisms are out of kilter with changed social realities.

The impotence of the 1950s is spelled out in a chapter in which Morris juxtaposes a critique of Walt Whitman with the twentieth century, symbolized by the Empire State Building. Foley encounters an "old man with a white beard," "bum and sage," "Out of cradle endlessly rocking, comradely and phony sage of the open road" (107). The tramp has a "soul powerfully sustained by envious, troubled glances of passers-by," but he is unable to do more than feed their guilt, offering criticism without constructive advice. This observation is followed almost immediately by Foley's reminiscences of his "Mystical Law," which reads, "When the world went up in smoke, the smoke would have this peculiar property. It would not, because of such eyes, be what it seemed. According to Foley's Law, what had been loved or created would be part of it" (108–9). The Law, however, is a sentiment; when Foley explained it to his students, he had taken out his father's watch, and they knew "he would now make a fool of himself." He goes on:

> *They* were not, *he* was not, the uncreated world itself was not, but what had been hammered out on the forge of art could be hammered to pieces, burned, bombed, or ignored, but it could not be destroyed. The outward form could be shattered, become smoke and ashes, but the inward form was radioactive, and the act of disappearance was the transformation of the dark into the light. Metamorphosis. The divine power of art. . . . When the world went up in smoke, as everyone predicted, the creations of the human imagination would be in that smoke and give it a peculiar property. Light. Bomb-strewn seeds of immortality. (110)

Foley's students take small comfort in this sentiment, and the novel as a whole questions its assumptions. Although Foley never wholly repudiates his Law, he recognizes that the private experience of art is of little immediate use against McCarthy and the cultural denial McCarthy represents.

As he often does when discussing soul-destroying realities, Morris employs the imagery of hellfire. Early in the novel, Foley is on the train to New York, and he observes

> A scene in hell, a cloud of sulphurous smoke dense and powdery as a pill dissolving, shot through with orange flames, burning like flares. . . . Along the train bank through the march grass a fringe of vomit-green froth, a signboard advertising clothes for fat boys, and a gray film of sewage on the surface of a river of pitted lead. The coach lights came on, the windows darkened; in the glass, as in a mirror, Foley saw His reflection—the Devil's horned profile and his leering smile of good fellowship. As the pressure built up in Foley's ears he closed his eyes, swallowed hard, and said "*Lasciate ogni speranza, voi ch'entrate*" ["Abandon all hope, ye who enter here"]. (77)

There is a distinct link between Foley's characterization of McCarthy as the "current Prince of Darkness" (161) and his recognition of the devil's face in his *own* reflection.

The convenient symbol of evil, of course, is McCarthy, but Morris suggests that evil is not merely an active force bringing darkness on the land; also to blame, though innocent of McCarthy's "crimes," are those "good" people who fail to perceive that the light requires active defense, who held that "[t]he doing of anything led to action, all action was blended with evil, but one could *be* good, one could only be good, by sitting on one's hands. Otherwise they would get bloodied in an earthly, temporal fight of some sort. Settling nothing. For what was ever settled here on earth?" (300). When Foley sees the "Devil's . . . leering smile of good fellowship" reflected back to him, he realizes that he, too, had been ineffectual. Described as "not committed. A state of mind that came to him naturally" (82), Foley is the first of Morris's bachelor protagonists. (Others include Howe of *Cause for Wonder*, Hodler of *In Orbit*, and Cowie of *One Day*.)

Noting the "steady erosion of the liberal mind" (290–91), Foley examines the inappropriate conduct that unknowingly aided McCarthy in his ascension to power. He probes his own models: Lawrence, who struggled for personal "perfection"; Proctor, who pursued makeshift causes; Lou Baker, the rejected lover who, like Foley, had tried to keep the record straight by writing it out; and another who is simply reduced to puerile gestures and the occasional *bon mot*. Significantly, Foley himself is not let off the hook. He sees himself as having whiled away his time in the ivory tower, preaching his "Mystical Law." He too had been sitting on his hands.

This discovery is given to him concretely when he recalls his physical examination at the induction center and his realization that his carefully prepared pacifist statement has little to do with the realities before his eyes. Ironically, the "man in charge" was unavailable, and Foley was declared 4-F before he could present his statement. The greatest revelation was his realization that his pacifism has been structured on a basis of ignorance of the human condition at large—embodied for him in the "several hundred [naked men] piled together, their pitiful drapery over one arm, herded like whores from one checkup to another one." When he left the induction center, he knew he had failed the army, but that he had passed "with flying colors, through the gates of hell" (294).

Morris links the McCarthy hearings to consumerism and "the heavenly Bazaar of America." Foley watches a father playing with his child, "in his kitchy-kitchy-kitchy, well-advertised concern and security for loved ones, long vacations with pay, carefree old age in ranch-style home, stone's throw from the ocean, cool, tangy breeze stirring flowers along the pickets, flaps on beach umbrella thrown up in the yard shading everfair bride from Time's cruel onslaughts. . . . In neat two-car garage, oiling the power mower, friendly head of house smoking his Kaywoodie pipe as up the driveway comes smiling mailman with Rock of Ages monthly insurance check" (187–88). For Morris such sentimentalism (derived from Norman Rockwell) is linked to acquiescence to McCarthy's attack on principles: both are perversions of the American Dream.

The Huge Season is in many ways an odd novel for Morris to have written, one that promises considerably more than his later emphasis on transformation of consciousness would allow. No doubt hatred of McCarthy's reign led Morris to these gestures, but he neglects to demonstrate *how* Foley will be able to convert his new understandings into actions. The novel closes with Foley's future uncertain, with the vague promise he will find the means to meet McCarthy on his own terms—for he knows he too is liable to questioning by McCarthy's committee. Foley concludes: "Destination unknown, resolution uncertain, purpose unclear, source undetermined, but a slit in the darkness where the eye of the chipmunk might peer out" (303).

The chipmunk to which Foley refers plays a minor but important role in the novel as a symbol of nature's revivifying powers, a sign that "Mother Nature was originating again." The chipmunk had been observed again and again by Foley—as in real life it had been observed by Morris and Loren Eiseley—as it actually danced, showing an intelligence beyond the powers of a typical animal. Foley, after observing the chipmunk, had gone to Darwin and spent time "brooding on a creative evolution of his own." It is not much to pin hope on, but Morris makes much of it: "If what Nature had in mind was survival, Man had ceased to be at the heart of Nature and had gone off on a suicidal impulse of his own. And Foley's chipmunk, among others, had got wind of it" (167–68). If men are suicidal, and if the chipmunk surpasses its normal nature, then the thing to do is to imitate the chipmunk—by surpassing one's own limited self. But this conclusion is too tenuous: The chipmunk appears to be something of a *deus ex machina*, smuggled in to shore up Foley's newfound, but fragile, determination.

Despite its weak conclusion, however, *The Huge Season* succeeds in its juxtaposition of two time periods and in its analysis of changes in consciousness from one generation to the next. This analysis is effected through Morris's observations of cultural conflict and the sense of loss felt when fine sentiments once having value are carelessly discarded. Foley's dilemma and the way he comes to an understanding of what has ailed him illustrate that a fine intelligence is required to deal with social malaise. The first requirement is a chastened and clear consciousness of one's own connection to essential issues.

Chapter Five

"Touching Bottom": Responsibility, Transformation, and "The Wisdom of the Body," 1955–1963

Much of Morris's best writing, including *The Field of Vision* and *Ceremony in Lone Tree*, comes from Morris at midlife, when he contemplated with renewed energies the workings of human consciousness and possibilities for effecting significant change. What made this time so productive was Morris's merging of consciousness, action, and a rationale grounded in the American literary past—as detailed in *The Territory Ahead*. In his fiction he worked out an imaginative theory of *transformation* of consciousness, based on biological evolution. Having pondered his umbilical relation to the Plains in earlier works, Morris was ready to use Nebraska as a *conceptual* setting.

In *The Huge Season* he had reconsidered his own criticisms of American life and contemplated possibilities for effective action—before finally leaving solutions to the reader. Foley's "Mystical Law" needed the validation of a theory capable of linking criticism to action. Morris's new satire was directed at a culture obsessed with youthfulness, with desire to overcome death through life insurance, and with the "harnessing" of nature in the creation of the bomb. In an essay entitled "Man on the Moon," Morris contemplated the grim irony of constructing "weatherproof" and "secure" fallout shelters for atomic war "survival," an irony much on his mind during this period.[1]

As G. B. Crump has shown, stressing immanence as the opposing pole to Booth's transcendence, Morris is indebted to D. H. Lawrence's "blood consciousness" (and Bergson's élan vital) in his major work. *The Territory Ahead* is obviously Laurentian, but it is balanced by Morris's interest in the very rational Henry James. The connecting link between Lawrence and James is supplied by the scientist Sir Charles Sherrington and his *Man on His Nature*, a book Morris's friend Eiseley might have been pondering. Sherrington provided Morris with the term—and the reasoning behind—"the wisdom of the body," as well as "a beautiful paradigm of the mind of Henry James," found in Sherrington's metaphorical description of the waking brain.[2]

The thesis of *The Territory Ahead*, Morris explained, was pertinent to his own experience of evolving consciousness. In his early life, he "had led, or rather been led by, half a dozen separate lives. . . . the only connecting tissue being the narrow thread of my *self*." In short, there was "[t]oo much crude ore. The hopper of my green and untrained imagination was both nourished and handicapped by it" (*TA*, 15). This led him ultimately to the realization that he would have to create his own order, establish his own identity, by a process of the imagination that was occasionally thwarted by lapses in memory. The refinement of this process, Morris implies, is evidence for his own purposes as a novelist. Through Sherrington, then through the creation of Leopold Lehmann, Morris linked himself to Henry James, "the most fully conscious mind and talent of the century" (*TA*, 189).

The Field of Vision

The character Gordon Boyd came into existence when Morris, with his third Guggenheim, traveled to Mexico to work on his next novel, having in mind a critique of American middle-class conformity. Mexico was ideal, providing rich contrasts with American life—so rich, in fact, that "the folly of capturing my complex impressions kept me from using the camera I had brought along."[3] Photography, however, found its way as allusion and image into the new novel and may have contributed its key metaphor, the "golden eye" of the Mexico City bullfight arena as both a lens to focus on the "field" of consciousness and a mirror to reflect "every gaze that was directed towards it."[4]

The Field of Vision is Morris's most difficult novel, weaving the lives of many characters into several thematic strands. The characters focus visually on the events at the center of the arena in which the matador and the bull are the predominant facts, but what they see are their own memories, desires, and fears. As Boyd says, "forty thousand pairs of eyes would gaze down on forty thousand separate bullfights, seeing it all very clearly, missing only the one that was said to take place" (59). This relativity of vision creates complexity, because Morris's multiple viewpoint *style indirect libre* technique makes it difficult to isolate a controlling authorial voice. It is necessary to puzzle out Morris's meaning from the sometimes conflicting reflections of the separate characters.

The novel explores the consciousnesses of seven characters, two of whom have no speaking parts. Five of these are Nebraskans: Walter and Lois McKee, Tom Scanlon (Lois's father), Gordon (the McKees' grandson), and Gordon Boyd (McKee's boyhood friend, who 30 years before had kissed McKee's fiancée, Lois, before McKee had kissed her himself). The McKees, Scanlon, and young Gordon had driven down to Mexico City for a vacation, where they had accidentally run into Boyd, who was visiting Mexico with the "psychiatrist" Leopold Lehmann and his psychotic patient, Paula Kahler. They arranged to attend a bullfight together, and most of the present action of the novel takes place in the stadium.

Morris makes the characters' spatial positions in the arena explicit; they are seated from left to right as follows:

| Walter | Lois | Leopold | Paula | Tom | Young | Gordon |
| McKee | McKee | Lehmann | Kahler | Scanlon | Gordon | Boyd |

Walter and Lois McKee, representing stifled consciousness and middle-class conformity, sit in opposition to the Tom Scanlon–young Gordon–Gordon Boyd triangle. Lois McKee appears to suffer from repression; her eyes have "the focus set, as it was in Lehmann's box camera, so that all the objects in the picture were relatively sharp. Or blurred. The selection was the work of another department. A hopper into which everything was thrown, but little came out" (76). Her fixed attitudes relate to her panic when confronted by Boyd as a sexual force 30 years before. She was not *supposed* to have been aroused by his impulsive kiss, but she was, and because Boyd's "wild streak" scared her, she married McKee.

The McKees are responsible for their grandson, young Gordon, but during the long drive, Scanlon had taken the boy in tow. Scanlon, who rejects the present by identifying with his father's heroic past, seeks to give young Gordon a myth to match the Davy Crockett coonskin hat the boy wears on his head. The old man, who "had frozen up the moment the boy began to talk to Boyd" (33), seems to recognize Boyd as his natural enemy. Although McKee is given the framework chapters, the protagonist is Boyd, whose youthful promise has been blighted by adult failures. Alienated from society, Boyd nevertheless seeks to escape solipsism by "touching bottom" through a meaningful *social* act. The plot concerns Boyd's struggle to influence the future through young Gordon. Boyd wants to bestow on the boy something more substantial than Scanlon's beguiling stories of the heroic past.

Young Gordon is subject to potential choice among the McKees' bland middle-class world, Scanlon's heroic past, and Boyd's "wild streak." Placing this choice into perspective are Leopold Lehmann and his patient, Paula Kahler, who sit *between* the present-minded McKees and the Scanlon-Gordon-Boyd representation of struggle between past and future. Two characters have no speaking parts, Paula Kahler because she *is* speechless, young Gordon because he is open potential to *become*.

The most "conscious" of the characters is Leopold Lehmann, the "therapist." Lehmann, presented auspiciously as a product of evolution, with "pronounced Neanderthal connections" (65), is a cosmic observer who conducts a philosophical speculation on consciousness and provides perspective on Boyd's impulsiveness. Morris's exalted opinion of him may be deduced from Lehmann's Weimar origin and his echo of Goethe's final cry for "*Mehr licht.*" Lehmann's primary patient, Paula Kahler, is, like Scanlon, a negative example, but whereas Scanlon has willed himself into an ossified past, Paula has willfully changed into something wholly new.

The Field of Vision is intentionally set in Mexico, where the ritual of the bullfight, with its primordial remnants of vital heroism, is still available. Boyd, a failed artist, seeks a means to reinstitute heroism in a world that no longer honors it, that exploits it for consumerist profit (he derides the notion that value can be determined by how much something costs). Scanlon's world of necessary heroism is dead, no matter how much he insists on reliving it, and according to Boyd, since the end of the frontier, American culture has been rendered *safe* in its drive for security; he is critical of American efforts to neutralize risk. Wanting to revitalize the heroic, Boyd muses on his own position: "Profession? Hero. Situation? Unemployed" (101).

In attempting to influence young Gordon, Boyd falls back on shenanigans. First he squirts soda pop at the bull, then he has the matador momentarily wear the boy's hat, making the *hat* heroic. But Boyd understands the distinction between *observing* and *performing* a daring act. Remembering a boyhood experience, when at a baseball game he had chased Ty Cobb and managed to rip a pocket from his uniform, Boyd decides to throw Gordon's coonskin hat into the arena, then send the boy to retrieve it. The whole novel may be read as a rationalization for this superficially puerile act. By throwing Gordon's hat into the ring and helping him over the fence, he means to free the boy from both cultural sterility and mythic nostalgia—to give him an experience of use in shaping his future.

That Boyd's act *appears* trivial is no argument against its significance. There is no guarantee that his small triumph or young Gordon's audacity will be efficacious for all time; as Boyd knows, a life of continuous transformations is necessary if meaning is to be sustained. By the end of the novel, however, McKee and Scanlon realize something significant has taken place. McKee hopes the events in the ring "might pass off like most of the things on a boy's mind" (249), but when he hears Gordon yelling, he knows a change has occurred: "McKee could tell you, even though he couldn't hear it, just what it was that boy was yelling, and that it wasn't for a bull, a bull's horns, or anything like that. . . . He was yelling for something, McKee could tell you, that he couldn't buy even if he had the money" (251). When McKee tells Gordon, "trying an old tack," to bring Scanlon along with him back to the car, "The old man popped up, like he'd heard that, and went along the rail by himself. It wasn't like him to move a foot without the boy, and McKee wondered if that was more of Boyd's doing" (244).

Earlier Boyd, seeing Gordon falling under Scanlon's spell, had determined to provide the boy with the prerequisite awareness to use his imagination in the interests of freedom. Boyd wonders what the boy understands:

> He was now a jigsaw [puzzle] loose in its box, the bullfight one of the scarlet pieces, but he would not know its meaning until the pattern itself appeared. And that he would not *find*. . . . The pattern—what pattern it had—he would have to create. . . . First, he would have to sense that parts were missing. . . . It called for transformation. Out of so many given things, one thing that hadn't been given. His own life. An endless sequence of changes, a tireless shifting of the pieces, selecting some, discarding others, until the pattern—the imagined thing—began to emerge. (154–55)

What Boyd sees as essential for Gordon is a creativity paralleling Morris's own, of learning to process "fragments" of experience through "an imaginative act of apprehension" (*TA*, 15).

The crucial philosophical support for this transformation of consciousness is provided by Leopold Lehmann as the psychiatrist of Paula Kahler and, more recently, of Boyd. Boyd had first turned to Lehmann when he understood that his will to failure was simply a perversion of the American success myth. As Lehmann had explained, as a therapist "he knew nothing of the body, little of the mind, but . . . he had an arrangement of sorts with the soul" (66). Instead of determinisms, Lehmann asserts a condition common to *all* humans, one central to all the mind's transactions between desire and reality. This condition is human frailty: *Help* is "a need shared by all men. No one was spared, no one was saved, none had a corner or a concrete shelter where the need of HELP would not one day raise its head. Each according to his nature—no matter what his nature—needed help" (202).

Lehmann's argument for transformation is linked dramatically to his relationship with Paula Kahler. Lehmann had taken her case after Paula, a chambermaid in a hotel, had murdered an "amorous bellhop" (74). When it was discovered that "Mrs. Kahler, as she was known, was not a *Mrs.* at all. She was a man, physically normal in every respect," Lehmann took her on, not merely as a patient, but as his "practice" (68). In time, he tracked her identity to a missing person once known as *Paul* Kahler at the Larrabee YMCA in Chicago. Lehmann traveled immediately to Chicago, where the train dropped him off "in the heart of the labyrinth." What he discovers about Paula Kahler is not wholly satisfactory, for Paul's motives in becoming Paula are ambiguous. Paul, as described by Shults at the YMCA, was a "saint" who influenced others to believe that everything had a purpose: The right thing was to act according to nature. Through Paul other lives are modified; his own nature prods them to sympathy (162–66).

The world, however, corrupts ideals. Paul had disappeared after his dead father's amputated hand showed up in an anatomy student's lunch pail. This incident is important, for it precipitates Paul's disappearance (and his reappearance as Paula); it is given as the cause for Paul's transformation from male to female. A purely psychological motive, however, is denied readers; Lehmann's ambiguous discussion with Shults pertaining to the change in Paul/Paula has to do with the nature of good and evil, not with psychological causation. Lehmann views Paul's transformation into Paula as *beyond* good and evil, much like the impersonal workings of nature.

Paula's refusal to recognize the male elements in her nature causes her to cry out in her sleep, indicating that her willed solipsism is existentially problematic. Nevertheless, Lehmann offers her to Boyd as an example of a "successful failure." Lehmann's purpose is to have Boyd use his talents to record and interpret Paula's transformation in his own "cure." "The words that Paula Kahler had made into flesh . . . called for a further transformation, back into words again" (72). Paula Kahler is psychotic, yet she continues to influence others, just as Paul had done at the Larrabee YMCA. Morris takes great pains to show this influence when Lehmann journeys to Chicago and enters "the labyrinth." Prior to visiting Shults, who will explain Paul Kahler's identity to him, Lehmann rents a room at a hotel—and there experiences one of those rituals by which Morris prepares characters for transformation. This particular ritual is elaborate, in several stages. When Lehmann enters the room, readers are pointedly told, "a warning bell on a drawbridge began to clang. Lehmann watched the shadow of the bridge, like a hand, move on the yellow blinds." In a moment, "[h]e could feel the building tremble, as if with rage, when a street car passed" (118–19).

Lying on the bed, Lehmann sees a calendar picturing "[a] red-cheeked child tirelessly licked by a long-haired dog. In the sky an airplane, symbol of his future, in the background a mother, symbol of his past, but in the eternal present he would go on being licked by his faithful dog" (119–20). Lehmann is moved to a meditation on the meaning of time:

> It struck Lehmann—it struck the person, that is, that he seemed to be at that particular moment—as if he had rented this room in a time capsule. Time—of the other variety—seemed to have stopped. Lehmann had been stored away, forever, with this small piece of it. A cord lumpy with flies, a bed that sang like a harp, a basin in the corner that smelled of urine, and a calendar dated May, 1931. These things, that is to say, were the eternal ones. . . . The changeless dreams of love and affection, licked forever the changeless face of the young, in which the changing past and future were always the same. In the dream, that is, began the irresponsibility. The sleeper awake, the shadow on the blind, the fly-clotted cord, and the drip in the basin that signified life, death and erosion in the mind. What one would find, that is, at the heart of the labyrinth. A hotel room, a guest for the night, the gift Bible with the red-stained leaves, and the figure in the carpet long ago worn into the cracks in the floor. The bed itself lipped with a spout, as if to pour out the sleeper, and the door with hooks on which to hang the empty days, the sleepless nights. And at the heart of this capsule was Leopold Lehmann, timeless man. (120)

Lehmann assumes Morris's burden of coming to grips with the "timeless" nature of reality: The objects, described with photographic preci-

sion, are both relevant to human use and representative of pure being—
like the objects in Morris's photographs.

At this moment Lehmann is "timeless man" seeking eternal truths,
one of which is the realization that life (including human life) needs the
support of pity—as shown in a scene involving a common fly. As
Lehmann lies on the bed, a fly falls onto his chest; he refrains from
killing it when he remembers how Paula had revived a "dead" fly with
salt and sunlight. Through Paula, Lehmann connects the fly explicitly to
human life, allowing it to live because it is "[a]s helpless, there on his
shirt front, as man himself" (122–23). These incidents move Lehmann
inexorably toward the revelation of Paula Kahler's identity. In the room
Lehmann mystically identifies with her and is conditioned for his final
movement to the "heart of the labyrinth." When he descends into the
street to meet Shults, he is prepared to see Paula's transformation as
beyond rationality. Just as her transformation is neither good nor evil,
his understanding of it must be neutral.

Lehmann's comprehension of the larger meaning of Paula's transformation is made manifest in his final section, in his meditation on consciousness. Here Morris's debt to Sherrington is most apparent, for the
quotation from Sherrington he had used in *The Territory Ahead* is now
clearly worked into *The Field of Vision.* Lehmann recalls how he and
Boyd had come out of the mountains to see an array of lights spread out
below them. "You ever see a sight like that?" Boyd asks. Lehmann says
no, but then he remembers:

> Not spread out in a valley like that, but trapped in his own head. The
> spectacle of the goings-on in his own mind. A labyrinth of lights, perhaps
> millions of them, so that it beggared any description, flickering with the
> current of every sensation, the pulse of every thought. A milky way in a
> rhythmic, cosmic dance, evolving and dissolving, assembling and dissem-
> bling, a loom of light where each impulse left its mark, each thought its
> ornament, each sentiment its motif in the design. . . . A mind that went
> back, that is, to the beginning, that in order to think had to begin at the
> beginning, since every living cell did what it had once done, and nothing
> more. It was *there*, then the word came, and it multiplied. In this manner
> the juices percolating in Lehmann, in the mind loaned to him that he
> tried to look after, had the same bit of froth on it that flecked the primor-
> dial ooze. So long as he lived and breathed he was connected, in a jeweled
> chain of being, with that first cell, and the inscrutable impulse it seemed
> to feel to multiply. On orders. Always on orders from below, or from
> above. The final cause erected the scaffold, ran the tubing up through

the framework, then called a halt when something like Lehmann finally emerged. (203–4)

This "labyrinth of lights," this "milky way" of a "cosmic dance," is borrowed directly from Sherrington's description of the waking brain that Morris connected to Henry James (*TA*, 103–4).[5]

But it is more than a matter of simply borrowing Sherrington's language. The assumptions underlying this passage—and many of Lehmann's poetic musings—benefit from Morris's reading of Sherrington. When Morris writes that Lehmann's is a "mind that went back . . . to the beginning, since every living cell did what it had once done, and nothing more," he echoes Sherrington's description of the formation of the human eye and the final cause that "motivates" each cell as its development takes place in the organization of a complex structure. According to Sherrington, "It is as if an immanent principle inspired each cell with knowledge for the carrying out of a design" (Sherrington, 94).

Armed with this view, Morris has Lehmann continue his thinking on the mystery of the mind and its relations, beginning with the brain:

> The *thinking* organ? So one would suppose. But if that pipe line to the lower quarters was broken, if the cables with the wiring were severed, *all* thinking ceased. Everything was there as before, but nothing came out of it. Some connection with the *first* cell had been destroyed, the cable that carried the protozoic orders, the word from the past, and without this word there was no mind. It seemed to be that simple. . . . There had to be connections, the impulse had to ooze its way through light years of wiring, *against* the current, since the current determined the direction. . . . In Leopold Lehmann the inscrutable impulse was reaching for the light. As it was in Paula Kahler. . . . But the thrust, even in reaching for the light, must come from behind. Out of the shoulders of the bull, on the horns of this dilemma, against the current that must always determine his direction, in reaching for more light man would have to risk such light as he had. It was why he needed help. It was why he had emerged as man. It was according to his nature that he was obliged to exceed himself. (204–5)

Here, then, Morris employs "the wisdom of the body" and builds his case. The cells making up the body are related to the mysterious functionings of the mind; mind is contingent upon body and the material factors conditioning it.

Consciousness is always potential in Morris's writing, depending on the needs of the particular human mind and on that "thrust from behind" that impels the individual to overcome habits and comforts that are self-imposed obstacles to change. The capacity for change is in everyone, but not everyone is similarly motivated. When Boyd protests that things are seldom as they seem, Lehmann responds:

> They were meant to seem different—each according to the nature that was capable of seeing, behind the spectacle of lights, the constellation in his own roof brain. The universe in the process of being made. . . . Here and there in the mind's sky, without warning, exploding nova like Paula Kahler, lighting up the far reaches, the space curve ahead, the spine curve behind. Emerging and dissolving patterns of meaning, seeding the world's body with cosmic rays that each according to his nature would absorb, resist, or lightly dust off. Each according to his lights, such as they were, if and when they came on. (205–6)

As for Lehmann, his last words in the book are *"Mehr licht,"* his own response to the cries of the watchers in the arena who, observing bonfires lighting up the dusk, shout "Luz!" and "Light! More light!" Receiving the light, "they stood and cheered for themselves, as if their yelling had brought it about" (206).

All of this metaphysical thinking has immediate bearing on Boyd. Boyd's perception that "[e]xcept for the still point there would be no dance" argues for a dynamic relationship between reflection and action. What is important for Boyd is the art by which the matador dominates the bull, his ability to control his impulse to move. But the "still point" does not last. No matter how much Boyd may cry out *"Slow it up"*—"it" being the action in the ring and the reflections it precipitates—return must be made to life, language, activities performed *within* time. "So many words," Boyd thinks wearily. Immediately afterward, however, he exonerates language: "But words had brought them together, and words indicated what had happened. Words wheeling around the still point, the dance, the way the bull wheeled around the bullfighter, the way the mind wheeled around the still point on the sand" (192–93). Making use of the ceremony in the ring, Boyd gives Gordon a new experience, a wordless ritual that nevertheless requires words to explain it. In so doing, he defeats Scanlon, who has only words and nothing more to offer. Scanlon's myth can no longer be *embodied*.

The lesson is clear: Boyd offers the boy a dose of heroic consciousness by giving him an active ritual rather than a dead myth. The boy attains a "wisdom of the body" that *may* help him overcome both the lure of nostalgia and the cultural repressions of the present and future. This elaborate rationale for Boyd's intervention in Gordon's life—his life-enhancing gift of "the thrust from behind"—is the crucial point of *The Field of Vision*.

Love Among the Cannibals

Morris's indebtedness to Sherrington continues in *Love among the Cannibals* (and in two other comedies discussed later in this chapter), a comic cultural critique linking "the wisdom of the body" to American "non-consciousness." Immediately following *The Field of Vision*, it was Morris's first attempt "to stand in the shifting and treacherous sands of the present, instead of fleeing into the past or the future,"[6] and it is therefore concerned with the immediate present." Morris's interest throughout is the nature of experience as cliché: he examines a natural means to transform the clichés of everyday life. The narrator, Earl Horter, and his partner, Irwin K. Macgregor, are "the poor man's Rodgers & Hart,"[7] who compose popular songs replete with clichés.

The novel's central metaphor is the elimination or stripping away of inessentials, a process echoed in the cannibalistic love relationship between Horter and Eva (the Greek) Baum, the ubiquitous roosting vultures, and the stripping of Horter's Hollywood studio car after it is ditched in Mexico. This last process not only provides the novel with much of its humor, but it reinforces the virtues of cannibalism as a mode of human conduct. The abandoned car is gradually dismantled (even as the Americans watch) by the Mexicans, and piece by piece it is carried off into the city and reassembled, leaving off "the little inessentials" unnecessary to its primary function. The point of the novel's treatment of process and repossession is made clear at the end when Horter tosses the Mexicans the keys. "I could see that it was their car now, rather than mine," Horter says. "Essential to them, but inessential to me, now, were the keys" (252).

In a similar manner, Horter is himself stripped down to essentials, a process carried on, with Horter's approval, through the agency of Eva Baum, a young woman with whom Horter becomes infatuated and whose existential philosophy is that "[t]he mind is in the body" (80). The crucial fact about Eva is that she is, explicitly, in "development." Having been revived from the dead at age 15, she views her life as a gift, and she gives of it freely; the only stipulation is that she be allowed to follow the course of her development, wherever that might lead. In the context of the novel, she is a life force and a bringer of light. Morris strengthens his case for Eva by directly contrasting her with Billie Harcum, a woman who reads Norman Vincent Peale and employs a calculative innocence to lure Horter's partner, Mac, into the bonds of matrimony.

The picture that Horter snaps of the couple at their wedding indicates his conception of the "phony" nature of that relationship:

> What I saw there altered my feelings—the way an assassin's might be altered—after he has pulled the trigger, and he sees what he has done. Had I got my man? No, he had escaped. The man I had shot was some sort of nameless stand-in for him. The man I wanted—Irwin K. Macgregor, first-class slob and second-class song writer—slipped out of focus when I pulled the trigger, when the shutter snapped. In his place, in his pitiful shoes, I had caught Adam Macgregor, most pitifully nude, with his ever-fair Eve green and swollen with the apple she had picked, but did not eat. Stand-ins, perhaps, but not people, figures in a frieze symbolizing the eternal bride, the eternal groom, and the eternal deception they played on one another—being true to one another in order to be false to everything else. (218–19)

Almost immediately after the wedding, Billie slips off her role as coy sweetheart and reveals her ambitions, informing Horter that she and Mac are turning over a new leaf: no more waiting for inspiration on the beach. In her Southern voice she tells Horter that "the beach is no place to wuk. It saps a puson's strength an I doan know what-all. We plan to wuk heah in the mohnin' and maybe take a li'l dip in the aftahnoon." Horter observes "Mac's head drop about an inch between his shoulders. He was squatted on the chopping block, head bowed, and I remembered that scene on the ground glass of the camera I had shot him once. I didn't have the heart to shoot him again" (232). He notes ironically that the tune Mac played on the piano the morning after the wedding was "Love for Sale" (230).

In contrast to Mac, Horter is not fooled by clichés, even though his livelihood relies on his skill in incorporating them into his lyrics. Horter is able to recognize the "real thing" ("roughly it's what Charlie Chaplin found, beginning with Paulette Goddard" [22]) when he first sets eyes on the Lachaise bronze-Madonna figure of Eva Baum; later, he is able to accept his emotionally risky role in her development because he knows, despite his desire for her as a long-term sexual partner, that she has something to offer beyond clichés. His indebtedness to her, even when he knows he is losing her, is expressed in the language of the book's title:

"I didn't know when I bolted with you that it was not to sleep with you in a warmer climate, but to love you in a language we could both understand. Earl Horter, the master of the cliché, did not say to you what he thought he was feeling, since he hardly knew, without the clichés, what it was he felt. If he talked about love in the language he knew, he cheated himself. He had to learn about loving and talking from scratch, and he saw that the first thing the lover destroyed was the mind in his body, since it had nothing to do with his body of clichés. The body was cannibal, the clichés were vegetable. Love among the vegetarians, that is, was verbal—it was made with participles, unmade with verbs, honored, cherished, and disobeyed with nouns. But love among the cannibals is flesh feeding on flesh. I've been living on your lips, the strings of your eyes, and you've been living on my heart, my lungs, and my liver. Essentials. The fatty inessentials cut away. If and when you get around to the hollow of my skull, I'll serve it up. If anybody asks us if these bones live . . . we can say yes, thanks to the essentials, thanks to the essential business of love. Such is the love song, Greek, of Earl Horter to his cannibelle."
(227–28)

Presented as a model of "essential" behavior, Eva teaches Horter something new about life. Bereft of her body and her physical presence at the end of the novel, Horter retains the impersonal gift of her being, a gift he has already put into practice in his own self-transformation.

The strength of her essential nature is manifested in her visit to the *Sea Beast*, a laboratory boat operated by Dr. Leggett, a marine biologist. When Eva swims to the boat, Leggett helps her from the water in much the same way he draws "primeval ooze" from the sea: "He was always turning up something unheard-of in the sea, and now he'd turned up this" (204). Morris carefully draws the parallel between the "primeval ooze" and Eva's "development." The ooze has the property of matter, having, in Sherrington's phrase, "the urge-to-live," in evolutionary formation; but Eva, nature made self-conscious, is capable of converting the "urge-to-live" into another of Sherrington's terms, "the zest-to-live" (Sherrington, 170–71). As for Horter, when later he sees the "sea-ooze sources of life" in a bottle, he understands the relationship of the ooze to Eva; noting Eva's hand in Leggett's, he thinks, "But what was it that disturbed the primeval ooze, what was it that got it to oozing, that is, if it was not a pair of deep-sea hands meeting like that? One platonic, the other pulsing with the juices of life. When I peered into that jar on the table, green and fermenting, what I saw was myself. If my sap was drained into such a bottle, it would look like that. Behave like that. And if the Greek's hands were then cupped around it, it would ooze life." Horter recognizes that the forces churning in Eva are as disinterested as the sea-ooze—and as potentially transformative; she too is "[a] solution of animal, vegetable, and mineral, in the process of becoming something else." Leggett's sea-ooze merely excites her to a further stage of her development (205 – 6).

Love Among the Cannibals, then, has as its chief trope the development by which, through embodiment in impersonal natural processes, life overcomes cliché and opens to cosmic consciousness. Morris is not opposed in principle to the ties that bind (although the book may be read as pertinent to his own collapsing marriage), but he wanted to explore the sexual ramifications of the "wisdom of the body." He called on Lehmann's musings on the nature of mind and evolution; in *Love Among the Cannibals* the electrical imagery of the current is reinforced with the organic notion of "ooze," which, like electricity, transmits energy. Lighter than *The Field of Vision*, *Love Among the Cannibals* makes quite as much use of Sherrington's assumptions about the relation between the evolved body and the transmission of vital energies.

Ceremony in Lone Tree

Whereas *The Field of Vision* is Morris's most conceptually complex novel, its "sequel," *Ceremony in Lone Tree*, is the most refined in dealing with the Nebraska milieu, an inquiry into Scanlon's myth of the heroic West carried into the midcentury present. It is arguably Morris's most "typical" book, bringing all his central themes together into one brilliantly realized and accessible novel. It is a complex portrait of Midwestern-Western life, carried on amidst—and deeply affected by—increasing evidence of social disorder and its effects on American consciousness. The most obvious signs of this disorder are the violence represented by the atomic bomb tests in Nevada and the murders providing the backgrounds to this novel.

The bomb and other forms of violence are ubiquitous in *Ceremony in Lone Tree*, linked to the ways the bomb culture and excessive security-consciousness threaten personal identity. Of major importance throughout is Charlie Munger (founded on mass-murderer Charles Starkweather, who in 1958 crossed Nebraska, choosing and killing his 10 victims indiscriminately). When Munger is captured, he gives as his motive that "he wanted to be somebody." Even though by the time of the "ceremony" he is safely in jail, Munger haunts the novel, continuing to give everyone "the jitters." Lee Roy Momeyer (who had worked with Munger and picked up some of his mannerisms), brings violence even closer to home. He runs down and kills, with his car, two of his peers who have been badgering him, explaining that "he just got tired of being pushed around."[8] Most people do not go to the extremes of Lee Roy or Munger, but the frustrations of the times breed, in Jonathan Baumbach's phrase, "violent atavistic preoccupations"; violence becomes "an assertion of identity, of being, the agonized death throes of life on the verge of extinction."[9]

Given Morris's views, expressed in *The Field of Vision*, that life without risk is meaningless and antiheroic, proof of loss of individuality, something might be said for *fear of* violence as a potential means of transformation. Morris said Starkweather had been a revelation to him—and it explains why *Ceremony in Lone Tree* focused so directly on violence in American culture: "Wasn't this America? Didn't everything happen for the best? To move from this state of ignorance to that state of disorder revealed by Charles Starkweather has been the mind-quaking move of my generation. Violence can be a life-enhancing release."[10]

As is often the case in Morris's sequels, *Ceremony in Lone Tree* deliberately questions the conclusions Morris had drawn in *The Field of Vision*. "[T]he comic despair of [Morris's] nihilistic vision" (Baumbach, 169) should be qualified by the suggestion that even as *Ceremony in Lone Tree* is a novel about threats to the American Dream, Morris shows the effects of violence on ordinary people who must cope according to their abilities; for that reason the novel evinces considerable empathy despite its satirical edge. In some ways, the novel is a defense of the myth-making imagination Morris had earlier criticized in Scanlon. If Starkweather and the bomb represent the quality of life in the future, then return to myth may be a desirable alternative—surely one way to account for the moonlight that Morris floods throughout this novel. If the American Dream is in disarray, the moonlight emphasizes the continuing dreams of human beings who must make do.

Ceremony in Lone Tree takes place several months after *The Field of Vision*, and carries the core of its cast from Mexico City back to Morris's haunted Nebraska. The novel is narrated through the largest cast in all of Morris's works. In addition to an omniscient narrator there are nine speaking parts: McKee, Lois McKee, Scanlon, Boyd, and young Gordon are carried over from *The Field of Vision*; additional characters from the Scanlon family are Maxine (Scanlon's daughter), Bud (Maxine's husband), and Etoile (their daughter); Edna (another of Scanlon's daughters) and Colonel Clyde Ewing (Edna's husband); Calvin (the McKees' grandson, young Gordon's older brother); Eileen McKee (Calvin's and Gordon's mother); and Lee Roy Momeyer (Bud's nephew).

Two other important characters are "Daughter," the young woman Boyd picks up in Nevada; and W. B. Jennings, the son of Will Brady (from *The Works of Love*), who travels to Lone Tree uninvited, apparently to get the story of Scanlon's life—more important, to inquire into the relations between his own life and the "ceremony" in Lone Tree. On the train, he sees a typical Nebraska windmill and recalls how, from one such windmill

> the man Jennings would have called Grandfather had hung head down, swinging on a length of baling wire. Had he leaped or fallen? Had he, too, dreamed of Santa Claus? What led a boy, born and raised in this soddy, to roll down the plain like a pebble to where men were paid to be Santa Claus? And another, a few years later, to leave at home his well-thumbed Bible; and another to take up his gun like Billy the Kid? In some way left to Jennings to discover, these lives seemed to be related, not merely to each other but to the man on the platform of the caboose. Local boys. Local boys who made—or unmade—good. (137)

Jennings wants to connect the disjointed elements composing mid-century life in Nebraska—and by extension, America. Although he is a taciturn man, he provides an aura of brooding that shores up the thematic elements and provides unity.

The novel has three parts. "The Scene," narrated omnisciently, opens dramatically: "Come to the window," readers are told, subtly urged to consider Matthew Arnold's injunction in "Dover Beach" to "be true to one another" in the face of cultural corrosion. This section introduces the characters, describes the setting, and places Scanlon at the window of the Lone Tree Hotel, peering at the mythic West through a flaw in the glass upon a scene that offers "no place to hide" and so encourages the imagination. "Scanlon's eyes, a cloudy phlegm color, let in more light than they give out. What he sees are the scenic props of his own mind. . . . The emptiness of the plain generates illusions that require little moisture, and grow better, like tall stories, where the mind is dry. The tall corn may flower or burn in the wind, but the plain is a metaphysical landscape and the bumper crop is the one Scanlon sees through the flaw in the glass" (4–5).

The second section, "The Roundup," brings the characters to the rendezvous at the Lone Tree Hotel. Boyd checks into a Las Vegas motel on his way up from Mexico and is asked if he would like to be awakened for the dawn bomb test; behind his name in the register the hotel clerk, dutifully wearing her atomic fallout monitor, writes "WAKE BEFORE BOMB" (31). This expression resounds throughout, setting up the novel's core question: Is it better to be fully conscious in a culture capable of such mindlessness—or instead, following Scanlon, to refuse such madness and take refuge in nostalgia? Boyd meets an audacious young woman he calls Daughter, inviting her to accompany him to the ceremony, perhaps to shock the others. After this Morris introduces McKee, Lois, Maxine, Etoile, Calvin, Bud, Lee Roy, and Jennings.

The first two sections set the scene and raise the crucial questions. In the long third section, "The Ceremony," Morris plays out the comic actions. The ceremony has a number of meanings. First, it refers to the family reunion and birthday party being given for Scanlon, who turns 90 in the course of the book—but, to everyone's satisfaction, sleeps through the party. The practical reason for the gathering, however, is "to let the women get together and connive about Etoile's and Calvin's marriage" (51), the idea being to let nature take its course with a little prodding from the conspiring women. The "courtship," followed by the offstage wedding, is the second ceremony.

There is a third and larger ceremony, a ritualistic replay of the American Dream in its heroic frontier guise, engineered by Calvin. He and Etoile make their way down the road to a justice of the peace, but the wedding designs are less important for Calvin than is his obsession to recreate for Scanlon one of the old man's Wild West scenarios. Calvin turns off to rent two mules and a wagon, in which he and Etoile return to appear at Scanlon's window—with himself in the role of Scanlon's remembered Samuels, and Etoile, unknowingly, playing the part of Samantha, the woman of Scanlon's father's dreams. In her bedroom, Lois—for reasons unrelated to Calvin and Etoile—fires a pistol into the moonlight; below, the mules break at the sound, and Samantha-Etoile stands up in the careering wagon trying to control them; at the sound of the shot Scanlon awakens—and then drops dead. Meanwhile Bud, hunting with bow and arrow in the moonlight, has managed to slay Colonel Ewing's prize bulldog.

But there is yet another ceremony. The birthday party, the courtship of Etoile and Calvin, and the revival of a mythic Western scene are followed by the ceremony occasioned by Scanlon's death and the initial preparations for his burial. The shot, in effect, kills off the chief avatar of the Dream in its atrophied form. When Boyd finds Scanlon dead, he says simply, "It died while we slept," and "The past is dead, long live the past" (284). Readers are left with a kind of Faulknerian celebration of the simple brute facts of human endurance within the cycles of nature and the ironic daily rituals of communal life.

Boyd's question—is it better to be asleep or awake?—is essential to Morris's portrayal of human actions; the answers are deliberately ambiguous. The fears besetting many of the characters come from forces over which they have no control; these fears are the very stuff of life, and the characters' strategies in coping are dwarfed by the events that precipitate the fears in the first place. Boyd's question is mirrored by the conflict between consciousness founded on the bomb ("this flash, then this pillar of fire . . . like a rabbit's ear" [31]) and another kind that takes its cues from the surreal light of the moon, which inspires dreams and softens the cultural absurdity that takes the bomb for granted. The moonlight suggests another form of consciousness founded in the imagination.

Individual acts of violence are reflections of the amorphous violence of the times, an ingredient of consciousness as "normal" as fallout. As such, who knows where it might not erupt next? The worst form of violence, expressed through the bomb, is de-individualized, expressive of a national malaise, and in their responses to it, people feel a loss of personal significance. This loss of identity is manifested in "sick" acts by which some seek release. In his random killings, it is apparent that Munger mirrors the psychology of the bomb: His victims, too, are anonymous. Munger's response is a form of unarticulated revenge against "representative" figures of a violent culture. In contrast to Munger, Lee Roy Momeyer at least has a visible motive: He kills those who have abused him. Asked if he had lost control of the car, Lee Roy shakes his head, refusing an excuse. " 'F—k the bastards,' he had said, and that was just what he had done" (127), linking the mechanisms of destruction to sexuality.

McKee thinks of Scanlon, a man who detests the present, as energized by recent violent events. "The very thing that scared the wits out of other people had given [Scanlon] a new lease on life. Those fool pistols he had from his father, that hadn't been fired for half a century, he oiled and polished, and carried one in a holster at his hip" (49). Bud is another example, a man taken to hunting cats—and later Colonel Ewing's Shiloh. Bud listens to Etoile's impassioned outburst on the reasons Munger went berserk. "You want to know why?' she yelled. 'It's because nobody wants to know why. It's because nobody wants to know *any-thing!* Everybody hates everybody, but nobody knows why anybody gets shot. You want to know somethin'? I'd like to shoot a few dozen people myself!' " Bud thinks, "After all that had happened, it was a comfort to him to know that she was right" (117).

Calvin, too, is aroused to passionate hatreds. His stutter, Etoile tells him, is a symptom of "his silly rebellion against a world where he couldn't ride horses, shoot guns and live just as he pleased" (93)—reason enough for him to love Scanlon's West. But in his trek west in search of gold, he had seen a mechanized uranium hunter who intruded on his pleasures. "Without having seen the face of this man he hated him. If he had had his gun along he might have taken a few pot shots at him. This was his grandfather's country, . . . and it was now Calvin McKee's country, to be defended from these cheaters the way you'd scare off cattle thieves" (99).

Finally, with Lois, violence is equated with males and the males' acquiescence in disorder. If she could, she would live in a world in which people were forbidden to point anything—including young Gordon's penis as well as guns and cars. More than anyone, she has the jitters, expecting Munger (or his current stand-in) to appear at any moment; this pervasive fear is related to her sense of evil as an amorphous sexual threat. She coddles Gordon, as if to overcome the male influence in his nature (as well as Boyd's influence over the boy; in this novel she continues to bear her grudge against Boyd as *the* male who aroused her sexual passion in her youth). She fears the evil that young Gordon is learning to express: "On how many occasions, rolling his sleepy head, he had given her a bite on the breast or the lips, and at the same time such a look as the serpent must have given Adam, sucking in his lower lip as if to taste the forbidden fruit" (242).

In the end it is Lois who, aware that the terror she feels is not because "something might happen, but after waiting so long it might not" (264), seizes the pistol as an instrument capable of alleviating impotence. She fires it out the window, a shot aimed at all her frustrations— but at nothing in particular. Across the room she sees young Gordon, "eyes like lanterns," gazing at her in "fear and admiration for the first time in his life" (268). The shot, of course, wakes Scanlon up only to scare him to death. Lois's act is more potent than she imagined, but nevertheless she gives no sign of regret. The shot kills off the dead past—and frees the present for new possibilities. In these terms violence can be life-enhancing. Shortly afterward the moonlight gives way to the red morning sky and the new day, its "light spread out on the plain" (293).

McKee has the last word in the novel. With the dawn he feels a sense of release: "He was just ashamed to admit—with the old man dead—he felt so good" (293). He recognizes that "something he had taken for granted in the world was no more," that "it took something crazy, good or bad, to pull a roomful of people together" (301, 297). The ceremony in the title is also a celebration of communal revivification, and the final purpose of the rendezvous that brings this motley assembly together is a kind of obeisance to life itself. The new day spreads out before them; for the moment at least, the violence has been dispersed, as has the moon light of surreal desire, and the business of the day is about to be enacted.

The first business is to get Scanlon's body to a mortician. Colonel Ewing, who might have provided transportation in his trailer, has abandoned them in his hurry to see the insurance representative about his dead dog. Eileen's car, Morris notes, is a sports car, inappropriate for the communal activity involved in getting a corpse to coffin. That leaves nothing large enough but the wagon with the mules Calvin had brought in during the night. The body is put under the canvas, and Calvin and Jennings ride on the buckboard with McKee, Boyd, and Daughter on the tailboard. With Scanlon's head facing forward, they ride into the West in parody of the frontier myth. McKee wonders, "How the devil did men ever cross the country in a wagon like it?" (303).

As the mules plod on, McKee takes a last glance at the Lone Tree Hotel. His mind on the future—real estate values, fields of wheat replacing the wild grass—McKee has a "queer thought": "Was it the sniff of that clover and the sight of that wheat—was it this that disturbed the old man's sleep? Was it this that led him to get up and die in the night? The last man in Lone Tree didn't want to smell clover, or see the wheat wave or the corn flower, or hear that the dust had blown itself out. No, he really didn't. Did McKee?" (304). McKee does not answer, but *Morris's* answer is surely no. The American Dream, built on past promise, remains necessary, providing a "metaphysical landscape" for the imagination capable of resisting entrapment in the mythic past. McKee is already thinking ahead. "It's going to be a hot one," he says, but no one hears him, for Boyd and Daughter have fallen asleep.

Boyd's quest for conscious meaning in *The Field of Vision* has given way in *Ceremony in Lone Tree* to a sympathetic understanding of the wear and tear of everyday life. Boyd's observations on the sterility of the culture in the earlier novel led him to seek an alternative in order to salvage his life; but in *Ceremony* Boyd is "stymied," as McKee says (296), reduced almost to silence. He does flail out at McKee's stifled emotional life, but McKee is able to respond that Boyd himself has taken refuge in the past. Boyd is forced to admit the truth of Daughter's observation that *everybody* takes consolation from their pasts. "It's been a long day," she says tenderly to Boyd. "Now you come lie down" (233).

Boyd responds by telling her the story of Morgenstern and Hyman Kopfman. Together in a hospital ward, Kopfman and Morgenstern dramatize the expectations in the American Dream. Kopfman, dying, blames his problems on America. Coming from Vienna, he had believed in the American Dream—so intently that it could never deliver all it appeared to promise. When Kopfman dies, Morgenstern has a relapse and is carried off to the "hopeless" ward (253–62). The lesson is that Morgenstern, having lived off Kopfman's narrative of the Dream, now has nothing left to live for. The Dream is life-enhancing—whether or not it is true. Morris apparently has Boyd tell this story to remind readers that Boyd, too, has held fast to the Dream, despite his failure to realize it.[11] In larger terms, the Dream is so opposed to the realities that mock it that this very opposition results in frustrations leading to violent acts, some of which are life destroying, others of which may have the power to provoke constructive possibilities.

Despite such abiding violence, however, the characters who come together in Lone Tree play out roles that ultimately have communal purposes. Violence has infiltrated their lives, but unlike Munger, the Scanlon clan understand the importance of social interaction and communal forms—even as the violence has weakened familial claims. Nevertheless, some of these characters make efforts to maintain civilized social processes. McKee's belief that real estate values are indicative of progress may be derided by Boyd, but McKee is at least stable and decent—as underscored by Morris, who tells us that when the shot is fired, McKee "finds himself doing just what . . . he had been doing all his life. He was up without a thought for himself" (278). The attempt to get Calvin and Etoile married may be a desperate gambit, but it nevertheless reaffirms marriage as a communal instrument. Against the forces creating such hatreds and forms of destruction, the rendezvous provides a cohesive strength that drains off violence innocuously.

The novel succeeds in affirming communal values (with the excesses of tradition burned off through Scanlon's death). Consciousness may be threatened—it may be better to be asleep than awake—but the ambiance of moonlight keeps the forces of the imagination alive, and after the long night the new day begins, spreading light. Life as organic process continues. Its central human function is consciousness; to be conscious is to live. *That*, Morris seems to imply, is the best we can do given the debilitating conditions caused by unthinking acceptance of the bomb and fallout shelters as viable security. Morris's ironic compassion is what makes *Ceremony in Lone Tree* memorable.

What a Way to Go and *Cause for Wonder*

In the five years between *Ceremony in Lone Tree* and *One Day*, Morris wrote only two novels, perhaps because of time and energy limitations imposed by the start of his teaching career. Both *What a Way to Go* and *Cause for Wonder* are epistemological in theme, distinctively Morrisian in their interest in exploring the nature of "bodily knowledge" or of the mind as a storehouse of images and memories. Because both novels are largely set in Europe, they have little to offer by way of social criticism, and deprived of the satirical commentary on American culture that is part of Morris's signature, they are of limited interest, with little to offer that Morris had not explored more profoundly in the Lehmann–Boyd–Paula Kahler sections of *The Field of Vision*.

What a Way to Go, published five years after *Love Among the Cannibals*, continues Morris's investigations into "the wisdom of the body." The protagonist is Arnold Soby, 47-year-old professor of Classics, who embarks on a voyage to Italy and Greece to pursue researches into a project, begun long before, that he calls "The Wisdom of the Body, . . . its causes and its cure."[12] His "researches" incidentally lead him to Cynthia Pomeroy, a 17-year-old who, like Eva Baum, is in development, although her development is decidedly more dynamic: She matures from day to day in physical transformation from adolescent to woman. She is the center of attraction to a number of men on the cruise. For most of the men, she is the embodiment of an ideal: for Pignata, struggling to become another Botticelli, she is Primavera; for Hodler, she is Nausicaa; to Perkheimer, a Jewish German-baiting photographer, she is Miss Liebfraumilch.

Each of these men seeks to pin Cynthia down in his imagination, transforming her, as Soby thinks, into "a fiction, possibly a work of art, an image of the heart's desire" (137). Soby alone retains the ability to see her as she is, without the blinders of stereotype; readers are led to believe that this ability is derived from an early understanding of the impersonality of love given him, along with the scratches on his back, by Sophie Demos, his long-dead but once passionate bride of seven months. She had taught him all he really knows about Greece—and inspired in him a profound curiosity about primordial wisdom. The novel is about love in the flesh in opposition to love rationalized in mythic, aesthetic, or sentimental terms.

This love in the flesh has its culmination in Soby's sexual encounter and marriage to Cynthia. Greece, to which Soby has journeyed to uncover the secrets of Sophie Demos's impersonal passion with him, is a land of transformation—in the terms of this book a "sea change" from the exigencies of the intellect to the "perilous sweetness" of a life dominated by the body. Whereas the other men want to make Cynthia over by way of their imaginings, Soby tries to see her in essential terms: to learn the "wisdom of the body" is to come to grips with impersonality, to free oneself from interpretations founded on presuppositions. Continual references to Thomas Mann's Aschenbach, from *Death in Venice*, serve as parallel to Soby's own "descent" into the urgings of the body—but whereas Aschenbach had not finally achieved Tadziu, Soby is successful in attaining Cynthia as a bride. Morris more than once links Soby's passion to primitive urgings and the firelit bodies of the dancing Ur-Mensch figures that populate Aschenbach's imagination.

In Soby's reflections, what Aschenbach had undergone was a process of transformation in which "[a]nother man, an Ur-Mensch, asserted his rights" (138). This reflection is linked to Soby's musings on the human eye and its relationship to mind and body—as anticipated from Morris's choice for one of the epigraphs to the book, from Darwin: "I remember well the time when the thought of the eye made me cold all over." Sherrington had used this quotation as an epigraph to "The Wisdom of the Body" chapter of *Man on His Nature*, in which he included a long discussion of the apparently teleological development of cells in the creation of the "final cause," the eye.[13] Morris borrows generously from this chapter, as the following passage indicates. Soby reflects on the "knowledge" and the "buried life" that the Ur-Mensch asserts in the affairs of conscious men:

> From whence did it come? One might suggest it was less of the mind, than the spinal cord. That living root that connected the brain of man with his primeval tail: the slimy ooze from which he emerged with his eyes. The eyes. Did they know about the eyes? . . . It was customary to speak of the mind's eye, but more accurate to speak of the eye's mind. For it had one. Yes, wonder of wonders, it had a small brain of its own. A tiny bud of the brain was attached to the back of it. At that point, not in the brain, the visible world was made visible, the facts became a fiction

congenial to man. Fiat lux! It was the eye that gave the command. A wisdom of the eye, so to speak, preceded that of the mind. Just to that extent certain tastes were determined long before the notion of choice existed; the mind merely ratified a choice already made. Free will? Did any smitten lover ever feel he was free to choose? He was chosen. His delight and despair lay in that knowledge. (138–39)

This "wisdom of the eye" (generalized in the text as a wisdom of the senses) is Morris's point: a return to reliance on the body for the "truths," the knowledge *it* knows.

In posing the problem in this way, however, Morris appears to reverse his position on the necessity for intellect in *The Territory Ahead*. Morris's case for the body here is one-sided, Soby's quest too successful, unmediated by inquiries into social obstacles. Morris closes the book off with Soby's marriage, leaving readers to imagine what may happen afterward when the rights of the intellect reassert themselves. Thomas Mann was wiser with Aschenbach than Morris is with Soby. By killing Aschenbach off in the midst of his Ur-Mensch passion, Mann promised nothing; Morris, on the other hand, concludes with a fulfillment of passion that readers may view with suspicion. The irony is that Morris's works have themselves enjoined readers to such skepticism.

The next book, *Cause for Wonder*, occasioned by Morris's return to Schloss Ranna after more than two decades, is a comic discursion on the meaning of time and the significance of consciousness in the ways time is perceived, processed, and stored in the mind. The protagonist is Warren Howe, another version of Boyd from *The Field of Vision*, but a Boyd without a mission and without much passion. Howe is a relatively curious but disinterested spectator who returns to "Schloss Riva" to excavate a portion of his past and try to come to terms with it—and because he was bidden to come to the Austrian castle by Dulac's funeral announcement. Dulac is not dead, as it turns out, but simply playing yet another of his notorious pranks.

The central image by which Morris conveys his theme is through "skull-time," time locked into subjective consciousness, duration telescoped into the immediate present. But the book attempts to do more than explore subjective consciousness; it also inquires into the nature of continuity of consciousness—through images that cut across generations and leap from one mind to another. Cameras and sound tapes, as metaphors of the recording processes of consciousness, are ubiquitous—and their constant repetition tedious.

The nature of the mind as a retrieval system of the past is given in an argument between Howe and his long-rejected lover, Katherine Brownell. Katherine thinks of the mind as an attic, "a big wastebasket": "[Y]ou can find in it what you want to." Howe insists, however, that images from the past may come to mind without direct reference to remembered reality—a sign that "there's more life in us than we're aware of. Maybe more sense. Somebody took that snapshot when my back was turned. It wasn't something I dug for, having buried."[14] In short, the mind contains memories that consciousness has forgotten. In this sense the "wisdom of the body" is also a kind of wisdom of the unreflective mind.

The means of generational continuity are worked out through the aged Monsieur Dulac and Katherine's young grandson, Brian, the recipient of sensations and perceptions, Dulac's chief hope for "immortality." Dulac wishes to impress on the boy a sense of audacity—at least this is Howe's interpretation. Just as Boyd turns to Gordon in *The Field of Vision* to inquire into consciousness, Howe observes Brian: "What was he thinking, that kid? What impressions had been made on his new, unused material [in his skull]?" (174). Again, Morris's language echoes *The Field of Vision*: "Turning his head slowly, like a panning camera, the boy took in the situation. Howe saw himself, somewhat underprinted, loose among the snapshots of [Brian's] mind. Part of the jigsaw scene he would one day assemble" (209).

The nature of this "jigsaw scene," of what the "panning camera" actually perceives or how what it perceives will be processed, is unclear. Readers only know that Brian does, in fact, perceive something—and he, like Gordon, is given totally from the outside; readers do not see into *his* consciousness. Between Dulac and Brian the past and the present interact. Morris returns to Sherrington's current to make this case:

> Through Dulac's hand, as through a cable, Howe sensed the flow of an alternating current. The past into the present, the present into the past. What had died of the past was dead, or more accurately put, was past—but what had persisted was now being taped, in some cryptic manner that would need decoding, in the head of the boy. From the old, the charge was now being passed to the new. *What* charge? That was what one never knew. The new, unused heads, like empty deep-freeze cartons, would not give up their meaning—if it could be said they had one—until thawed. The present would prove to be whatever proved to be unexpendable. (185)

Time, in this sense, is skull-time, "[a] form of daylight time salvage, a deep-freeze where time was stored like the mammoth in the Siberian cake of ice" (268–69).

The book has little more than this to offer: a view of the exigencies of consciousness as it accumulates sensations for future processing—if and when such processing will take place. It is not clear precisely what Dulac has to offer the boy, other than an audacity unrelated to particular needs. There seems no urgency in *what* Dulac communicates. The urgency of consciousness working toward a particular goal, as found in *The Field of Vision*, is lacking in *Cause for Wonder*. The novel does little more than orchestrate the thesis that "The pile of new, unused material between those ears soaked up what [Brian] saw like a blotter. To hell with understanding. First one soaked it up. The understanding would come, if at all, years later when it dripped, like a bright red fluid, from the tip of his brush or his pen" (172–73). This idea, however, had been expressed more cogently in *The Territory Ahead*; nothing in *Cause for Wonder* gives reason to believe Brian will employ brush or pen in the future.

Morris had come some distance since he urged the necessity for greater American consciousness in *The Territory Ahead*. By the time of *Cause for Wonder* he seems subject to his own charge that American writers—always excepting James—tend to depreciate the intellect. Readers may agree with Marcus Klein's observation that in *Cause for Wonder*, Morris appeared to be "blinking at everything he has known."[15] But it is possible to take a kinder tack by assuming that *What a Way to Go* and *Cause for Wonder* (and to a lesser extent *Love Among the Cannibals*) are something like Graham Greene's "entertainments," as distinct from his novels. It is true, too, that *Cause for Wonder* had been on Morris's mind ever since his winter in Schloss Ranna in the mid-1930s; this novel was Morris's fifth attempt to deal with that experience.[16] It is possible, too, that Morris was casting about for new ways to approach the American cultural condition—and that these novels constitute a kind of moratorium during which he replenished his reservoir of raw materials. Morris returned to American themes in his next novel, *One Day*, his attempt to come to terms with the assassination of John F. Kennedy.

Chapter Six

"How Things Are":
Grasping the Present, 1964–1979

In a speech at the University of Chicago in 1967, a speech "vividly and wittily and unhappily describing the absurdities of contemporary culture,"[1] Morris provided the key to his writing of the late 1960s and 1970s. Referring to the current "science-fiction content of our factual lives," he said: "We say *that's how things are*. And how are they? That is precisely what we would like to know. *How* they are is the essence that escapes us. In this embarrassment we turn to the scientist, the artist, and to Madame Sosotris, famous clairvoyante. All deal a wicked pack of cards. All tell us or conceal from us the same things. And how are they? It seems as if nothing is as it seems."[2]

Morris might have been referring to his own condition when he wrote, "The grain of what we call the American mind, over which thought passes with a rasping lisp, is peculiarly unsympathetic to the man who thinks."[3] As a "man who thinks," Morris increasingly saw American culture as a culture of disorder, one that evaded easy definition and comprehension and that threatened to overwhelm all intellectual effort. The catastrophic event in Dallas on November 22, 1963, exacerbated Morris's sense that chaotic forces and manifold selfish interests were loose upon the land. At the time, he was in the midst of a novel that he "might have entitled *How Things Are*,"[4] suggesting that simple clarity was his goal in the more complicated post-1950s world. The purpose of the author, he now seemed to suggest, was not to change reality but principally to serve as a seismograph for cultural tremors. "This is not a happy time to be an artist," he said, "but it is even worse not to be one. He *is* how things are. His function is to sound out how he is" ("Things," 35). But this purpose is different from what he had espoused in the 1950s; his works show that he was coming to distrust the intellect and to accept cultural fragmentation as an entrenched contemporary reality.

One Day, Morris's longest novel, was his final attempt in fiction to gauge the American temper as a whole (although he continued his social criticism in the essays published as *A Bill of Rites, A Bill of Wrongs, A Bill of Goods* three years later). Thereafter, in his *fiction* of the 1960s and 1970s he experimented with countercultural assumptions, based on his view that "[b]ehind the frequently theatrical facade of rebels who are now preoccupied with causes, I am struck by how remarkably sane their daydreams are. Far-fetched, it's true, but appallingly sane" ("Things," 47). His language there suggests the ambivalence he felt about the countercultural "theatrical facade," so contrary on the surface to the rigorous logical mind. Morris, following his own advice, was entering "the territory ahead," prepared to examine his own assumptions and willing to take risks.

Starting with Alec in *One Day*, Morris put a tenuous faith in "natural" or socially marginal characters—rebels and outsiders: in *In Orbit*, the inspired hoodlum Jubal E. Gainer; in *Fire Sermon* and *A Life*, the octogenarian curmudgeon Floyd Warner, two hippies, and a mysterious Indian; and in *The Fork River Space Project*, a pair of mysterious men who may or may not be space travelers. Kelcey's manner of dealing with the world surrounding Fork River involves his recognition that just as he can change visual perspectives by applying pressure to the lids of his eyes, so also can he achieve new perspectives of the imagination through contemplation of the NASA photograph of the earth taken from space. In the end, however, Kelcey acknowledges the costs of emotional distance: "The immense pathos of my situation was part of the cosmic perspective, as if I shared with the cosmos the vast indifference of the prime mover. In this way, momentarily, I had learned to live with things as they are."[5]

One Day

The major concerns of *One Day*—time, death, and consciousness and how these are connected in American culture—are derived from Morris's "brooding on the role of Death in a deathless culture." This novel was one Morris had begun before the assassination of John F. Kennedy, one he considered calling *How Things Are*: "I wanted to know. Writing a novel is one way of finding out. I wanted answers more complex, and more gratifying, than previous novels had been able to supply me. I was ambitious, that is. I wanted to put up or shut up." The assassination temporarily took Morris away from the novel—the event "overpowered my fiction and paralyzed my imagination"—but later he decided to include the assassination as one of the novel's focal centers, and so it became *One Day* ("OD," 26, 12, 14).

One Day is a meditation on the meaning of Kennedy's assassination for American culture, specifically in the lives of the inhabitants of Escondido, California, who represent aspects of the malaise that inhabits (and inhibits) them. The purpose of the novel is to account for the significance of disorder in the culture at large and to comment on the various strategies by which people arrange their lives to deal with it. In contrast to McCarthy in *The Huge Season*, the "Prince of Darkness" in *One Day*, Lee Harvey Oswald, cannot be explained in political or social terms. Oswald represents (in extreme form) a psychology of disorder that in this novel is rampant in American life.

Shortly after the assassination, the newspapers account for Oswald as a loner, and those who knew him as a child claim that the seeds of his destructive act were already discernible then. The media, that is, simplify Oswald by reducing him to manageable clichés—leading Cowie to recognize that *he* has better credentials as a loner than Oswald does. In contrast, Alec Cartwright, the audacious avatar of change in *One Day*, cries that she *never* wants to understand Oswald's motives; such explanations fail to consider the social conditions—from which Oswald emerged—for which everybody must take some responsibility. "*His* hands may be dirty," Alec cries out, "but our own lily-white hands are clean. It lets us off the hook."[6]

One Day probes the characters' commonplace complicity in the assassination. The chief indictment is one of misanthropy: the animal pound, with its central location in the town, reinforces the motif that many humans prefer animals to people. Most of the characters relate directly to the pound: Evelina Cartwright is the owner (and Alec's mother); Wendell Horlick ("People are no damn good" [54]) is the superintendent; Ignacio Chavez is the local dogcatcher; Harold Cowie, the novel's central reflective figure, runs an animal clinic across the road. Other characters include Miriam Horlick (Wendell's wife), who despises people *and* animals and prefers vegetables to both: "Vegetables were beautiful. People were not" (217). Miriam and Wendell's son, Irving, goes one step further, spending much of his time rooting through trash cans for castaway *things*.

The most sympathetically drawn portraits—besides that of Alec Cartwright—are those of transplanted immigrants: Luigi Boni, originally from Venice, a barber and minor artist; and the Mexicans, Chavez and his wife, Conchita. But even Chavez, "a God-fearing man, came to know that he too shared the guilt of the godless. . . . What next? When and where would God strike?" (37). Conchita, who "seemed to have little use for her mind" (35), is called in to nurse a "discarded" child and does so not out of a sense of responsibility but simply because to do so is natural. Another character is Adele Skopje, Evelina's odd astrologer friend, who had announced early in the day that "under Scorpio" it was unwise to travel because of the "danger of accidents" (91–92)—and who by the end of the day is dead.

It is the mortician, Holmes, who speaks out most concretely on human dignity in "his 'sermon' on death," a tone poem revealing Morris's "long admiration for the *Devotions* of John Donne, and the Knights who speak out in Eliot's verse dramas" ("OD," 20). Whereas in earlier books Morris had treated morticians satirically, in *One Day* Morris has Holmes defending the funeral industry, even through a blunted attack on Jessica Mitford's "American Way" of death (242). Holmes's critique of how people live "dead" lives is a defense of the dead in terms that link him to Muncy in *The Home Place*: "Alone with the body I am always aware of its charge of life. Does that seem strange? You are familiar with it yourself. It's that feeling you have when you enter an abandoned house. It's life you feel. The life of the inhabitants" (255–56). In another place Holmes reveals a trace of misanthropy: "In the presence of the dead I often feel what I seldom feel among the living. The presence of life. The dead seem to respect it as the living do not" (249).

As in most of Morris's novels, *One Day* is primarily an exploration of consciousness to which plot is secondary. Morris hangs the novel on the assassination, but the key event is the shocking discovery that a human child has been abandoned at the pound. Morris moves skillfully through the day, weaving his characters' personal stories with the discovery of the child's parentage and, more subtly, with the news from Dallas. Adele Skopje's warning to avoid travel echoes through the book. The main victim is the president, but travel is unwise for others as well: Luigi Boni is pinned to the street by Holmes's hearse; Cowie, thinking of a car accident years before, is stopped for running a red light; and the prophetess is herself found dead in a runaway car. The opening scene—looking back on "the disordered events of the day" from late night—deliberately incorporates fog as an emblem of human captivity to contingency: "That we are such stuff as fog is made of is hardly a fresh impression, but events have a way of making it new" (21, 24).

The day begins with Chavez's discovery of the abandoned baby, followed by the town's responses. Evelina takes the child home with her to the house once again occupied by her daughter Alec, who during the night has returned from her brief career as a freedom rider in the South.

The baby, as Evelina intuitively knows, belongs to Alec, who had left the child in the pound in order to shock Americans into living more responsibly. But by the time the assassination is reported, Alec already doubts the efficacy of her effort. Morris devotes the last long chapter to an explanation of Alec's motives—in which she is seen as an audacious, if misguided, exemplar of ongoing consciousness.

The novel, then, is primarily a record of the battle between social awareness and the numbness of "non-consciousness"—or the guilt imposed by consciousness when the will is stymied. This struggle is worked out largely through the contrasted attitudes of Alec, a young woman who persists in making fresh starts, and Cowie, a man who has "given up." Harold Cowie is the novel's focal reflective character, another of Morris's ineffectual protagonists, described as a "decent, sympathetic, reflective dropout who does not have (or does not *choose* to have) what it takes to make the scene" ("OD," 17).

Cowie is fully conscious of the costs of his self-imposed impotence, but this knowledge only increases the guilt he wears like a protective cloak to absolve him from social interaction. He appears to represent a kind of death-in-life. Like Oswald, Cowie reflects, he is a loner, but Cowie accepts his guilt as a condition of modern consciousness. Nevertheless, he is an able critic of the culture; among his convictions is that there is an implicit *Bill of Wrongs*,

> the small print at the bottom of the Bill of Rights. Chief among these wrongs was the right to give up. In each man's weary pursuit of happiness this right to give up loomed larger and larger. Cowie had given up people, Alec had given up her child, numberless lovers had given up love, and increasing numbers had given up their conscious lives. A nonconscious life they still lived, and the future looked bright for nonconscious dying. But to be fully conscious was to be fully exposed. Cause for alarm. As a matter of survival one gave it up. At one and the same moment this was an act of salvation and an act of destruction. Miltown. A cemetery with stop and go lights. (365)

Suffering from insomnia, Cowie broods on his condition. To cope with his world, he relies on rationalizations that provide a sense of order. One of these rationalizations is that the past has determined "his natural tendency to see everything from the sidelines" (65). As a child he had received a chameleon as a gift. One day it disappeared into a huge sandpile, its protective coloration rendering it invisible. Cowie spent the rest of the day and the following morning searching for it, to no avail.

Finally his guardian called to him, "For chrissakes, kid, . . . when will you give up?" Now Cowie reflects: "Was there something in Cowie, older than his boyhood, that gathered the import of such a question, and knew that his life would not come up with an answer to it?" (83–84). While Mr. Ahearn had led him back to bed, Cowie had resigned himself—and now, when asked to guess what is in the basket at the pound, Cowie responds, "I gave up long ago, son" (89).

Cowie, however, does not give up consciousness; rather, consciousness plagues him, but self-knowledge is no cure for what ails him. The manner in which his attitudes have hardened into defense mechanisms is described through a series of events after Cowie, at 23, had been jilted and fled to Mexico; there the car he was driving struck and killed two workers. Cowie escaped with injuries "peculiar, but slight. His hands were broken. The ankle of the foot he had applied to the brake was badly sprained" (177), indicating that he had *tried* to avoid the collision. In the hospital, he had time to consider conflicting interpretations of the crash. The Mexican version was that Cowie was innocent; the "accident" was a matter of fate: "The Indian with the red flag was admittedly at fault, but his crime was no crime since it was time for the siesta. Nature was nature, just as fate was fate. Cowie had merely been a wheel in God's mysterious plan" (181).

This explanation, however, was not acceptable to Cowie. For him the philosophical issue involved the problem of time. Mexican time, symbolized by the cathedral bell outside his window, is foreign to him, as detailed in Cowie's observations from his hospital bed, when

> it occurred to Cowie that the bell, sounding the hour, had nothing to do with the hands of the clock. It sounded in a world entirely its own. The clock itself sometimes ran, sometimes stopped, so that the time it told was not time in Matamoros. Nobody seemed to care. . . . If one ignored the ridiculous time on the clock's face, a more sensible time seemed to emerge. . . . The steps of the cathedral, flooded with light so they might be seen from the highway, seemed to be the stage, the predestined setting, for a time less arbitrary than that on the clock's face, or Cowie's wrist. But why bother? There was this problem of Cowie's guilt. There was this phenomenon commonly described as an accident. No true sense could be made of human events if one accepted the illusion traced on the clock's face: every clock told time that was out, not the time that was in. Cowie preferred to believe in a time wherein it was clear, and in no way accidental, that he would round a predictable corner and responsibly wipe out the lives of two men. Better guilt than pointless murder, meaningless events. (188–89)[7]

Cowie is attracted to this cathedral, or celestial, version of time, but he also knows that his preferred guilt is a terrestrial phenomenon. Cowie's problem is one Morris had dealt with before—beginning with the mixed terrestrial and celestial evidence procured by his camera and continuing in his fictional explorations in *The Huge Season* and *The Field of Vision*—a problem of the conflict between Platonic desire and mundane reality. Cowie, however, unlike Foley or Boyd, is unable to reconcile the terrestrial mundane and the celestial freedom *from* mundane time.

When a young woman, Concepción, approached Cowie in his hospital room and "placed her lips on his mouth," Cowie ran for his life— because his plans to match her up with his very willing physician were shattered. She upset his desire for order by wanting Cowie, not the doctor. But now Cowie sees the whole matter as more complex. He suggests that his "generous impulse to provide the poor girl with a suitable lover" might have been his own "artful dodge," "[a] respectable sensible way to give up" (200)—a means, that is, to allow him to escape human connections. He turned down the celestial connection Concepción offered because it required mundane responsibilities. Instead Cowie returned to the States, gave up medicine, and settled for being a veterinarian.

Cowie refuses the consolations of both celestial and terrestrial time precisely in order to accommodate guilt: To involve oneself in earthly causes is simply to be defeated; on the other hand, it is impossible to escape the mundane. Cowie's compromise is to withdraw, to make an adult fetish of the child's giving up. Cowie continues to give up because he understands contemporary life as an impossible dilemma. This ubiquitous sense of impotence, in Cowie's view, is also responsible for Oswald's murder of the president:

> So this senseless crime not only made history: it made American sense. In each American ear the word from Dallas would acquire its own troubled burden of meaning, and its own intolerable burden of meaninglessness. What word was it? How well Cowie knew it. *Impotence*. The assurance that nothing said, nothing written or cabled, nothing accepted or rejected, nothing suffered or felt, nothing now up before Congress or still in the blueprints, nothing dug out of the past or prescribed for the future, would restore to a man his belief in his power to affect the course of human events. He might exert it, but believe in it he did not. (366)

The murder, then, can be explained in other than personal, psychological terms, and Cowie, like Alec, sees Oswald as merely another symptom of a cultural disorder stemming from frustrated individualism.

Although Cowie explains Oswald as in many ways similar to himself, Oswald's own peculiar sense of impotence led him to take up the gun. In contrast to Cowie, Oswald had not given up; rather, he had seized the day, whatever his personal motives. Oswald and Cowie represent different sides of the same coin: One withdraws, the other refuses to withdraw, but both are motivated by impotence. Of Oswald Cowie thinks: "A free man, he testified to the horrible burden of freedom: how connect with some*thing*? How relate to some*one*? It was no accident that he singled out the man who represented the maximum of human connections, and displaced this man, this symbol of connections, with himself. Lee Oswald had merely deprived another man of what, in his opinion, he had been deprived: his right to the pursuit and possession of happiness" (366). Part of Morris's intention is to show that Cowie, as a representative contemporary, may seek releases of his own in a culture disordered by materialism, solipsism, and excessive consumerism.

But more important, Morris posits Alec Cartwright as an implicit critic of Oswald—and she has a great deal to do in this novel. In a discussion with Wayne Booth, Morris noted that Alec displays an audacity similar to that of a number of his female characters: Daughter in *Ceremony in Lone Tree*, Cynthia in *What a Way to Go*, and Lou Baker in *The Huge Season*. Of Alec, Morris said: "There is nothing in any of the other people in *One Day* that can compare with Chickpea—she is the most open, experiences the most that is contemporary; and she is a foil to the most sympathetic of the male characters, Cowie."[8] "Chickpea," the section that details Alec's education, closes out the book, in formal opposition to the opening scene in which Cowie reflects on the day in its closing hour.

At *her* end of the book, however, Alec is given to us *prior to* the events of the day; she represents time seized and used, in process of changing from one moment to the next; her experiences are in dialectic with her reflections on them, unlike Cowie's continual references to "meaningful accidents" and the past as determinant. Alec is open to change; she *must* exert herself to effect change, within both herself and the culture she despises. The novel closes: "Her mission was accomplished . . . and if her eyes were wide as those of the oracle at Delphi it was because she, too, held the future in her hands" (433). Her mission, of course, was to deposit her child in the pound, thereby to shock humanity out of its "non-consciousness."

By this time readers know that Alec's mission is a failure; nevertheless, its significance for the future is not that it was futile or silly, but that it was performed out of a sense of outrage and daring. Morris describes her inheritance as a mixture of order and disorder: Her father, "prepared" and predictable, had nevertheless "a latent, even dangerous, sense of disorder, a lust for it," in opposition to her "disordered" mother's "lust for order." Her parents were "[a] perfect match. What was their child to do but take a step for order in reverse?" (140). This "step for order in reverse" is the key to her character. Alec is given to social involvement, to acts of protest against "the way things are," first as a demonstrator, then as a freedom rider in the Civil Rights movement.

On a trip to Europe she had met an American black, Lyle "Protest" Jackson, and prior to his return to the States (to the front, as he calls it), they had a brief affair. After his departure, she found herself pregnant. While awaiting the birth, she learned of the death of Ruth Elyot, a young woman who had been Alec's college roommate. This information led her to recall her emotions from years before when she had learned that Ruth, while on a train taking her home, had "managed to give birth to a child but failed in her attempt to dispose of it" in the train lavatory. Ruth's motive was "to protect the father of the child from scandal, and the child from shame" (405 – 6). The child was dead, and Ruth Elyot was arrested; the newspapers reported the incident as "an all but unmentionable crime." For Alec the event was horrible, but she recognized in her attitude toward it a feeling of admiration as well:

> Her mouth went dry to think of it. That such a brutal act impressed her so favorably was not a good sign. Was she perverse? Was it cruelty she loved, and not tenderness? Not until the crime and the punishment faded did she sense what enthralled her was the will that made the crime possible. In one breath it was horrifying and fine. At a given moment the Elyot clan, countless generations of them, had possessed little Ruth Elyot, like a demon, and given her the strength of Gods. It was not pretty. But it was what one meant by that culprit life. (407)

The Ruth Elyot–Alec Cartwright connection is important to the novel, partly because it is consistent with Morris's views of the often peculiar ways people are influenced by others—as in the Foley-Lawrence and Boyd–Paula Kahler relationships, in which the *failures* of others are instructive. More important, in *One Day* the Ruth Elyot incident is to Alec Cartwright what Oswald's deed is to Cowie—something horrifying and "daring" at once. Alec completely rejects Ruth's act (just as Cowie knows Oswald's act is wholly destructive). For Alec, "Ruth Elyot had simply been too far out, or too far in. Her example did not apply to the commonplace world where people lived" (408). Like Cowie, Alec realizes she lives in terrestrial time and that she has to make do with it, but unlike Cowie, she does not surrender her options to perform celestial deeds of her own.

Alec follows Jackson to the States and becomes a freedom rider. When she is sexually assaulted by rednecks, however, her sympathy with Jackson's antiwhite ideology is tested. She begins to hate the whites, to envy the blacks. She is led to wonder why Jackson wants to have what the whites have—if the whites have nothing worthwhile. "White people looked to her worse, but toward the black her vision was clouded. For what incredible folly did *he* desire to look white? For what conceivable reason did *he* want to integrate? With what? With men lower than the animals? Had the black man been invisible so long he thought this deathly white was a desirable color? He should be told to bless his luck that he was black. That the laws of the country prevented him from being something worse" (414). When she finally catches up with Jackson, she mocks his "revolution" against the whites: "You want to sell him used cars and use his filthy crapper and drive one of his ugly cars into the suburbs? You want a house full of shit and wall-to-wall carpets? . . . Give a shit where the bus is going, what you want's a good seat. Well, I don't" (418–19).

To nurse her hurt feelings and sense of loss, Alec takes refuge in a movie theater and sees *Mondo Cane*, with its "theme of dog-eat-dog." She is horrified: Dogs *are* better than people; it is people who perform savagery on animals. She concocts her plan: *Her* child would live with the animals, "The first to be immortal in this preordained way. The first, if not the last, to resign from the damned human race," a new "Moses in the bulrushes." By placing her child in the pound, she would give the world "[a]n unheard-of thing, a protest to be *heard*. Who could misunderstand it? Who would not believe in his soul the child was right? It was—as nothing else in her life could be—on a level with the protest of Ruth Elyot: it would horrify people. They would want to burn the mother at the stake." So she flies to Escondido, and in the early hours of the morning, with the fog burning off and in the sky "the pale dawn of a new day," accomplishes her mission (429–32).

However, Alec has made two naive miscalculations. She has, first, failed to take into account the "what next?" of history and its strength to overpower her protest. Oswald's act renders her gesture meaningless. Second, she has failed to consider the powers of apathy. Even an event as earthshaking as the president's assassination is taken in stride. Beginning to understand the depth of her naïveté, Alec realizes she must love her child, not merely use it. The futilities and frustrations of love that Morris incorporates into the novel—Cowie's rejection of Concepción, Cowie's jilting by Eleanor, MacNamara's refusal of Evelina, Miriam's unrequited love for Cowie, and the ongoing war between Alec and her mother—are central to the problems of contemporary culture: humans must learn again to fulfill their domestic and communal responsibilities.

Alec and Cowie are the two "philosophical" poles in *One Day*. Only these two characters are capable of converting sensations, feelings, and perceptions into knowledge. Alec and Cowie make sense of events by recognizing what these events cost in human terms. But Cowie can make no real advances; only Alec is able to forge into the future. The other characters do not so much reflect on events as respond to them in ways they have made typical. Evelina is too busy in her pursuits to have time for reflection; she *does*, rather than thinks. Miriam Horlick, the intellectual, gives seminars in art, but refuses to relate the art to human concerns and thus fails to possess it. Luigi Boni is content to make trivial drawings for sale in Evelina's shop. They are caught up in everyday-ness—yet Morris deals sympathetically with all these characters.

The structure of *One Day* helps Morris make his case for consciousness. The opening presents time already past and reflected through a mind that has given up. This position may be considered realistic. But the next sections of *One Day* return in time to examine the events Cowie has outlined. The final section questions both Cowie's opening reflections and the events of the day, positing Alec as a character who *may* have potential to change her world. This conclusion is more satisfying than Foley's fragile optimism in *The Huge Season*. *One Day* promises nothing, but it does offer a variegated, carefully textured portrait of culture in the 1960s—and an audacious young woman. Readers are left with the conviction that "that culprit life" is itself an astounding essential value—in opposition to the death-in-life that Cowie represents and that Holmes uses as the basis for his defense of the dead.

In Orbit

One Day had shown Morris's loss of confidence in thought as a means to mend the social scene; if Cowie represented the thinking man, American culture was in a bad way. Morris's next novel (his last of the 1960s) was *In Orbit*, a response to *One Day*, taking Morris a step beyond Alec Cartwright in his experimentation with countercultural possibilities. *In*

Orbit was well received as an attempt to focus on "how things are" in the heady atmosphere of the mid-1960s: George Garrett, for one, praised Morris's ingenuity in trying "to make both sense and art out of the brute, raw, flashing, shifty facts, the material of the American present."[9] Leon Howard called it the "most perfect of his short novels" and believed its unlikely dropout hero to represent the artist who takes his being from motion, "wheeling in an unpredictable orbit."[10]

In contrast to *One Day*, *In Orbit* posits a world disengaged from civic responsibilities. In the Indiana town of Pickett, contingency and anarchy rule. Morris gives vent to another side of human nature, that side seeking freedom from social responsibility by acting according to "nature." In dramatic contrast to Cowie's need to deny the accidental and outlaw contingency, the characters in *In Orbit* give themselves more or less over to randomness. In a world of pure contingency, human thought would have little to do but place events into retrospection. Hodler pays for tips about the news, but the news itself is made by *events* falling out by chance—and by impulsive human nature.

When one acts "according to nature," however, the rules of civility and morality are rendered null and void. In his amoral world, Jubal acts as he pleases—so long as he evades capture. Many others in the town recognize his complete anarchy, but at the same time they are envious of his freedom. That envy seems the point of the novel, for Jubal gets away with things the townspeople desire to do themselves but cannot because of the social contract into which they have been uneasily socialized. The result, however, is a shaky Freudian pact between id and superego—one that makes for a struggle of conscience between duty and desire.

Given this condition, *In Orbit* is a comedy about chance (though, of course, it undercuts chance by virtue of its conveyance through carefully ordered language). The premise of *In Orbit* is that "nature abhors a vacuum"—obliquely suggesting that American culture is itself a "vacuum" that welcomes whatever can come along to fill it. The tornado that hovers threateningly is the central symbol: The characters are associated with it to the degree that they embody something similar to its natural—but mindless—forces. The novel reflects Morris's earlier views on "the wisdom of the body," now tempered by his more recent thought on disorder in American life; certainly it is Morris's greatest departure from his argument for the conceptual imagination in *The Territory Ahead*. Here, having given Cowie his chance, Morris inquires into the significance of amoral, "natural" forces as expressions of the countercultural, emphasizing sensation and energy and downplaying reflection, reason, and order.

The plot of *In Orbit* is once again primarily a study of the characters who appear in the cast. Jubal E. Gainer (Jubilee: cause for celebration), "the boy on the loose," a runaway fleeing the draft that might send him to Vietnam, steals his friend's motorcycle, helmet, and leather jacket and flees, only to run out of gas in the college town of Pickett, Indiana, where he has bizarre encounters with a number of the town's citizens. The citizens on whom Morris focuses include Curt Hodler, *In Orbit*'s reflective male character and writer-editor of the *Pickett Courier*; he is a bachelor, but readers are told that "[i]f the needle hadn't skipped in the making of Miss Holly," Hodler might *not* be a bachelor.[11] The other principal characters are Pauline Bergdahl, Hodler's friend, who provides him with chance news tips and is the first to recognize that the boy on the motorcycle is a runaway; Holly Stohrmeyer, a feeble-minded woman whom both her guardian, Sanford Avery, and Hodler find sexually attractive; the Vienna-born Felix Haffner, a teacher at the college and sponsor of "happenings"; Charlotte Hatfield, an uninhibited woman who loves to dance and to whom Jubal is attracted; her husband, the poet Alan Hatfield; and Oscar Kashperl, who runs the Army and Navy Surplus Outlet.

Much of the novel is given through Hodler's perceptions—not all of it, however, for much of the seductive power of the work comes from Morris's method of structural discontinuity in which he dismembers chronological time and by turns follows Jubal and the other characters' moves across the novel's stormy landscape. The novel works through suggestion and almost casual repetition of elements that gather meaning through accumulation—such as the twister, the "historic elm," the bees, and the crop-duster plane that sprays a number of the characters. Once again, as David Madden says, "The task of imaginative synthesis is mainly the reader's."[12]

In a short span of time, on a day of threatening weather, Jubal runs out of gas, encounters the feeble-minded and at the moment half-naked Holly Stohrmeyer and on an impulse sexually assaults her; he assaults the giggling Haffner by crushing a bag of cherries over his head; he stabs Kashperl in the Surplus Outlet store; and he is attracted by the "natural" Charlotte Hatfield, following her home and watching her "twirling, swirling" dance through the windows of her house. All this time Sheriff Cantrill is after Jubal, but Morris pointedly remarks how unwilling the townspeople are to give the sheriff precise directions: "Didn't anybody want to pin this public enemy down? . . . Did they all dream of being a man on the loose? Envied by inhibited red-blooded men, pursued by comical galoots like the Sheriff. He went that-a-way.

With the thoughts, fantasies, and envious good wishes of them all" (105 – 6). Finally the tornado swoops down and puts Jubal literally "in orbit" before setting him down, reinforcing the relations between the title, nature, and the ramifications of the novel's design.

Randomness, chance, contingency, the natural are the thematic keys to *In Orbit*. The twister is the primary symbol, but the motif is echoed everywhere. The randomness in nature is appealing to almost all the characters, mostly because it reduces the ennui of everydayness and adds excitement to life. Jubal personifies the amoral and unpredictable; of boys like him, Pauline Bergdahl says: "They don't mean no meanness, Mr. Hodler, and they don't mean no goodness either. They just couldn't care less" (110). The boy is deliberately paralleled with the twister as a dangerous, unpredictable, energetic force of nature. Kashperl is a lover of disorder, his three thousand books having no visible title or author on their spines: "A few have numbers, applied by Kashperl in a moment of weakness, a hunger for order, but this soon passed" (77). Haffner is bored by the predictable and prefers "happenings" over more structured artistic activities. Charlotte Hatfield prefers both her cats and her friends "non-fixed," pooh-poohs her poet-intellectual husband's observation that the power in a twister should be "harnessed" for use, and "prefers creatures who don't think" (134).

Even Hodler, the reflective newspaper editor, sleeps well during twisters, despite his "gentle nature": "The worse the storm, the better he sleeps. Something in his nature, as well as in nature, seems to find release" (150). In Hodler's mind even American civilization is comparable to a twister. He had once written a book on the role of the Swiss in shaping American culture: "What, if any, *shape* has it? On Hodler's troubled mind's eye, it seems a mindless force, like the dipping, dancing funnel of the twister, the top spread wide to spew into space all that it has sucked up" (15). Comparing the twister to "the boy on the loose," Hodler thinks:

> a twister had certain obligations that he felt this boy did not. There were these opposing forces, high and low pressures, moist and dry air in unpredictable mixtures, great heat and cold, fantastic combinations that built up like nuclear fission, and most important of all there was the element of chance that dissolved it in vapor, or brought it to perfection, a tube that dipped from the sky and rearranged most of the matter it touched. . . .
> Is this why he feels a pleasurable apprehension in the knowledge of this potential killer [Jubal]? . . . Destructive elements are not merely on the loose, but some of them are rubbing off on Hodler. (122–23)

Everything in the novel is connected to the arational natural, and those characters who submit most thoroughly to its mindlessness are those who have the most freedom and who draw others' envy to them.

The tale seems almost a commentary on Freud's *Civilization and Its Discontents*, with Morris taking the position that the psychic costs of civilization are repression, guilt, and ennui—from which humans seek release in eccentric, antisocial, or instinctual behavior. Sheriff Cantrill receives no help in his efforts to track Jubal down, which suggests that the townspeople see Jubal as acting out *their* forbidden wishes. Alan, the intellectual, often explains "the importance of inhibitions in civilized life" to Charlotte, telling her "that without them the people of Pickett would be like a bunch of middle-aged delinquents." Charlotte understands him, but she insists these inhibitions keep people from acting naturally and that they seek release in *un*natural ways, like those people who "go to church just to work up an appetite" and then gorge themselves. Alan points out "that eating like pigs kept them out of worse mischief. They weren't out killing people on the state's highways, or in concentration camps." But, as Morris says, "That argument carried little weight with Charlotte, based, as it was, on reason" (31).

In addition to the twister, many objects and events in *In Orbit* appear frequently enough that they carry the resonance of symbols. The first of these is the airplane first seen "spraying the orchards" (26) and last mentioned as a roaring sound covering Jubal's escape after his encounter with Holly Stohrmeyer. Although Morris does not emphasize this, the plane's function is to spray chemicals on the orchards to retard blight by worms and insects. Carl Bredahl argues that this activity of spraying serves, along with the bees circling Holly and the cherries dripping from Haffner's head, to emphasize the sexual energy that Jubal carries into "the suppressed sexuality of Pickett, . . . a natural world ripe for fertilization."[13] Bredahl's argument helps readers see the array of sexual symbols in the novel, but it is just as likely that the plane, because its purpose is ultimately *anti*natural(to destroy natural inhabitants of apples), is one of the "mechanical" devices that David Madden places in contrast to the "animal-sexual-natural" thrust of the novel (Madden, 142). Perhaps the plane is best seen as a complicating factor supporting the novel's thought-provoking ambiguity: The plane destroys "lower" life forms in order to preserve the fruit for human consumption.

A more important, and perhaps equally ambiguous, object in *In Orbit* is the historic elm tree that has been "felled" on the college campus— not by the tornado, but intentionally by humans. Morris calls it "the day's major event. . . . Small fry stand in a circle anxious to be hit by falling branches" (74–75). Afterward, parts of the tree are made into souvenirs, and by nightfall, a wedge of the tree has found its way into a place of honor in the Pickett Inn. One interpretation of the tree is that it represents tradition and that its removal is emblematic of the loss of tradition. That at one point some of the townspeople gather about the spot of the removed tree "as if at a burial" (94) suggests that its loss is mourned. But Morris also says that the tree goes back in time to "when the Indians scalped the first settlers, hardy, stubborn men who worked liked slaves to deprive their children of all simple pleasures, and most reasons to live" (75). In this way Morris links the tree first to violence, then to a "hardy" persistence that is void of humane value.

A third repeated element in *In Orbit* is the presence of William Holden and his role in the movie *The Bridges of Toko-Ri*. Jubal and his friend LeRoy Cluett see the movie on their way to be inducted into the army, but what happens to Holden's character changes Jubal's mind. Instead of the heroics Jubal expected, he sees Holden left behind in China, with "no place to hide," when his plane—and the planes of his rescuers—run out of gas. To Jubal this is an ignominious ending to what had been to that point a successful mission, and he is outraged with the navy for abandoning William Holden. Jubal "was no fool, he knew war was hell, but nobody had told him it was crazy. Nobody had told him it was up to Jubal if he ran out of gas" (23). When he quarrels with his friend, he dons LeRoy's helmet, takes off with LeRoy's motorcycle—and runs out of gas himself, in Pickett.

All these elements—the crop duster, the historic elm, and William Holden's impact on Jubal—are successful unifying devices. The last is in some ways the most useful to Morris. Jubal's adventures lead him to another place where there is "no place to hide," and his progress through the town is an item of much anticipation. The helmet, looking like the one worn by William Holden, allows for Hodler's potential headline that there is a spaceman loose in the town, and the spaceman image links to the novel's title and connects the boy all the more firmly to the twister. There is also a delightful irony in having the draft-evading Jubal show up at the Army and Navy Surplus Outlet: Does he not believe William Holden is "surplus" in China? The novel's ending alludes again to Toko-Ri: "If the army is no place for a growing boy, neither is the world. Bombed out are all the bridges behind him, up ahead of him, treeless, loom the Plains of China, the cops, LeRoy Cluett, and the sunrise on the windows of the Muncie Draft Board. There is no place to hide. But perhaps the important detail escapes you. He is in motion. Now you see him, now you don't" (153).

In *In Orbit* Morris experimented with a philosophy often contrary to his previous work. The American culture of the 1960s appears to have outdistanced his interest in attempting to cope realistically with it. The evidence of *In Orbit* suggests that to combat this disorder, Morris wanted for a time to experiment with larger forces functioning *through* disorder and providing it with cosmic coherence. So Morris composed a carefully designed novel, small and concise, with images ramified in a complex series of interweaved patterns: a *personal* demonstration that the erosions of culture can be combated through art. The book departs from Morris's interest in intersubjective relations and the meaning of the social scene. In making Jubal the "hero" of the novel, Morris wished to play with the idea of disorder as providing, if not social benefit, at least evidence of sentience—certainly a different kind of gesture from the one he had made in *One Day*.

In so contrasting "natural" behavior to Cowie's tortured thought in *One Day*, Morris once again risks being misunderstood. Readers alerted to social attitudes may think Morris sides with Jubal's amorality and may consequently find his "natural" attitudes *anti*social. In *In Orbit* Morris abandons the cautions of *One Day*—which so carefully counter-points Cowie with Alec Cartwright in giving us a version of "how things are" and details the costs to Cowie of his self-imposed impotence. In *In Orbit*, by contrast, civilization has no one to defend it, nor is Morris interested in showing that acting "naturally" may be insufficient for the needs of communal life. His next book, *A Bill of Rites, A Bill of Wrongs, A Bill of Goods*, was a collection of essays, more acidic than humorous, on the futilities of contemporary intelligence; its litany of complaints seems odd after the crafted abandon of *In Orbit*.

Fire Sermon and *A Life*

After *In Orbit* Morris did not publish another novel for four years. When he did the result was interesting and provocative: two small and care-fully crafted books that suggested Morris was feeling his age. Although he did not intend from the outset to write two complementary novels, *Fire Sermon* and *A Life* are unified by virtue of their focus on 82-year-old Floyd Warner, their attention to vision and visual perception, and their relatively uncomplicated employment of mythic elements. In Warner, character is less important than a kind of mystical connection with Life that he only half-understands. These books are extraordinary in their simplicity; like Hemingway's *The Old Man and the Sea*, they are statements that appear to be capstones of a career. The books, and the lives within them, are stripped to their essentials; the stories unfold slowly, and every word counts. The humor is seasoned and sharp-eyed, as in this archetypal example of generational dissonance: "At the boy's age . . . the Uncle got up at dawn, harnessed the horses, plowed forty acres of corn and alfalfa, fed and watered the team, then milked five cows and separated the cream before he sat down to supper. Thanks to a big bowl of oatmeal he was able to do that, although he preferred eggs."[14]

After the more "objective" *In Orbit*, these novels have close autobiographical connections. Although Morris had, to a degree remarkably uncommon in American literature, dealt with senior citizens almost from the beginning of his career, these novels are his first to have an elderly protagonist. Warner is based, thinly disguised, on Morris's Uncle Dwight, his mother's brother. Warner shares with Dwight a sister named Viola (but the character is probably based on another sister, Winona, who died in 1973 and to whose memory Morris dedicated *A Life*), a hatred of his father (and his father's heavy-handed Adventist religion), and a deliberately ambiguous agnosticism supported by readings from Colonel Ingersoll, "the great agnostic."[15] The hippie Stanley in *Fire Sermon* connects both to Jubal E. Gainer in *In Orbit* (although Morris extends Jubal considerably more sympathy) and to Morris's purported friend Luke in "The Leaning Tower of Pizza" from *A Bill of Rites, A Bill of Wrongs, A Bill of Goods*.

Fire Sermon has the look and feel of a book that developed organically, Morris first laying out a pair of characters and the situation of their lives, then allowing the characters to engage their settings and assert their identities. Floyd Warner, age 82, had, a little more than a year before the action of the novel, become the guardian of then 10-year-old Kermit Oelsligle, whose parents had been killed in a car accident, leaving Warner the next available kin. Kermit had come to live with Warner in a California trailer camp where Warner is a handyman. The relationship is a difficult one, mostly because Warner "does not like kids. He thinks they are all a pain in the ass" (10). Obviously, Warner gives Kermit reasons to be embarrassed by him, including that in his cap he "looks like either a bug or something worse" (11). The readers' first glimpse of Warner is given through Kermit's eyes, of an old man who "gleams in the sun like a stop sign," wearing "a yellow plastic helmet and an orange jacket with the word STOP stenciled on the back of it" (3).

After an extended exposition, a telegram arrives announcing the death of Warner's sister (and Kermit's aunt), Viola. This announcement is a shock to the old man because he was close to Viola and she was witness to his running argument with their father; her letters to him ("my darling old scoffer") over the years have sustained him in his agnosticism, allowing him a "religion" he otherwise denied himself in his hatred of his father. He and Kermit prepare for the trip to Nebraska to "settle her affairs": they decide to drive, taking the ancient car and trailer down from their blocks. The 1927 Maxwell coupe is considered an antique by several observers on the road, one of whom makes Warner an offer of $3,000 for it.

The journey by car—Kermit figures it out to be 1,948 miles—does not begin until more than a third of the way through the book, and the book's countercultural antagonists, the hippie pair Stanley and Joy, do not appear until near the middle. After passing Stanley and Joy a number of times on the highway, Warner finally picks them up, as if he comes to some mystical understanding that they have roles to play in his and Kermit's life. This does not mean he likes them. The two are nuisances, and the young man takes considerable delight in antagonizing Warner. For Stanley there are only two kinds of people, and he classes Warner characteristically with the "non-fuckers" of the world (109).

Kermit, however, is fascinated by Joy's "big, warm, friendly smile" (155), and he recognizes Stanley as looking like "the Lord Jesus of the jigsaw puzzle sent to him by Aunt Viola, with the eyes that were said to follow you wherever you went" (97). From the beginning, Morris emphasizes Kermit's position on the edge of adolescence, so the road journey, the meeting with Joy and Stanley, and the "fire sermon" are components in his initiation—just as, in Morris's characteristic balancing act, the same events mark Warner's experiential "initiation" into an acceptance of death.

When they arrive at the home place outside Chapman, Nebraska, Warner reverently revisits his past, going into the house and examining Viola's many objects (things that have turned into antiques). In his careful cataloging and description of these objects (once again reminiscent of his photographic reverence for such artifacts), Morris appears to reattach them to human life: Viola's collection is a sign of her longevity and her role as earthly protectress (as "the others died . . . they left to her those things they valued" [142]). To enforce this quality, Morris notes the panes of "red, blue, and yellow church glass" accounting for "the curious color of the light" in the room. Upstairs Warner finds an empty room, where he sits in "a rocker facing the open window where the blind was half raised" (135–6). There he has a near death experience and is rescued by Kermit.

Later, Warner is outraged to find Joy and Stanley naked in Viola's bedroom, and he assaults them with a mop, accidentally knocking over the kerosene lamp, which leads to the burning of the house. Everything in *Fire Sermon* leads to this ritual destruction of the home place and of the objects attached to Warner's past, then to the symbolic action of giving the boy up to his adolescence and future adulthood. Somewhat like Sarty Snopes in Faulkner's "Barn Burning," Kermit runs off from the fire, hides himself through the night, and arises in the morning, his new life lying open before him—like Sarty, having cast off his affiliation with his blood relation. Joy's mantra verifies the burning of the house as a ritual occasion: "Fire transforms," she says (154).

When Kermit returns he finds the Maxwell missing and hears Joy's explanation that "old birds" go off to die when it is their time. Typically cynical, Stanley says that Warner abandoned them to the fire, but when asked by Kermit why Warner left the trailer behind, Joy says, "For us, silly" (153), suggesting wider implications. Because Warner had noted the boy's developing acquaintance with Stanley and Joy at several points, it comes as little surprise that he leaves Kermit behind, believing Kermit's place is with them rather than with an old man in search of his death.

This extraordinarily accessible and paradoxically profound book could only have been created from deep experience of the world, and it has a certain wisdom in it. Once again, this is a book about knowledge, in this case, the transmission of a message across generations, the title suggesting the presence of powers beyond the rational mind. The crucial theme of *Fire Sermon* is the passage from the past into the present, including the initiation of Kermit, the ritual destruction of the past, and the shift of power from old to young. The "fire sermon" entails the burning of objects that have been gathered there, in the terms of the ritual, *as if to be burned*, just as the young have arrived just at the right time to inherit responsibility for the future.

Warner's life is continued in the most archetypal of all of Morris's novels, *A Life*, published two years later. Here Morris steps up the mythic elements and provides the purest example of a ritual of entry to transformative experience, step by step taking Warner closer to his death in the hands of a "shaman," closing out the experience of withdrawal first made clear in *Fire Sermon*. In Morris's recap (in *A Life*) of the events in the first book, intended to connect present and past events, he embellishes the ritual and makes clear the meaning of the "sermon":

> Just before the house had burned down, and he was still in it, like a ghost in the upstairs bedroom, he had experienced a similar sensation. The weakness in his limbs had led him to sag to a chair, facing the cracked blind and yellow light at the window. The impression had been that his eyes, his *own* eyes, hovered above him like a presence, seeing the things of this world about him for the first time. The view from the window, framed like a painting, impressed him as timeless and unchanging, the old man seated on the armless rocker was within the scene, not outside of it. For a fleeting, breathless moment he took himself for dead. (15–16)

The experience, that is, had prepared him for the fire and the wholesale destruction of his past by clarifying his vision. The fire had served to strip him of the things of this world in preparation for the events that now follow in *A Life*: his approach to an appropriate death, as "one of those chosen not merely to grow old, but to grow ripe" (152).

A Life begins in Chapman the day after the fire, when Warner attempts to locate kin of Kermit on his mother's side. He finds a Miss Effie Mae, "old now and a little dim-witted," living with Amanda Plomer. Effie Mae's brother Ivy is known to be "the last [white] man in the county to be killed by Indians" (4), so it is significant when, gripping Warner's arm, Effie Mae cries out, "God protect him from Indians." In the house, Warner finds himself involved in a prayer circle with four old women: "Warner could not explain the tremor, like a chill, that began at his fingers and passed through his body, affecting him so powerfully that his knees trembled. He glanced upward to see, pinned to the rafters, postcards and pictures of a religious nature, the details somewhat blurred by the film on his eyes. For the second time in twenty-four hours what Warner knew to be commonplace seemed strange, and what he knew to be bizarre seemed commonplace" (13–14).

The importance of the prayer circle is emphasized by its aftereffects, leaving "his mind fuzzy, like a blow on the head" (15), and it reaffirms the significance of "Warner's impression, the day before, that he had lost in the last few days a part of himself, measurable as weight" (8). Immediately thereafter, he stumbles on Ivy's grave and (in yet another Morris doubling) identifies with him. Warner finds himself on a road he had traveled years before to pick up his bride-to-be, then to his old homestead where he had raised sheep near the Pecos River in New Mexico. As he travels, he feels himself unraveling, shrinking, removed further and further from life. The road seems to be bringing the past back to him rather than leading to a future, and memories crowd his mind, linking him to some of the objects and structures—abandoned houses, a schoolhouse pump, an outdoor privy, a grain elevator—portrayed in Morris's photographs. As Warner gets closer to the center of life, he feels an "unmanly concern for his dwindling remains" and is gratified to find that "an emotion so frail, so womanly, had overcome his stubborn will" (36).

His tenderness for life is shown when, stopping for water at the pump near a quiet schoolhouse, he rescues a kitten that had been thrown into the filth under an outhouse and thinks of the "goddam kid" who put it there: "The vileness of man made his eyes film over, and aroused his fury against heaven" (61). He takes charge of its welfare, and deciding to buy it some food, stops at a restaurant. The importance of the stop is manifested in Warner's observation: "Of all the things in this world, or almost all of them, there was nothing that Warner disliked more than a day full of happenings like so many leaves blowing. Since morning, one thing had led to another, and they had all led to this seat at the counter" (74).

In the restaurant Warner encounters George Blackbird, a Hopi Indian recently returned from Vietnam. Blackbird immediately senses Warner's existential condition. "Old man, what you want?" he asks (80), but Morris gives every indication that Blackbird already knows, and he tells Warner he will accompany him. Blackbird does this in such a way that Warner feels "he had been chosen" (90). Warner buys a can of tuna for the kitten, but once they are in the car, Blackbird finds the kitten dead and unceremoniously throws it out the window. Warner has

> a notion so strange it made him smile. The moment coming up, the one that came toward him like the line on the highway, then receded behind him, was something he had no control over. He could watch it coming, he could see it receding, but he could do nothing to avoid it. The Indian, the cat, and the prayer ceremony had come out to nowhere to take him somewhere. He could see it happening. He could see that it was not an accident. He had come this way by his own free choosing, and having chosen as he pleased, he was right where he was. One thing led to another, to another, to another, like the count of the poles that passed his window (95).

In the end, having arrived at the homestead he had shared with his bride and feeling spent and dazed, Warner has his rendezvous with death. Blackbird comes to him out of the darkness, light glinting from the tuna can cover in his hand. He holds Warner's hand and slices his wrist, and Warner, with no alarm, watches the blood pulse forth. This event is presented as a ritual in which both parties have specific roles in a larger scheme: "It was not Blackbird's intent to do this for him, but Blackbird, too, has been shaped to this moment, the ceremonial opening of the vein in Warner's wrist" (152). And so Warner dies, willingly removed from life, his death presented as a natural event closing out a complete life. Together *Fire Sermon* and *A Life* show the gradual stages of Warner's withdrawal in significant detail and without sentimentality.

Both these novels develop slowly and with a great deal of attention to acts of perception and to objects and events closely observed. In Morris's cataloging of Viola's objects seen by both Warner and Kermit, readers are constantly led to remember the etched character in Morris's photographs and the patina on the objects within them. Raymond Neinstein notes that in the openings of both novels and the closing of *A Life*, Morris "appeals to our sight, as if a painting or a photograph were being described in each case. Not only is a picture described, but we are told where we, as viewers, stand."[16]

In addition, the novels contain surprisingly frequent references to frames and reflections à la Morris's method in *Works of Love*. When in *Fire Sermon* Morris wants to affirm the new relations between Kermit and the hippie couple, Kermit sees not through a window to the world beyond, but sees a mirrored reflection, one that "revealed it was just the three of them against all the rest" (111). Later Kermit, following Warner into the house just prior to the fire, looks, not directly into the room, but through the "open half of the door" that "framed the bureau mirror at the foot of Aunt Viola's bed, reflecting the glass shade and the smoking chimney of her lamp" (146). That Morris, rather than simply describe these scenes, requires such emphasis of focused and framed visual complexity suggests the depth of emotion he must have experienced in composing these books. These scenes may only be viewed through the safety of deliberate indirection.

The Fork River Space Project

Given the rich visual significance of *Fire Sermon* and *A Life*, it seems no coincidence that in his next novel, *The Fork River Space Project*, Morris should deal *directly* with the epistemology of perception. *The Fork River Space Project* is a slighter, somewhat self-indulgent, near–science fiction novel that places its focus on the relationship between reality, the imagination, and the connection between perceptual vision and conceptual understanding. As Craig Watson observes, Morris had increasingly focused in his novels on "the observer himself, the quality and limitations of his ocularity,"[17] and he links this book to Morris's photography. *The Fork River Space Project* is indebted to Stanley Kubrick, to NASA, and to Morris's friendship with Loren Eiseley. The novel includes images found also in Morris's homage to Eiseley, "The Origin of Sadness" (also set in northern Kansas), and in the first of the *Time Pieces* essays, "In our Image."

The observer-narrator of *The Fork River Space Project* is another writer, Kelcey, as he widens his horizons courtesy of his young wife, Alice; a house painter named Dahlberg; and the proprietor of the Fork River Space Project, Harry Lorbeer. Lorbeer's point in this project is to restore a sense of awe to human existence: "[W]ithout awe we diminish, we trivialize, everything we touch" (113). Lorbeer's project, that is, is a version of Morris's: to transform consciousness through efforts of the imagination. The problem is that Lorbeer's project is conveyed flatly through words; readers are told *about* the imagination at work, are more or less onlookers who watch Kelcey's excitement without being able to share it. The book remains an intellectual exercise, not an active experience. But what readers watch is nevertheless interesting and leads to contemplations of their own.

The main point of the novel is precisely the consequences of expansion of consciousness to produce thoughtful transitions to unknown futures—more important, to do so without fear. This idea is sketchily worked out through the friendly alliance that Kelcey's young wife (who is a generation younger than Kelcey and thus in Morris's revised vision easily susceptible to change) finds herself in with Dahlberg. Kelcey's need for an accommodation provides him with an immediate motive for coming to terms with change and for changing *himself*. By the end of the novel, in a feverish hour of understanding, Kelcey realizes that he is in some brave new world of the imagination: "For the first time I felt that I was part of the solution, rather than the problem. . . . Would it surprise them if I said that it did not strike me as peculiar that two men shared the same woman?" (178).

The project, located in a schoolhouse in a mysterious ghost town in northern Kansas, is a presentation designed for the senses: a loud playing of Strauss's *Zarathustra* (that Kelcey had last heard in Kubrick's movie *2001*), an eerie light "that appeared to come through panels in the roof and had a curious subterranean dimness, as if filtered through water," and a slide show consisting of photographs taken from space, beginning with one of "the earth just above the moon's horizon. The upper half only was illuminated, so that it resembled the cranium of a human skull" (105)—probably the NASA photograph (*View of Earth Rise, 1969*) that Morris discussed a decade later in "The Camera Eye," and that he says he contemplated "[f]or many months, on the wall facing my desk,"[18] indicating its personal importance.

What is most interesting, perhaps, is Morris's imaginative idea of time and space derived from contemplation of this photograph. At one point the photograph leads Kelcey to think of viewing earthly motion from space. The farther out in space one goes, the less motion is perceivable; therefore, it follows (imaginatively) that there *should be* some point in space at which motion stops, thus making space equal to time. Two corollaries follow: first, if one then proceeds even deeper into space, one will by that fact go back further in time; second, if such return in time is possible, then it is possible also, by moving laterally in space, to insert oneself as a perceiver into the past. Thus Kelcey can imagine the lives of the primitive cave artists alongside his own past as seen from space. "Now if you just carry that to its conclusion, at some point in space time has stopped. It's all in suspension. My game is to zoom in from space on the Mesozoic period" (155).

A decade later, in "The Camera Eye," this conceit remained much on Morris's mind when he speaks of an "unearthly double vision" achieved from "pondering a view of the planet from space":

> Through rents in the cloud cover I saw the Great Plains, the pattern of fields and right angles, the dry bed of a river . . . and where flecks of green indicated a village, I strained to see who it was who returned my gaze. A child, clothed in rompers, sat in the talcum-like dust beneath the porch of a house. Wide-eyed and entranced, he dreamily gazed through the porch slide slats in my direction. . . . If I would peer at this child from far enough in space, where earthly time was in abeyance, would not the child who sat there, recognizably myself, return my gaze? (18)

This is an interesting and telling image, this view of the author contemplating his former self in an intersubjective act of mutual recognition. This image, it might be argued, is emblematic of what Morris had been doing in much of his fiction for more than 40 years: visioning himself as an other—his double—to create his work, and in doing so, to come to terms with the meaning of his existence.

Morris had moved a considerable distance from the early 1960s, when he had pondered "how things are" and attempted to answer that first with his longest novel, *One Day*, then through the anarchy of one of his shortest novels, *In Orbit*. The evidence of *Fire Sermon* and *A Life* suggests that Morris was no longer interested in addressing the "arrears" of American culture. In *The Fork River Space Project* Morris's characters conclude that the world can be changed simply through a change of perspective (*not* a change in social or cultural conditions)—an interesting, and perhaps consoling, idea, but a solipsistic one. "How things are" in *The Fork River Space Project* is a bad dream from which escape is possible only for those able to mobilize a self-centered consciousness.

Chapter Seven
Retrospection: Ordering the Past, 1980–1997

Having recounted the final days of the octogenarian Floyd Warner, perhaps leading his audience to conclude that he was winding down, Morris nevertheless continued to be productive throughout the 1970s. Although his novels were short and infrequent, he published a variety of other books—including colored snapshots and texts in *Love Affair: A Venetian Journal*, a collection of short stories, and two books having the stamp of the professor: one on reading as a civilized value, *About Fiction*, the other a collection of pieces on the American penchant for images, *Earthly Delights, Unearthly Adornments*.

By the end of the decade Morris appeared once again to be immersed in visual imagery, writing several new essays on photography that dwell on both the magic of the medium and its dangerous cultural appeal when its products are taken for granted. Sometimes he linked the magic of photography to one of his concerns at the start of his career, as in this haunting sentence from an essay first appearing in 1981: "Photographs considered worthless, time's confetti, slipped from their niche in drawer or album, touch us like the tinkle of a bell at a séance or a ghostly murmur in the attic. And why not? They are snippets of the actual gauze from that most durable of ghosts, nostalgia."[1]

In the 1980s Morris became increasingly retrospective, looking back over his career and putting the finishing touches to it in a gradual withdrawal from public life. This process gives the appearance of careful planning, as if he were deliberately preparing his case for the judgment of posterity. Making this case involved the privileged emotional freedoms of those who have lived long lives—although he remained thoroughly on guard against sentimentality. From *Plains Song*, his final novel, published just before his 70th birthday, through three volumes of autobiography, to his collected essays on photography and photographic epistemology, *Time Pieces: Photographs, Writing, and Memory*, Morris's work has a polished finality about it. This finality is obvious, too, from the evidence of his collected short stories, in which one of his subjects was the transitory territory of old age.

There is visible in Morris's writing from this decade a kind of mellow-ness, as if Morris were feeling comfortable in his role as a senior literary statesman. His retrospection shows an acceptance of his situation as an aging man. What appears most remarkable is how thoroughly his inter-est in visual images once again penetrated his prose, so that in the case of *Plains Song* and some of the short stories readers must pay attention as much to the play of images as they do to the narrative. Two images that recur in the novel, the memoirs, and the short stories are the merging of "lampglow and shadow" and glimpses of sky framed by tree branches—as in Hazlitt's near-vision as he lies in his hotel room in "Glimpse into Another Country": "In the play of reflections on the ceiling he glimpsed, as through a canopy of leaves, the faraway prospect" of "bustling figures swarming" in a "station lobby"[2]—an archetypal image of the crowded flow of life Hazlitt is about to leave behind.

It is fitting that Morris concluded his career with such renewed atten-tion to the visual. In *Time Pieces* he sounds a warning that Americans are too careless of photographic images, and he still insists on distinctions "between photographs that mirror the subject, and images that reveal the photographer."[3] Morris's attachment to American objects makes him uncomfortable with the idea of "reading" photographs, as if they could be detached from strong emotion, and he prefers "icon" to "art." That he was given two major retrospectives of his photographs in the 1980s is a testament to his continuing appeal as a photographer of "things about to disappear."

Plains Song for Female Voices

It is appropriate that in his final novel Morris should circle back upon himself to commemorate the Nebraska home place and the life of his Aunt Clara in an apparent farewell to his novelistic craft. In this novel Morris refined his views of women in a dense and conciliatory prose: It is at once one of his most complex books and his most compassionate toward women. *Plains Song for Female Voices* functions through counter-point, layers and layers of female voices (in third person and omniscient narrative) swelling into a chorus. Through these voices Morris writes of the emotional lives of women in a manner close to social history. *Plains Song* is a paean to womanly endurance as well as a panoramic view of

American social history (the century ending with Vietnam) from the viewpoints of women.

Plains Song covers three generations of women in the Atkins family, focusing most on the trio of Cora, the mother; her daughter, Madge; and her niece Sharon Rose. It is Cora's emotional presence that haunts the novel; it is she, for better or for worse, that the other women in the family measure themselves against. The novel begins—like Katherine Anne Porter's "The Jilting of Granny Weatherall"—with the mother on her deathbed, nudged to memories of her past. Like many another woman in late nineteenth-century America, Cora had married (to please her father) and moved west with her husband, Emerson, then lived out her life in Nebraska. Cora is an unlikely matriarch, having little experience in the world and a culturally stifled consciousness, but she is a woman who courageously endures, faithful to the principles of her heritage.

She and Emerson have one child, Madge, but equally important to the novel is the daughter of Emerson's brother, Orion, and his wife, Belle Rooney. This daughter is Sharon Rose, and she is reared by Cora after the death of Belle; Madge and Sharon grow up nearly as sisters. Whereas Cora represents the stifled, but valiant, life on the Plains, Sharon Rose is the chief opposing force, for she rejects the Plains—but even as she rejects the people who inhabit the Plains, she finds herself attached emotionally to them. This attachment is the largest issue the novel probes.

In time Madge marries her man and Sharon leaves for the university, then for Chicago and a career in music. Madge finds satisfaction in her role as wife and mother, although she is reluctant to admit her pleasure in sex; Sharon, on the other hand, never marries, finding her emotional satisfactions in music, and she overcomes loneliness in friendships with women. Later she brings Blanche, Madge's oldest daughter, to live with her in Chicago, but sends her back when it becomes clear that Blanche carries too much of the half-submerged farm environment with her. During her life, Sharon returns three times to Nebraska, the last time for Cora's funeral, by which time the home place has vanished and the Atkins family is into its fourth generation.

Whereas Cora and Sharon Rose embody the principles of two distinct ways of life, there are two central events that receive symbolic meaning through reiteration and, finally, through combination in Cora's memory. The first of these occurs early in the novel. Cora, having sexual intercourse for the first time (and apparently the last) with Emerson, is so aghast at the brutality of the experience that she bites her knuckle, to the bone, in order to keep from screaming out. Emerson's explanation to the doctor is that a horse bit her; this explanation is acceptable to all, including Cora, who senses the need for a public explanation for something that cannot be discussed.

The second event takes places years later, and it is used to clarify Sharon Rose's relationships, specifically to Madge, but indirectly to all the other women: The event precipitates her departure for Chicago. Already appalled by the social understanding that girls are reared only to become wives, Sharon Rose finds Madge spooning with a boy. "Is he looking for a wife or a housemaid?" Sharon screams out, within hearing of Cora.

> Cora had been on the screened-in porch, ironing; she had stood leaning on the iron, speechless. Nothing had prepared her to believe that Sharon Rose had such resentment, such bitterness, in her. Cora had . . . seized her by the wrist, and whacked her palm with the back of a hairbrush, sharply. How well they knew what Sharon Rose thought of her hands! "That will teach you!" Cora cried, knowing that it wouldn't even as she said it. Not Sharon Rose. She had turned from Cora and run up the stairs.[4]

Cora's anger in striking Sharon Rose with the hairbrush is remembered well by both women. For Sharon Rose it symbolizes both Cora's rigid acceptance of the limited role women are allowed to play and her half-stifled understanding of human motivations.

Ironically, the physical act itself draws the women closer together in their understanding of their separate realities; certainly the act forces Cora to reexamine her life with Emerson. Two-thirds of the way through the novel, Cora remembers Sharon's words on seeing Madge and Ned Kibbee kissing, and she sees Sharon Rose's similarities to herself: "It might have been last summer, it might have been this morning, Cora standing in the pickle-sharp draft off the kitchen, except that now she knew, as she hadn't before, that Sharon Rose had meant it just as she had said it. It had not been a horse that bit her; she had bitten herself" (164). What Cora understands in this juxtaposition of memories is that both she and Sharon Rose are casualties of a culture that limits women's potential. Sharon's rebellion is more open and concrete than Cora's biting of her hand. Sharon realizes later that what she resents most is the power of the culture to sever close relations between women—especially between herself and Madge.

When later Sharon invites Madge's daughter Blanche to Chicago, supposedly to "save" her from the Plains, she does so out of "suppressed feelings of guilt" (146) and a determination to make amends for her neglect of the folks on the home place. But she takes Blanche under her wing for personal reasons as well: "Sharon could no longer bear the thought, nor avoid it, that this girl child would soon appeal to some loutish youth stimulated by the seasonal fall of pollen, and be thick with child. The thought almost sickened her. . . . Before the cocoon of Blanche's childhood had peeled away she would be locked into the trap that nature and man had set for her" (148). Blanche stays with Sharon for an extended time, but when the girl is discovered to have an interest in boys, Sharon returns her to Nebraska. Sharon tells Madge that Blanche is simply "not a city girl. Madge was relieved to hear her say so, because her father had been wondering why they had her in the first place if she wasn't at home where they could enjoy her, before she got married" (161).

There is a third epiphany in *Plains Song*, showing the ambivalence in Sharon's motivations for moving away from Nebraska. Returning east after one of her home visits, Sharon sits next to a young man on the train. The young man clears a spot in the window to catch a last glimpse of what is outside—to see, that is, the place he will in the future be from, having escaped it.

> Sharon . . . saw nothing but his reflection. "Boy, am I glad to see the last of that!" he said, happy in his freedom, in his expectations that whatever life held for him in the future, it would henceforth be his own life, it would not be the life of Battle Creek or Colby, it would not be the trauma of birth or burial, or mindless attachments to persons and places, to kinships, longings, crossing bells, the arc of streetlights, or the featureless faces on station platforms, all of which would recede into the past, into the darkness—wouldn't it? (137)

The question adding doubt at the end is Sharon Rose's, based on her own understanding that the past is not so easily jettisoned. In the young man, Sharon sees herself. The passage reflects her own ambivalent misgivings.

The major issue of the novel receives crucial treatment in yet another of Sharon Rose's returns to Nebraska, this time for the funeral of Cora. Sharon is met by Caroline, another of Madge's daughters, who drives her past what had once been the home place, but which is now being bulldozed out of existence. Caroline and Sharon Rose have a conversation that puts their relations with Cora into perspective:

> "Poor Cora!" Sharon blurted.
> "I'll never forgive her," said Caroline. "Never."
> "Caroline!" Sharon cried. She almost barked it, but her eagerness to hear more shamed her.
> "She never complained. An animal would have complained. She would still be in all that rubble if they hadn't moved her."
> A hand to her eyes, Sharon felt her head was splitting. The air trapped about her face smelled of flint.
> "At least I can complain," Caroline said. "She couldn't."
> With an effort, Sharon said, "She *could* have, Caroline, but she simply *wouldn't*."
> "Could or wouldn't, she didn't," said Caroline, "and now she's dead."
> (201)

Caroline prides herself on being modern; she is one of the interim results of an expansion of consciousness in women, as least able to articulate her feelings. But Sharon is appalled by the savagery of Caroline's rejection of Cora's life. By this time Sharon has come to realize that Cora's strength of character is useful to all women: The animal qualities of the Plains people speak to traditional forms of faith and endurance that the younger generations appear carelessly to reject out of hand.

All of this has final relevance when after the funeral Sharon returns to the motel to keep her appointment with a woman she had met earlier in the Boston airport, Alexandra Selkirk, described as similar in appearance and character to Cora. Alexandra is a feminist of some reputation, dogmatic in her belief that "[w]omen's previous triumphs had been by default. Men had simply walked away from the scene of the struggle, leaving them with the children, the chores, the culture and a high incidence of madness" (188–89). With Alexandra, Sharon hears a rooster crowing:

> The sound was piercing, but cracked, shrill with young male assurance, transporting Sharon to the hush of a summer dawn, the faint stain of light between the sill and the blind at her window, the house dark as a cave, in the stairwell the sounds of stove lids being lifted, shifted, the pungent whiff of kerosene spilled on the cobs, the rasp of a match, and in the silence following the whoosh and roar of the flames the first clucking of the hens in the henhouse, all of it gone, vanished from this earth, but restored to the glow of life in a cock's crow.

"You hear that?" said Alexandra. "The same old tyrant!" Was it a smile she turned to share with Sharon or a grimace? This would be a young tyrant, not an old one, but it seemed unimportant in the context. (227–28)

Like *Ceremony in Lone Tree*, *Plains Song* ends with dawn providing a reinvigorated sense of the fullness of life. This ritual of rebirth supports the theme of continuity of womanly strength (represented by Cora and by Alexandra's assured self-mockery). With Sharon, the reader comes to acknowledge Cora's example—what she has made of herself, despite the cultural limitations imposed on her. Morris implies that fidelity to one's nature is essential to overcome the rationalized and privileged forces of culture.

With Cora's death now in the past and the home place inexorably plowed under, Sharon makes manifest her realization that if she has rejected Man's culture, she has not rejected humanity. The burden of her life might have been easier to bear if she had been able to come to terms sooner with the rural past into which she had been thrust. Her rejection of the Plains carries with it the knowledge, accumulated through time, that women on the Plains, as elsewhere, are to be valued for their integrity and their refusal to submit wholly to male culture. In the end, accepting Cora as well as Alexandra Selkirk, Sharon is able to accept the meaning of the past as reshaped in the present: Alexandra, that is, has her own nature that links her—and Sharon—to the past as embodied and identified in Cora Atkins. Sharon's feminism, then, is this complex understanding, not to be simplified in Alexandra's terms.

As in all his novels, much of Morris's meaning is carried through his style and narrative method. As Ellen Serlen Uffen writes, in *Plains Song* Morris "chooses to suggest depths, but not to plumb them. The result is a book of nuances."[5] The narrative presentation is complex. *Plains Song* is told from multiple perspectives, as suggested by the plainsong of Christian music history. But more important than music, more closely related to narrative method, is photography. As discussed in previous chapters, the assimilation of Morris's camera eye to prose is largely responsible for the obliquity of his style, an obliquity carried fully into *Plains Song* in a narrative method that necessarily adheres to essential human time but also emphasizes how past events are freshly interpreted and imbued with new meaning. This idea of the mind as a selective repository has supported Morris's major themes since his discovery in the 1940s that he could in fact reconstruct the past. The style he devised for *Plains Song* makes room both for necessary chronology and a para-doxical timelessness based on the mind as receptor, processor, and reviser of images.

That photography is crucial to the conception of *Plains Song* is imme-diately suggested from the photograph Morris employs to separate the 14 "chapters."[6] In the original photograph, *Reflection in Oval Mirror* (fig-ure 2), the oval is framed within a rectangle. For the novel, however, Morris removes this frame, causing ambiguity. Readers must pause to study what they see: Is it a window, a mirror, or merely a photograph similar to those pictured within the image itself? The photograph enhances the novel's theme of the necessity for rethinking the past as well as the continuous process humans must undergo as they reshape memory to serve present needs.

Beginning with this photograph and its obvious ambiguities, *Plains Song* is insistently visual. Morris consistently zooms in on the eye, the agent of visual perception: Madge's eyes are like buttons or "raisins stuck into the dough of a raw sugar cookie," Sharon Rose's are large, unblinking, direct, intense (65); Cora's are "luminous" and "lustrous" (200–203) and are perceived by Sharon Rose as "[t]he intense staring eyes . . . of icons" (88). Belle has "darting blackberry eyes" (46); Blanche has eyes "like lanterns" (139; "If a lighted candle could be placed in her mouth, would she glow with an inner light?" [147]). In addition, there are ubiquitous references to "lidded" or "averted" eyes, signifying knowledge refused or social collusion denied, offset by "knowing glances" between people, signifying the sharing of "secret" knowledge. One comic example of the complications of intersubjective visual exchange involves Sharon's observation of her sister's beau, who plans to be a "veter-nary": "The way he stared at her, as he chewed, upset her less than his unawareness that she was gazing at him" (127). It is char-acteristic of Morris that sometimes he even notes when these glances are *not* exchanged.

It might be suggested that what Morris does in the prose of *Plains Song* is similar to what John Berger and Jean Mohr attempt almost entirely through a sequence of 150 photographs in *Another Way of Telling*: to "follow, for a few minutes, the mind of an old woman consid-ering her life."[7] Just as Berger and Mohr wish to encourage readers to deeper contemplation of the interior realities of French peasant life, so Morris asks readers to get inside the lives of these archetypal American women. Reading *Plains Song*—like reading *The Works of Love*—is similar to viewing photographic sequences—"extended, sustained bodies of

work, where single images refer to others and alter their visual and cog-
nitive weight and significance," in patterns sometimes so demanding
"they can wear you out with their subtle intricacies."[8] Morris, too,
makes enormous demands, providing a great deal of information to
remember and to reconsider when he alludes to pieces of it in fresh con-
texts.

This intricacy can be seen by comparing two passages—one at the
beginning, the other at the end—of *Plains Song* involving Morris's use of
mirrors. Early in the novel Morris links Cora's "religious nature" to her
feelings about mirrors: "She never lacked for self-knowledge in the matter of vanity. Mirrors impressed her as suspect by nature in the way they
presented a graven image. She keenly and truly felt the deception of her
reflected glance. . . . She had never held a mirror in such a manner that
she might see [herself from behind]. . . . Neither had she (since a child)
gazed with open eyes on what the Lord had created below her neck" (4).
Clearly Cora's sense of self is not derived from self-conscious visual evidence. Her reluctance before the mirror is another way of averting her
eyes, believing that reflection on the body is indecent. Sharon gradually
comes to admire Cora's ability to maintain a sense of self without need
of social validation.

The mirror image at the end of the book is linked to the earlier passage regarding Cora. The image reflected is that of Alexandra Selkirk:

> Against the light of the bathroom her flat, skeletal figure appears to be a
> resurrection of Cora. She faced the mirror to draw a comb through her
> short coarse hair. As if hallucinating, Sharon seemed to see a wire-
> handled syrup pail dangling from her hand, weighted with eggs. . . .
>   Still facing the mirror Alexandra said, "I'm going for a walk. I want to
> see the sunrise. Do you know the sun is perpetually rising? Every
> moment somewhere. Isn't that awesome?" What she saw in the mirror
> led her to smile. She turned to say, "You want to join me?"
>   What expression did she surprise on Sharon's face? For a moment it
> shamed her it was so open, betraying her customary independence.
>   Alexandra said, "Do I look a sight? Who is there to see me but God?"
>   Sharon had already moved to rise from the bed. "I'm coming," she
> said. "I've not seen a sunrise since I was a child." (228–29)

The mirror is the most obvious link between the two passages: what
the private (and socially invisible) Cora and the public (hence highly visible) Alexandra Selkirk see reflected back to them is not so very dissimi-
lar, at least from Sharon's viewpoint. But what they make of what they

see is intensely different, marking a change of social and political consciousness. Cora's tacit role in this evolution is essential, for carried through her is a strength of character that Sharon must recognize and cherish; Sharon's "evolution" is concluded when she relinquishes her pity of Cora and accepts the lesson of Cora's life. Her success is marked by her observation of the similarities between Cora and Alexandra, when she seems to see Alexandra carrying Cora's egg pail.

Much of this meaning is carried through religious imagery. Cora's reluctance before her mirror is represented by her fear of "graven images." To focus on the human body would be to worship a false god, deflecting from the God she appears never to question. Alexandra, on the other hand, has been "liberated" from exterior interpretations of her body. She accepts her body with self-assured humor. When she says to Sharon, "Who is there to see me but God?" she puts God into context with the "same old tyrant" rooster who has been crowing outside the window; she believes the meanings of both God and the rooster have been culturally coded—and are open to humorous critique. Her allusion to the rising sun of Ecclesiastes supports the intergenerational theme of the book and connects her thoroughly to Cora.

But what of Sharon Rose's transformation? At the funeral service for Cora, Sharon had listened to "Abide with Me" and brooded on the hymn's meaning: "But what, indeed, had abided? The liberation from her burdens, the works and meager effects of Cora had been erased from the earth." In the church Sharon thinks of this erasure as a "violation" and an "ultimate rejection" (214–15), a view she must overcome. Morris's use of symbolism is particularly significant in the concluding chapter in which Sharon transcends mere independence and appears to achieve release from guilt into a state of freedom, centered in the rebirth-sunrise. Marilyn Arnold writes that in *Plains Song* "the language and imagery of redemption proliferate. Morris not only provides the suggestion of the crucifixion in the name of the motel [The Crossways], but also interjects a 'cock's crow' into the scene."[9]

When the two women approach the dawn, Sharon says she has "not seen a sunrise since I was a child." This echoes the passage quoted earlier that "since a child" Cora had not gazed at her naked body. What the novel completes is a journey through Cora's life, then through her death and resurrection in Sharon's perception of Alexandra; the novel carries a message of evolutionary continuity that links Cora's strong-willed and nearly celibate asceticism to Alexandra's unconcern for limited cultural codings. Linking generations, the book connects deaths to births. Then when Sharon sees the sunrise, she accepts both Cora's resurrection and enters into freedom from a self-abnegation she had criticized in Cora but failed earlier to see in herself.

Finally, it is pertinent to ask how Sharon's transformation of consciousness is brought about in *Plains Song*. In many of his novels Morris inserts a ritual "thrust from behind" that impels his protagonists to seek life-affirming change. Such an event occurs in *Plains Song* when Sharon is concluding her second visit. She had been extremely critical, to the point of rudeness, of the "animal-like" existence of people remaining in Nebraska. As she sits in the car after the family meal, she experiences a "drugged," "drowsing," "confused" condition: "The heat drone of the insects, the stupor of the food, and the jostle of the car seemed to blur the distinction between herself and the swarming life around her." Morris adds, "Her soul (what else could it be) experienced a sense of liberation in its loss of self" (134–35). This event prepares her for her final visit, when her liberation through full acceptance occurs.

Morris suggests preparation for knowledge in *Plains Song* another way, one much in keeping with his use of visual imagery to suggest conceptual interpretations and one that gives Blanche a role in the evolution of consciousness. When the book ends, Blanche's future remains unknown, but she is described as having Cora's "wraith-like figure" and "lustrous eyes" (203). Earlier Sharon had sought to save her by bringing her to the city; the scene in which she recognizes her folly is worth recalling. Blanche is supposed to meet Sharon at the zoo, but Blanche fails to appear. When Sharon finds her, she is with a boy who has given her "some sort of exotic chicken"; the boy slips away as Sharon approaches, but Blanche continues to stroke the chicken's "plumed, brightly hued topknot" (159). The scene, with its phallic suggestion, horrifies Sharon: She sends Blanche home. Later when Sharon returns for Cora's funeral, she is given Blanche's room, where painted on the wall are Blanche's artistic efforts, including "an exotic-looking bird, with a dishevelled topknot" and eyes "open, and bright as hatpins" (205).

But the crucial event, occurring directly before the family's departure for Cora's funeral service, takes place during one of Morris's inimitable family meal scenes. Sharon looks up to see a bird fluttering. "The bird, a parakeet or a canary, hovered as if it intended to nest in Sharon's hair. Did she gasp? The startled bird rose toward the ceiling, then in a faltering, bobbing flight it moved from head to head, circling the table, pausing as if confused over the head of Caroline" (212). The bird is Blanche's, but it finds Blanche's place at the table occupied by Sharon,

and thus it circles "from head to head." It may be suggested that in this
bird Morris extended his religious imagery to incorporate a veiled image
of the Holy Ghost, intended to bestow enlightenment on the assembled
before they make their final farewell to Cora. This is a book, after all, in
which God the Father is explained by Alexandra Selkirk as a cultural
concept supporting the male status quo. Alexandra asks, "Who said let
them have dominion over the whole shebang? *He* did. We've been living
under him all of these goddam centuries" (224). Those words—the
"He" in charge of the shebang—are loaded with meaning.

   Plains Song has many similarities—30 years later—to *The Works of
Love*, despite the passivity of that book's protagonist, Will Brady. Both
The Works of Love and *Plains Song* deal with deeply submerged emotions
and the problems involved in the articulation of complex feelings resulting from Plains upbringings and subsequent inabilities to find the city
sufficient to quiet the yearnings for a better life. The problem
announced in the opening pages of *The Works of Love* is crucial also to
Plains Song: "This desolate place, this rim of the world, had been God's
country to Adam Brady, but to his wife, Caroline Clayton, a godforsaken
hole. Perhaps only Will Brady could combine these two points of view.
He could leave it, that is, but he would never get over it."[10] Like Brady,
Sharon Rose could leave the Plains environment, but she would never
get over it.

   But whereas the earlier book dwells in pathos on an isolated individual, *Plains Song*, through its counterpoint, works out its themes through
the family; and rather than emphasizing failure, *Plains Song* stresses
endurance and the growth of consciousness through interplay with family members and an intelligent use of memory. In *Plains Song* consciousness and intelligence triumph. *Plains Song* serves as an archive of Morris's experience and judgment as well as a repository of visual images
through which he emphasized the process of seeing as a means of making meaning.[11]

Autobiography, Photography, and Morris's "Camera Obscura"

Immediately after *Plains Song* Morris turned to memoir, completi[...]
story of his own life—to the publication of *Ceremony in Lone Tr[...]
marriage to Josephine Kantor—in three volumes. As [...]
expected, these volumes tell many stories similar to those [...]
fiction, and they produce further detailed proof that Mor[...]

a significant extent his autobiography. In the first, *Will's Boy*, Morris tells the story of his boyhood as his father's son. The second, *Solo*, recounts Morris's *Wanderjahr* and his "captivity" in the medieval castle near Vienna. The third volume, *A Cloak of Light*, is more dutifully conventional, detailing Morris's writing career, his domestic situation and friendships, and his later travels to Mexico and Europe. Between the first two memoirs, Morris produced *Photographs and Words*, an account of his adventures with photography, which included laser-scanned reproductions of many of his photographs. Photography was obviously much on Morris's mind as he prepared for retirement.

The memoirs, written more or less as capstone volumes when Morris was in his 70s, have significant bearing on Morris's aesthetics. Retrospection served to narrow his focus, and what he was most interested in pursuing were those formative images and events that conspired to make him into an artist. This focus is why *Will's Boy* is the best of the three, a book rich with visual imagery, at times approaching poetry in its lyricism (flawed only by the insertion of long quotes from his fiction). This book provides hints to Morris's aesthetics that relate his boyhood experiences to his choice of photography as a means of coming to terms with emotional needs.

In a provocative essay, G. B. Crump describes Morris as an author who had to overcome *in his fiction* his personal inclinations to "evasion, willed isolation, and failure of feeling."[12] Noting the many references Morris makes to concealment in his memoirs, Crump suggests that Morris's childhood was something of a disaster in its emotional contractions and had to be *overcome* in the author's adult life. Morris's own explanation of the emotional costs of his childhood suggests an extreme introversion: "*I had little or no suspicion that my true feelings were precisely those that I would learn to conceal.*"[13] But by emphasizing that he *learned* to conceal "true feelings," Morris appears to underscore this process as usefully educational, all but denying its psychological trauma. No doubt Morris's boyhood was emotionally confusing, but in *Will's Boy* (and to some extent in the other two volumes) Morris chooses to focus on how e transformed the personal into the transcendental imaginative.[14]

Through memoir, Morris in effect moves the emphasis from his per- psychology to his learned ability to create art—emphasizing both and the *activity* of artistic creativity. Perhaps an appropriate his model of the creative mind (and its activities) is that of the ura. The camera obscura—in which images of the outside ied by light, mysteriously upside-down, into a darkened interior—is appropriate to Morris's aesthetics because of his frequent references to contrasts of light and dark in a variety of permutations. Morris's repetition of this chiaroscuro effect strongly indicates that something in his mental makeup desired this image for a basic human fulfillment.

This deliberate contrast of light and dark in Morris's work comes in two different versions. First, in his photographs Morris used stark contrast, perhaps because he wanted to downplay "documentary" content and to convert the pictured objects into mental images. In the second version, most pertinent here, that contrast between light and dark is soft and muted, and it is the province of prose. But perhaps *contrast* is the wrong word entirely, because what is remarkable in this approach is the way light and dark *merge* into each other. This effect is found most dramatically in the opening pages of *Will's Boy*. In his introductory comments, Morris presents two organizational images, the first an Emersonian metaphor of "radiating circles," representative of creative *methodology*; the second a picture of "lampglow and shadows," representing a vibrant memory at the core of Morris's aesthetic *motive*.

Because this image is dense and complex and is echoed in later pages, it is useful to quote it at length: "The first of my childhood impressions is that of lampglow and shadows on a low ceiling. But under my steadfast gaze it dissolves like tissue. It resists both fixing and enlargement. What I am left with is the ache of a nameless longing. On my child's soul lampglow and shadows have left radiating circles that a lifetime drizzle, of lapping and overlapping, have not washed away."[15] Several images and phrases in this passage reveal connections between memory and method. First, because this memory is "the first," it must assume not only temporal but essential priority—whether it occurred first in time is less relevant than that Morris *now* thinks of it as foundational. Second, the memory is *elusive*—and its elusiveness is seductive. In order to explain its nature Morris chooses metaphors of "fixing" and "enlargement" that are drawn from photography, in this way linking the movements of memory to the mystery and magic of the photographic dark room: As the memory resists final processing, it calls for recursiveness that gives art its ritual quality.

Finally, Morris relies on the language of emotion to sugg image's power over him: The memory entails both an *ache* and This kind of oxymoronic language to describe emotion (ech like *Real Losses, Imaginary Gains* and *Earthly Delights, U ments*) states Morris's view of the human condition, in w mortality are balanced by the powers of imagination. But Morris is not deceived by vain hope. Loss is real and death is ultimate—and because they are, life is a bittersweet affair. That bittersweet quality is found in both "the ache of a nameless longing" and the compensatory image "lampglow and shadows."

It is important that Morris's light is not a light found in its natural state, but rather one he recreates for its emotional release. The *glow* of a lamp—not the scene lit by the lamp—is the primary point. Odd as it might seem, the writer who appears most to share Morris's interest in such light is Edgar Allan Poe. Richard Wilbur, who wants to see Poe's tales as "more than complicated machines for saying 'boo,' "[16] notes the frequency of "enclosed or circumscribed" places in Poe and says Poe intends "the isolation of the poetic soul in visionary reverie or trance. When we find one of Poe's characters in . . . a claustral room, we know that he is in the process of dreaming his way out of the world" (104). Poe's "claustral" rooms contain no natural lighting—if there *are* windows they are tinted "so as to transform the light of day" into a condition pertinent to "the portrayal of those half-states of mind in which dream and reality are blended." Such light is appropriate to "the timelessness and placelessness of the dreaming mind" (115).[17]

Such light for Poe is a means to, and a ritual condition of, imaginative poetic transcendence. References to light often serve the same purpose for Morris. As "[f]lickering candles, wavering torches, and censers full of writhing varicolored flames" characterize Poe's lighting (Wilbur, 115), so Morris's work contains ubiquitous images of caves lit by flame, of dimly lit séances, even of the mind as a darkroom. For Morris such images are important to the making of art: "There is a history of darkness in the making of images. At Peche Merle and Altamira, in the recesses of caves, the torchlit chapels of worship and magic, images of matchless power were painted on the walls and ceilings" ("Image," 1). These quasi-religious effects of light are closely associated for Morris with photography: "The camera eye partakes of the supernatural, of the miraculous. It is no accident that it is a gift of light and that its alchemy ˙es place in darkness. At work in the darkroom or under the hood of a ⸳ra, the photographer is in the charmed world of the séance, of ˙ and unearthly expectations" ("Eye," 21).

⸳age laden with significance is that of the egg candler as Mor-⸳rs it from his youth. The room in which the egg candler is ˙stinct similarities to the camera obscura: it too is a dark chamber in which light provides essential illumination. Morris describes it in some detail: "My father's candling room was like a dark, narrow pantry, the only light coming from the two holes in the candler, a Karo syrup pail with a light bulb in it" (*WB*, 28–29). Morris clearly associates the room with the process of image-making: "The candling-room image is an assembly of overlapping, shifting memory impressions. It is one I have constructed to reaffirm and stabilize a fading impression."[18] In describing its effects, Morris sounds the same note that he uses for "the séance" activities of the photographic darkroom:

> In the candling room, smelling of cracked eggs and excelsior, the scorched smell given off by the candler, my father was a ponderable presence, more than a voice, more than a father. The light flashed on, then off, his face. I heard the eggs drop into the fillers. In the intense beams of light from the candler the air was thick as water. Many things swam in it. Inside the egg the yolk twirled, there was an eye like a hatpin, there was a lumpish cloud soon to be a chicken, there was a visible shrinkage, indicating age, all revealed in the light beam. I was not well paid, but I was well schooled, and would not soon forget what I had learned. (*WB*, 30)

Morris associates the candler with his father and with successful accomplishment and knowledge—thereby positing the otherwise distant father as a significant contributor to Wright's being "well schooled." Morris's father is described as "more than a father," suggesting archetypal significance.

In creating these chiaroscuro images, Morris often links the *social* idea of attempted concealment to the *aesthetic* interplay of images in which darkness is dissolved by light. Early in *Will's Boy*, he quotes from the opening paragraph of an earlier essay:

> *The small creatures of this world, and not a few of the large ones, are only at their ease under something. The cat crawls under the culvert, the infant under the table, screened off by the cloth that hangs like a curtain . . . in the Platte Valley of Nebraska, street culverts, piano boxes, the seats of wagons and buggies, railroad trestles, low bridges, the dark caves under front porches were all favored places of concealment. . . . Seated in dust as fine as talcum, my lap and hands overlaid with a pattern of shadows, I peered out at the world through the holes between slats.* (*WB*, 6 [Morris's italics])

To this list one might add barber chairs, caves real and ⸱ including "the dark cave of the theater,"[19]—and even th heading out on the road in search of the scenes that, photographed, would reveal America.

Of his aesthetics Morris writes, "If my training had been religious, my participation would surely have spoken of 'voices,' of visitations, of materializations, and called on the resources of the 'séance' to give substance to my sensations." He specifically links the "space beneath the porch" to "more orthodox holy places." By the time Morris and his father moved to Chicago, he goes on, he had "grown too large for concealment," and he established "routines that emphasized recurrence" and "ritual observation" (*Cloak* 226), suggesting a ceremonial involvement in his environment. Such images and metaphors appear with such frequency that readers might be alerted: whenever they find one of them in Morris's work, they should be prepared for the possibility that the author is employing a ceremonial image of consolatory, life-enhancing aesthetic significance. That Morris so emphasizes them in his memoirs suggests their importance to him as he approached old age.

From the child's need for safety Morris developed a camera obscura aesthetic, a theory of that mental room where memory and emotion-driven imagination conspire in the creation of art. It is a place of invention, where details are concocted in a magical ceremony, requiring hushed voices and "lampglow." If under the blazing sun there is "no place to hide," then safe places are needed where the light is muted. If such havens imply an antisocial self-protectiveness, they also make possible the movements of the imagination. Just as the limitations of photography gave way to Morris's need for clarifying narrative, so his earlier fascination with "lampglow and shadows" may suggest a predilection for the chiaroscuro of photography. But at the starting point, at the very core of experience, there existed a glow of light illuminating a primal scene, making the dark bearable and the consolation of art a life-enhancing possibility.

Morris's Short Stories and the Subject of Aging

e of the last fiction Morris wrote went into his short stories, making ppearance in *Collected Stories: 1948–1986*. Eleven of the 26 works *ed Stories* were first published in the 1980s, suggesting that as ` his powers diminish, he turned to the smaller demands of `. Of principal interest here is that some of these stories are `rris's interest in the lives of the elderly is hardly new, as `ervations on aging linked to the photographs in *The*

Home Place, his portraits of Tom Scanlon, and his attention to Warner in *Fire Sermon* and *A Life*. What is new, however, is that these short stories have the vantage of personal experience, Morris's observations derived from his own aging process.

Morris brings to his stories of old age a seasoned pictorial imagination that relishes closely observed and experienced details, a characteristic ironic tone, and a wry humor blended with an oddly mellow world-weariness. The almost unexpected poignancy that results suggests that in these stories Morris's temperament found its most appropriate expression. Five of these stories focus explicitly on protagonists making intimate accommodations to old age: "The Customs of the Country," "Victrola," "Glimpse into Another Country," "Fellow Creatures," and "The Origin of Sadness."[20] Although virtually unknown and rarely discussed, these stories are among the finest—subtle, humorous, and unsentimental—short stories about aging in recent literature.

Perhaps the best entry to Morris's treatment of the effects and consequences of old age is "The Origin of Sadness." Schuler (based on Loren Eiseley), an anthropologist who comes to doubt Darwin, is the prototypical Morris protagonist. His "appealing melancholy" and bearing as "a banished warrior who knew himself to be doomed" are signs of the haplessness Morris has pictured frequently in his fiction. Visiting "the great ape Massa" in a zoo, Schuler's recognition of Massa's "despair at his place in a cul-de-sac of evolution" elided the differences between them, and Schuler acknowledged an "unspoken kinship" with the animal.[21]

The story takes its title from Schuler's perception that sadness is an inevitable corollary to consciousness in the world. When his wife dies unexpectedly, then when he visits his aged mother and finds "little sign of recognition," Schuler desires "to slip time's noose" by encasing himself in the polar ice cap—where in the fullness of time he might achieve *timeless* distinction as a fossil. Thus Schuler comes to consider imaginative means to transcend life's confinements. Beset by new evidence of mortal pain, Schuler has an experience that begins to alter his consciousness. In his grief at his wife's death, Schuler is driving in the dark, and he comes upon a house being moved along a road (an apt s
for his losses). He sees "the glitter of a cat's eyes at one of the
The rays of reflected light pierced his own like lasers. I
Schuler, more than it disturbed him, that these encounters
itations, the confirmation of his disordered feelings. A v
high would not have surprised him. In the winter sky

zling, and on the balls of his eyes he could feel the prickling rain of light." The story ends with Schuler waiting for death, having "accidentally" fallen into one of the Kansas arroyos he had explored as a child; now, "under the covering of snow, he found the familiar fossil fragments" that link him both to his own past and to the expanse of the geological record (271–74).

Although none of Morris's other stories posit solidarity with creatures from the geological past, Schuler's relationship with Massa marks the kind of reciprocity between humans and other animals found frequently in Morris's writings—especially in "Fellow Creatures," in which the retired Colonel Huggins responds sympathetically to a variety of animals. Morris draws attention to the lives of animals by asserting Huggins's kinship with them (the name Huggins is entirely appropriate). Huggins's evolution begins insignificantly: "Nothing special," Morris says, referring to Huggins's discovery that the neighbor children's leghorn pullet has taken refuge in his garage. As if for the first time, Huggins pays close attention, "amazed to note the range of emotion in the cluck of a chicken." He is led to consider the duplicity in human behavior toward animals: pet-loving people are capable of referring to *fryers, chicken-fried rabbit, roast spring lamb*—or *filet de cheval américain*. Huggins remembers feeling the judgment of a "congress of cows" adventitiously converged on a neighbor's deck ("like guests at a cocktail party") and his refusal to eat the spare ribs he had been cooking—and the time his wife notes the similarity of the "plump bird" in her pan to a newborn human. "[N]ow that Huggins had been alerted," he sees animals, "[e]scaped or missing pets," everywhere (228–33).

These recognitions remind Huggins of yet another experience—the point of Morris's comic accumulation of examples. One day Huggins had observed a flock of grackles perched above him. When he hooted at them they flew off; when they landed, Huggins detected a change of tone in their "discussion." The grackles flew off again, congregating in a tree under which Huggins would pass. Suddenly Huggins had the "impression" "that the gabble of the birds caused the leaves to tremble, as if ~ed by a breeze." It is not their *movement* but their *voices* that stirred first ~ves, then Huggins's imagination. As he moved beneath the tree, ~kles departed once again. But Huggins was attentive: "Bits of ~eathers rained on him. The agitation Huggins had observed in ~ow felt within himself—a tingling, pleasurable excitement. ~rd, he could see strips of sky as if through cracks in leaky ~he top, perched at an angle, was a single black bird.

Either that bird or another just like it—among birds it seemed unimportant—fluttered along with Huggins, its hatpin eyes checking on his interests and curious habits." In memory, this communication links Huggins's withdrawal from exploitation of animals to a mystical communion with them, his ego more or less eclipsed. The story ends with the grackle accompanying Huggins to his driveway, from where he heard "the expectant clucking of the little pullet, and he responded in kind" (234).

In another story, "The Customs of the Country," Hapke experiences reciprocity not between animals and people but with another generation. Hapke has come to America from Switzerland as a handyman, later working as janitor and gardener at a school. Over the years he is relatively content at his work, enjoying the children's voices and the company of friendly dogs when he eats his lunch on the playground. In time, however, the school has to accept older as well as younger children, and this means that Hapke must learn to deal with older, "idle boys." He is baffled by those boys who, while "loafing about, strike at flowering plants with sticks, or absentmindedly break off buds and twigs" (178). After Hapke complains, he finds one of his shrubs intentionally destroyed, and he takes it as a warning: The destruction was symbolically intended for him.

Hapke now lives with fear and incomprehension. One day one of the older boys accosts a small girl who is wading in a shallow creek bordering the playground. The boy pushes the child into the water, where she drowns. Hapke hails a passing jogger, but it is too late. At the ensuing interrogation, Hapke is accused by the "prankish" boy's father of failure to intervene. The outcome causes Hapke to withdraw, "no longer [feeling] responsible for young waders." But even in such melancholy circumstances, compensations exist. Leaving the playground one day, Hapke is accompanied by a small boy, and finding himself "part of the boy's deep brooding," he experiences "a tremor of fear." But the boy comes up to him and puts "his small, soft hand into Hapke's big rough one. For a moment he held it like an injured bird." In neglecting to identify the antecedent to "he," Morris is deliberately ambiguous, suggesting the "injury" might pertain to both participants; in flowing ways, sympathy consoles young and old. Hapke's empathy is broad when as they walk, "the boy's free hand absently plucked the leaves and twigs from the bushes they were passing. He did that as if it went with his thinking, as Hapke was sure that it did" (181–83).

Another story involves a bond between an old man and a potential for pathos controlled through humor. "Victrola" the protagonist's dog, though Bundy thinks the name absurd, finding any resemblance to the RCA mascot "feeble." Theirs is a "close relationship," but only because they have grown old together; Bundy sees himself as a "human parallel" to the dog. One day (during Whole Grains Cereal Week, Morris notes), Bundy walks the dog to the supermarket and ties it to a bicycle rack. While Bundy is in the store the dog is attacked by other dogs—and dies, apparently from fright. Morris guards Bundy's response: we are told that recently Bundy's "eyes had filmed over" while he watched the Royal Wedding on TV. The emotion in the conclusion is also carefully controlled. The first word of the story is "Sit!" as Bundy commands the dog to an action, Morris says pointedly, it has already performed. The story concludes with someone suggesting to Bundy that *he* sit. But Bundy finds that *told* to do so, he *cannot*; his knees will not flex. That he feels his loss is reflected only indirectly in his focus on a revolving police car beacon, then on the care provided by a chaperone to "[o]ne of those women who buy two frozen dinners and then go off with the shopping cart" (184–93).

In varying degrees these four stories deal with protagonists who, from the perspective of advanced age, attain a wisdom that allows them to transcend certain limitations in their earthly life and to achieve acceptance or renewal amidst diminished circumstances. Despite their indirection, abbreviated narrative, and reliance on compiled examples, these stories offer few interpretive challenges. The same cannot be said for "Glimpse into Another Country," which may be Morris's finest story precisely because of its density of imagery, richness of suggestion, and agreeable ambiguity.

The protagonist of "Glimpse into Another Country" is an old man named Hazlitt, who journeys alone from San Francisco to New York in quest of "life assurance" from a medical specialist, apparently to get a second opinion on a first opinion left unspecified. On the plane he encounters a Mrs. Thayer, among whose eccentricities is her manner of scanning the final pages of her book before reading the beginning. At ~~ne~~ point, appalled by the pervasiveness of crime in the world, Mrs. ~~ver~~ exclaims, "There is no place to go!" to be safe (196). Afterwards, ~~Thayer~~ shows up, with quiet coincidence, in some of the places ~~visits~~ in New York.

~~otel,~~ Hazlitt finds "the impression he had of himself" in the ~~d~~" (199), suggesting he is being prepared for an alteration ~~He~~ enters a state similar to "having a buzz on" (201). ~~litt~~ attempts to purchase a bracelet for his wife at

Bloomingdale's, but while his driver's licence is being verified (and his Visa card significantly refused), the store is evacuated because of a bomb threat; Hazlitt finds himself on the sidewalk feeling "an obscure elation" because he now carries "no driver's license, no positive identification" (203)—and no Visa.

The next day Hazlitt keeps his appointment with the specialist, whose manner implies Hazlitt's case is hardly worthy of attention, but an elderly assistant tells him "a reprieve is the best one can expect, at our age." Upon his departure, Hazlitt feels "free of a nameless burden." Back at Bloomingdale's to complete his interrupted transaction, he decides instead to purchase a strand of pearls—"Was it some trick of the lighting that made them seem to glow?"—at a cost that "astounded but did not shock him." Because his wife "kept her jewels in pouches," Hazlitt asks for a pouch for the pearls (204–6).

Elated, Hazlitt walks to the Metropolitan Museum, recalling his past visits there with his wife. In the book department, Hazlitt once again spies Mrs. Thayer. Remembering the pleasures he used to take in the museum's Fountain Court lunchroom, Hazlitt makes his way there, only to find that it has been disappointingly renovated: Its cool, refreshing elements are gone. Hazlitt finds the stairway descending to the lavatory, and there he is accosted by several small boys, who deprive him of the pearls. Curiously, Morris relates this theft in a matter-of-fact tone, as if to suggest that what occurs there offers Hazlitt no surprise.

In the lobby shop Hazlitt pauses to buy a pin "of Etruscan design, that he felt his wife would consider a sensible value." Outside, he pauses beside a bus, and one of the riders inside taps at the window. It is Mrs. Thayer yet again; Hazlitt can see her face only dimly, but he understands that she is signaling—or waving farewell?—to him. Although "[w]hat appeared to be tears might have been drops of water" on the window, her eyes are "mild, and gave him all the assurance he needed" (209). As he watches, the bus carries her away.

Morris's broad archetypal allusions demand that this story be interpreted mythically. The journey structure appears to frame an elaborate rite of passage, and the symbolic loss of identity serves as a means mythic entry into new experience. The story recounts an old man's ney by air from one coastal city to another, then of the events in him on the surface and in the underground of that city. The jou be interpreted as Hazlitt's initiation into understanding. He to accept one of the final conditions in the human cor from life's center to its periphery. This ritual is given in detailed "glimpses." At the heart is the thoroughly platonic relationship between Hazlitt and Mrs. Thayer, a relationship suggesting a mythic need for a witness-guide to see the ritual through.

Mrs. Thayer may be viewed as the presiding goddess of Hazlitt's journey—overseeing his rite of passage. Her "there" (Thayer) appears to respond to the loss of "where" in the world at large, for, as Morris concludes his myth, she gives Hazlitt "all the assurance he needed." Deprived of a meaningful world such as had existed in the past and now stripped of final vanities, Hazlitt in reentering reality has the assurance of this odd goddess that his existence ceremonially reaffirms the human condition.

Given this interpretation (many others are richly possible), Hazlitt's journey in quest of "life assurance" concludes with his chastened understanding of the vanity of human wishes for immortality. He learns that, though desire for immortality is understandable, it is misguided because it ignores necessity and the tacit contract made at birth. He knows now it was vanity that drove him so to clutch to life. The old man who walks away in "Glimpse into Another Country" achieves a wisdom allowing him to buy his wife an Etruscan pin that *she* "would consider a sensible value." In these terms, "Glimpse into Another Country" is a bittersweet parable of final acceptance of the inevitable, in which an old man, tempted by desire, is enabled to find his place once again in the coils of mortality.[22]

Chapter Eight

"The Territory Ahead": Wright Morris and American Literature

Morris's new short stories were the last original fiction Morris published.[1] In an interview on the occasion of his photography retrospective in 1992, Morris made it clear that he had ceased writing,[2] and perhaps his last public appearance was his address at the San Francisco Museum of Modern Art in September of that year. By that time, many of his books, including the fine reprints from the University of Nebraska Press, were out of print, and the rising market value of first editions had depleted many bookstores of choice Morris titles. Yet even under these conditions new readers continue to get hooked on Morris's work. Morris's major champions in the late 1990s are readers of fiction who are appreciative of subtlety and sensitive to nuance; people who are drawn to the mysterious qualities of Morris's photographs and the intertextual ambiguities of the photo-texts; and Black Sparrow Press, which has been reprinting, in omnibus volumes, some of Morris's works.

It is appropriate now, at the end of Morris's career, to inquire into his fortunes in the future. What is it about Morris's work that makes it worthy of continued attention? Certainly, despite the length of his career, it is not because Morris is able to explain the historical significance of particular events in the twentieth century. Morris has focused rather on everyday events, on commonplace, domestic relations. Morris's major importance lies in his emphasis on nuances of consciousness and on his meditative approach, derived in large part from the subtlety and sensitivity of his early contemplation of photography. Impelled as a young man to *look*, he created, like no other writer, a rich visual pro style that to be fully appreciated requires close attention from wi readers. "The reader's pleasure," Morris wrote, "is often in propor what is left unsaid, or ambiguously hinted. To read such fiction grasp some of the skills involved in its creation. As in music calls for this response, playing on the sensibility of the rea

Wright Morris deserves serious attention because his plary: Morris was a writer who lasted the course a admirable adaptation. Relishing independence, he belonged to no school; he was willing to defy limits and presuppositions of writers who preceded him. Much of his early work challenges the assumptions of local color regionalism; his considerations of Midwestern-Western life have none of the sentimentality associated with regionalism. His work—poised *between* rather than representative *of*—requires the kind of disciplined concentration demanded by such masters as Henry James, Willa Cather, and Ernest Hemingway. Leslie Fiedler's caveat is to the point: "Perhaps [Morris's] subject matter is a little too American for those who can appreciate the subtlety of his form; the subtlety of his form a little baffling to those with a real taste for his provincial subject matter."[4]

Readers remember Morris's characters—a large and redoubtable cast, characters who grapple intimately with "that culprit life."[5] His obvious concern and care for these characters—despite his comic satirical edge—reflect his need to come to terms with their real-life doubles, and his irony keeps him from sentimentality. Joe Flower's view of Morris is useful: "What he learned to do was write about people—normal, complex, not particularly noble, unpredictable but as regular as the day, people we might know, people we might even be—to write about them with sympathy, with mercy, with a painful kind of depth, with neither surprises nor limits, with something approaching love."[6] His characters may appear puerile, soft-headed, or impotent in their particular settings, but they remain human—and sometimes capable of audacity.

Moreover, Morris focused on characters often downplayed in American literature, as he put it himself, often "speaking up for people who would rather remain silent."[7] He wrote intuitively of the lives of the elderly even when he was young and should have known that writing about old folks in a youth-obsessed country was distinctly *not* prudent if he wanted an audience. Morris has also written well and with perspicacity about women, leading to testaments such as Linda Ferguson's that Morris is one of two "writers who have taught me the most about women,"[8] and such as the description of *Plains Song* as the "best feminist ˌel of the past fifteen years."[9] Finally, what male writer has focused so   ˌ and intimately on the small domestic dramas staged around the ˌn dinner table—where, leaves added as necessary, families ˌthe wondrous inanities of social intercourse. The set tables in ˌ *one Tree* and *Plains Song* provide ample evidence of Morris's ˌf the comic burdens of human communication.

In his photo-texts Morris advanced the intertextuality that has become one of the marks of postmodernism in the arts. His photographs show—for those willing to look closely—an abiding concern for the lives of "the inhabitants." In Bruce Nixon's words, Morris's photographed "objects provoke rich and complicated stories about their owners,"[10] and as I have suggested, Morris's characters often exhibit the curious, mysterious patina of his photographs. Yet work on the photo-texts has only begun: Connections between image and word in Morris may have much to tell Americans about their lives. Mary Price's introduction of a third term, "clue"—beyond "mirror" and "window"—for discovery of meaning in Morris's work will be of value.[11]

Morris's themes are interrogatory ones, questioning the views of reality held by his characters and often assumed by readers. His version of the American Dream is a perfect example. Morris was born 20 years after the 1890 census closed the American frontier, but he followed Frederick Jackson Turner in questioning what the closing of the frontier meant for American life. Morris's work spans that important period during which pioneer values were finally pushed aside by rampant consumerism and a shift in cultural values. Morris has written more than once of how "[a]t some time during my lifetime, the individual person has ceased to be the standard unit of measurement. . . . The new unit is the aggregate, a system of dealing with sums and totals. In this way the gross national product has replaced the personal human image."[12] This is a late statement, yet it speaks to Morris's preoccupation with "salvage" as one of his motives for photography. As Bruce Nixon eloquently put it: "Morris stood along the shoreline of time, gazing through his camera at the receding tides of manifest destiny and the democratic optimism that accompanied westward expansion" (20).

To Raymond Neinstein's observation that "It is hard to find grounds for optimism in Morris's work" because "the very act of imaginative transformation can create and trap us in a metaphysical landscape"[13] of little power in the real world, it must be responded that Morris's approach to the American Dream is a wholly realistic one. What the Dream offers is a cure for compacted nostalgia for the might-have-be a hoped-for resolution to yearning of such magnitude that it car burden of impossible idealism. Morris's major early theme, the s between nostalgia and nausea, quite perceptively speaks to the addressed in the American Dream, the impossibility of its and the costs of disappointment in human failures to

Hyman Kopfman story Morris apparently *must* tell again and again (in *War Games*, in *Ceremony in Lone Tree*, in the story "The Safe Place"), is emblematic of this condition of shattered idealism. It is this disappointment that haunts so many of Morris's characters—even as it challenges other, more audacious characters to fresh efforts toward human fulfillment.

But Morris understands and gives voice both to the *need* for such hope and desire, and as evidenced by his spirited attack on Norman Rockwell, to the abuses that nostalgia is heir to. Rockwell addresses the "paradox of our situation"; Rockwell "understands the hunger, and he supplies the nourishment . . . for the Good Old Days . . . sensations we no longer have, but still seem to want, dreams of innocence, as a rule, before they became corrupt."[14] Morris's whole career as a novelist, it might be argued, comes from his understanding of that "paradox" and his sympathy for those who are nevertheless captive to it. His ability both to criticize American culture for its excesses *and* to empathize with those making do within that culture is often what attracts thoughtful readers to him: such readers have *experienced* both the fog and the moonlight.

Morris's work is finally valuable for its carefully orchestrated—if sometimes unconscious—response to autobiographical realities. The death of his mother and the frequent absences of his father left an emotional gulf that Morris learned to fill with creative energies, comprehension of the past, and the resolutions inherent in narrative structures. Morris's life as "half an orphan" drew him irresistibly toward the formulations and consolations of art—first to grasp the visual memories, then to explain through narrative the importance of carefully *seen* objects to the ongoing flow of life. This synthesis *is* Morris's work, as his work is his life. Because of the fragmentations in his experience, the many separate lives he lived, Morris wanted to restore life to its primordial wholeness and purity.

Morris's work is rich and rewarding, and because it is, many of his novels and photographs have a good chance of surviving into the ʾenty-first century as successful works and as portraits of mid- and twentieth-century Midwestern American life. It is unthinkable that such as *The Home Place*, *The Works of Love*, *The Deep Sleep*, *The Field Ceremony in Lone Tree*, and *Plains Song for Female Voices* will cease ʾeaders and scholars. There is a good deal of critical work yet ʾhotography and photo-texts, and much more light needs ʾhe short fiction, on Morris's biography, and on the nature of his bittersweet comic vision, especially in light of its accommodations to loss. As for Morris's own critical views, the central arguments of *The Territory Ahead* should continue to give Americans and American writers pause. Above all, Morris's view of the struggle between nostalgia and nausea must be remembered for its continuing importance to future reconstructions of the essential American Dream.

Notes and References

Chapter One

1. G. B. Crump, "Wright Morris," in *A Literary History of the American West* (Fort Worth: Texas Christian University Press, 1987), 781.

2. Wright Morris, "Being Conscious," in *Voicelust: Eight Contemporary Fiction Writers on Style,* ed. Allen Weir and Don Hendrie Jr. (Lincoln: University of Nebraska Press, 1985), 23.

3. David Madden, *Wright Morris* (New York: Twayne, 1964), 170; hereafter cited in text.

4. Wright Morris, *A Cloak of Light: Writing My Life* (New York: Harper & Row, 1985), 137; hereafter cited in text as *Cloak.*

5. Chester E. Eisinger, "Wright Morris: The Artist in Search of America," in *Fiction of the Forties* (Chicago: University of Chicago Press, 1963), 330; hereafter cited in text.

6. Wright Morris, *The Home Place* (New York: Charles Scribner's Sons, 1948), 174.

7. Wright Morris, "Of Memory, Emotion, and Imagination," in *Earthly Delights, Unearthly Adornments: American Writers as Image-Makers* (New York: Harper & Row, 1978), 3.

8. Wright Morris, *Will's Boy: A Memoir* (New York: Harper & Row, 1981), 35; hereafter cited in text as *WB.*

9. Wright Morris, "How I Met Joseph Mulligan, Jr.," *Harper's Magazine,* February 1970, 83.

10. Wright Morris, "Babe Ruth's Pocket," *Ford Times,* September 1972, 50–54.

11. Wright Morris, "Made in U.S.A.," *American Scholar* 29 (Autumn 1960): 486.

12. Wright Morris, "The Cars in My Life," *Holiday* 24 (December 1958): 47.

13. Wright Morris, *God's Country and My People* (New York: Harper Row, 1968), not paginated.

14. Wright Morris, "Real Losses, Imaginary Gains," in *Real Losses inary Gains* (New York: Harper & Row, 1976), 6.

15. Wright Morris, *Solo: An American Dreamer in Europe:* (New York: Harper & Row, 1983), 1; hereafter cited in text as *Sol*

16. Wright Morris [and Jim Alinder], "Interview," in *Str facts: Photographs 1933–1954* (Lincoln, Nebr.: Sheldon Mer 1975), 115.

17.   Wright Morris, *Photographs and Words* (Carmel, Calif.: The Friends of Photography, 1982), 27; hereafter cited in text as *P&W*.

18.   Wright Morris, *Structures and Artifacts: Photographs 1933–1954* (Lincoln, Nebr.: Sheldon Memorial Art Gallery, 1975), 122; hereafter cited in text as *S&A*.

19.   Howard Devree, "A Reviewer's NoteBook: Brief Comment on Some of the Recently Opened Group and One-Man Shows," *New York Times,* 26 October 1941, sec. 9, 10, col. 2.

20.   John Szarkowski, "Wright Morris the Photographer," in *Wright Morris: Origin of a Species* (San Francisco: San Francisco Museum of Modern Art, 1992), 13.

21.   Wayne Booth, "The Two Worlds in the Fiction of Wright Morris," *Sewanee Review* 65 (1957): 377, 397.

22.   Carolyn Nelson, "The Spiritual Quest in the Works of Wright Morris" (diss., University of Chicago, 1967), 153.

23.   G. B. Crump, *The Novels of Wright Morris: A Critical Interpretation* (Lincoln: University of Nebraska Press, 1978), 9, 22–25.

24.   Irving Howe, "Mass Society and Post-Modern Fiction," *Partisan Review* 26 (Summer 1959): 433.

25.   Marcus Klein, "Wright Morris: The American Territory," in *After Alienation: American Novels in Mid-Century* (Cleveland: World Publishers, 1964), 30.

26.   Leslie Fiedler, *Love and Death in the American Novel,* 2d ed. (1966; New York: Dell, 1969), 502.

27.   Alan Trachtenberg, "The Craft of Vision," *Critique* 4 (Winter 1961): 42.

28.   A. Carl Bredahl, "Wright Morris: Living in the World," in *New Ground: Western American Narrative and the Literary Canon* (Chapel Hill: University of North Carolina Press, 1989), 133.

29.   Raymond I. Neinstein, "Wright Morris: The Metaphysics of Home," *Prairie Schooner* 53 (Summer 1979): 143–44.

30.   Ralph N. Miller, "The Fiction of Wright Morris: The Sense of Ending," *MidAmerica* 3 (1976): 69–76.

31.   G. B. Crump, "Author in Hiding," *Western American Literature* 25 (May 1990): 5; hereafter cited in text.

32.   Roy K. Bird, *Wright Morris: Memory and Imagination* (New York: ᵊter Lang, 1985), 57.

33.   Ruthe Stein, "A Freeze-Frame on Eras Past," *San Francisco Chronicle,* ᵊmber 1992, B3.

Wright Morris, *The Man Who Was There* (1945; Lincoln: University ᵃ Press, 1977), 132.

Wright Morris, "How I Put In the Time," in *Growing Up Western,* ᵊes (New York: Knopf, 1989), 117. Oddly, this refrain is found in the following: "How do I explain that all the mirrors and windows of Paris had not returned to me one remembered reflection. What did this young American really look like?" (*Solo*, 194).

36.   Wright Morris, *War Games* (1972; University of Nebraska Press, 1978), v; hereafter cited in text as *WG*.

37.   C. F. Keppler, *The Literature of the Second Self* (Tucson: University of Arizona Press, 1972), 11–12.

38.   Wright Morris, *The Deep Sleep* (1953; Lincoln: University of Nebraska Press, 1975), 124, 131.

39.   This argument is presented in much greater detail in my "Dualism and Doubling in Wright Morris's *War Games*," *Centennial Review* 37 (1993), 415–28.

Chapter Two

1.   Wright Morris, *Photographs and Words* (Carmel, Calif.: The Friends of Photography, 1982), 18; hereafter cited in text as *P&W*.

2.   Wright Morris, "Made in U.S.A.," *American Scholar* 29 (Autumn 1960), 494; hereafter cited in text as "USA."

3.   David Madden, *Wright Morris* (New York, Twayne, 1964), 29; hereafter cited in text.

4.   G. B. Crump, "Author in Hiding," *Western American Literature* 25 (May 1990), 3.

5.   Wright Morris, *Conversations with Wright Morris: Critical Views and Responses*, ed. Robert E. Knoll (Lincoln: University of Nebraska Press, 1977), 111; hereafter cited in text as *CWM*.

6.   Wright Morris, *About Fiction: Reverent Reflections on the Nature of Fiction with Irreverent Observations on Writers, Readers, and Other Abuses* (New York: Harper & Row, 1975), 54.

7.   Hiram Haydn, *Words and Faces* (New York: Harcourt, 1974), 232.

8.   Wright Morris, "Being Conscious," in *Voicelust: Eight Contemporary Fiction Writers on Style*, ed. Allen Weir and Don Hendrie Jr. (Lincoln: University of Nebraska Press, 1985), 24.

9.   Wright Morris, *The Territory Ahead* (1958; Lincoln: University of Nebraska Press, 1978), 96–97; hereafter cited in text as *TA*.

10.   Granville Hicks, "Introduction," in *The Wright Morris Reader* (New York: Harper & Row, 1970), xxxi.

11.   Charles Baxter, "Stillness," *Doubletake* 4 (Spring 1996): 89.

12.   George Garrett, "Morris the Magician: A Look at *In Orbit*," *Critic* 4 (June 1967): 6.

13.   Wright Morris, *Fire Sermon* (New York: Harper & Row, 11, 47.

14.   Wright Morris, *The Works of Love* (New York: 221–22; hereafter cited in text as *WL*.

15. Wright Morris, *Ceremony in Lone Tree* (New York: Atheneum, 1960), 286; hereafter cited in text as *CLT*.

16. David Madden, "Wright Morris' *In Orbit*: An Unbroken Series of Poetic Gestures," in *The Poetic Image in Six Genres* (Carbondale: Southern Illinois University Press, 1969), 141.

17. Wright Morris, *"One Day*: November 22, 1963—November 22, 1967," in *Afterwords: Novelists on Their Novels,* ed. Thomas McCormack (1968; New York: St. Martin's Press, 1988), 26.

18. Wright Morris, *The Home Place* (New York: Charles Scribner's Sons, 1948), 76; hereafter cited in text as *HP*.

19. Wright Morris, *A Cloak of Light: Writing My Life* (New York: Harper & Row, 1985), 10–11.

20. Wright Morris, *A Bill of Rites, A Bill of Wrongs, A Bill of Goods* (New York: New American Library, 1968), 175–76.

21. Wright Morris, *God's Country and My People* (New York: Harper & Row, 1968), not paginated.

22. Wright Morris, *A Life* (New York: Harper & Row, 1973), 15–17.

23. Wright Morris, *Plains Song for Female Voices* (New York: Harper & Row, 1980), 102; hereafter cited in text as *PS*.

24. Wright Morris, *Solo: An American Dreamer in Europe: 1933–1934* (New York: Harper & Row, 1983), 49–51.

25. Jane M. Rabb, ed., *Literature and Photography: Interactions 1940–1990* (Albuquerque: University of New Mexico Press, 1995), 352.

26. Colin Westerbeck, "American Graphic: The Photography and Fiction of Wright Morris," in *Multiple Views: Logan Grant Essays on Photography, 1983–89,* ed. Daniel P. Younger (Albuquerque: University of New Mexico Press, 1991), 273; hereafter cited in text.

27. Wright Morris, *Structures and Artifacts: Photographs 1933–1954* (Lincoln, Nebr.: Sheldon Memorial Art Gallery, 1975), 4; hereafter cited in text as *S&A*.

28. Sandra Phillips, "Words and Pictures," in *Wright Morris: Origin of a Species* (San Francisco: San Francisco Museum of Modern Art, 1992), 30–31.

29. Wright Morris, *The Deep Sleep* (1953; Lincoln: University of Nebraska Press, 1975), 10.

30. Wright Morris, *The Huge Season* (New York: Viking, 1954), 77; ᵉreafter cited in text as *HS*.

31. Mary Price ("Wright Morris: Three Photographs," *Raritan* 14, no. 2 ᵗ: 28) reads the door as "leaning against the wall," "not attached to any-   ᵗnd she draws interesting conclusions from it; but I would argue that   ᵗ a *folding* door, that we see only one of two doors attached by hinges   ᵗ; the visual evidence shows hinge hardware on *both* sides of the

ᵗ Morris, *Cause for Wonder* (New York: Atheneum, 1963), 31.

33. Walker Evans, "Photography," in *Quality: Its Image in the Arts,* ed. Louis Kronenberger (New York: Atheneum, 1969), 180.
34. Wright Morris, preface to *The Inhabitants,* 2d ed. (New York: Da Capo Press, 1972).
35. Linda Hutcheon, *The Politics of Postmodernism* (New York: Routledge, 1989), 1–2.
36. Wright Morris, "Privacy as a Subject for Photography," *Magazine of Art* 44 (February 1951): 53
37. John Szarkowski, *Looking at Photographs: 100 Pictures from the Museum of Modern Art* (New York: Museum of Modern Art), 148.

Chapter Three

1. Wright Morris, *The Territory Ahead* (1957; Lincoln: University of Nebraska Press, 1978), 15.
2. Wright Morris, *Structures and Artifacts: Photographs 1933–1954* (Lincoln, Nebr.: Sheldon Memorial Art Gallery, 1975), 122; hereafter cited in text as *S&A.*
3. Wright Morris, "The Inhabitants," *New Directions in Prose and Poetry 1940,* ed. James Laughlin (Norfolk, Conn.: New Directions, 1940), 148; hereafter cited in text.
4. Alan Trachtenberg, "Wright Morris's 'Photo-Texts,' " *Yale Journal of Criticism* 9, no.1 (1996): 114.
5. Wright Morris, *A Cloak of Light: Writing My Life* (New York: Harper & Row, 1985), 80; hereafter cited in text as *Cloak.*
6. Wright Morris, *My Uncle Dudley* (1942; Lincoln: University of Nebraska Press, 1975), 96; hereafter cited in text.
7. Wright Morris, *Photographs and Words* (Carmel, Calif.: The Friends of Photography, 1982), 26–27.
8. Donald L. Miller, *Lewis Mumford: A Life* (New York: Weidenfeld & Nicholson, 1989), 425.
9. As noted in Morris's *Will's Boy* (New York: Harper & Row, 1981), 5, Fayette was born in 1904 and lived only a few days. A "little brother Fayette" is also noted in the text of *The Man Who Was There* (1945; Lincoln: University of Nebraska Press, 1977), 125; hereafter cited in text.
10. Wright Morris, preface to *The Inhabitants,* 2d ed. (New York: Da Capo Press, 1972); hereafter cited in text. There are 52 photo-texts but no pa numbers in this book, so I provide photo-text numbers to guide inter readers to the specific material discussed.
11. David Madden, *Wright Morris* (New York: Twayne, 1964)
12. G. B. Crump, *The Novels of Wright Morris* (Lincoln: U Nebraska Press, 1978), 54–55.
13. Jefferson Hunter, *Image and Word* (Cambridge, Ma versity Press, 1987), 59.

14. Raymond L. Neinstein, "Wright Morris: The Metaphysics of Home," *Prairie Schooner* 53 (Summer 1979): 124, 126.

15. Peter Halter, "Distance and Desire: Wright Morris' *The Home Place* as 'Photo-Text,'" *Etudes Textuelles* 4 (October-December 1990): 86.

16. Wright Morris, *The Home Place* (1948; Lincoln: University of Nebraska Press, 1968), 87; hereafter cited in text.

17. See "The Untold Lie," in Sherwood Anderson, *Winesburg, Ohio: Text and Criticism,* ed. John H. Ferres (New York: Viking, 1966), 202–3.

18. David E. Nye, " 'Negative Capability' in Wright Morris' *The Home Place,*" *Word and Image* 4 (January-March 1989): 164; hereafter cited in text.

19. John Hollander's view—that Muncy's reference to his "camera eye" confirms he has brought his camera with him—oversimplifies the book's intertextual complexity. See "The Figure on the Page: Words and Images in Wright Morris's *The Home Place,*" *Yale Journal of Criticism* 9, no. 1 (1996): 96.

20. Linda Hutcheon, *The Politics of Postmodernism* (New York: Routledge, 1989), 10, 119.

21. The most accessible evidence for this disquietude is to be found in Morris's essay "Privacy as a Subject for Photography," *Magazine of Art* 44 (February 1951): 51–55, in which Morris differentiated between photographic *revelation* and *exposure,* finding the latter a violation of privacy.

22. James Agee and Walker Evans, *Let Us Now Praise Famous Men* (New York: Ballantine Books, 1966), 169; hereafter cited in text.

23. This argument is developed at greater length in my "Photography and Privacy: The Protests of Wright Morris and James Agee," *The Midwest Quarterly* 23 (1981): 103–15.

Chapter Four

1. Marcus Klein, "Wright Morris: The American Territory," in *After Alienation: American Novels in Mid-Century* (Cleveland: World Publishers, 1962), 207; hereafter cited in text.

2. Wright Morris, *A Cloak of Light: Writing My Life* (New York: Harper & Row, 1985), 145; hereafter cited in text as *Cloak.*

3. Wright Morris, *Photographs and Words* (Carmel, Calif.: The Friends of Photography, 1982), 49–50.

4. Wright Morris, *The World in the Attic* (1949; Lincoln: University of Nebraska Press, 1971), 44; hereafter cited in text.

5. Wright Morris, "Letter to a Young Critic," *Massachusetts Review* 6 (Fall-Winter 1964–65): 99.

Leon Howard, *Wright Morris* (Minneapolis: University of Minnesota 17; hereafter cited in text.

ight Morris, *The Deep Sleep* (1953; Lincoln: University of '975), 125, 131; hereafter cited in text.

8. Wright Morris, *Man and Boy* (1951; Lincoln: University of Nebraska Press, 1974), 17; hereafter cited in text.

9. Sigmund Freud, *Civilization and Its Discontents*, trans. James Strachey (New York: Norton, 1961), 50–51.

10. Henry James, quoted in Wright Morris, *The Territory Ahead* (1958; Lincoln: University of Nebraska Press, 1978), 201–2.

11. David Madden, *Wright Morris* (New York: Twayne, 1964), 64.

12. Charles Baxter, "Stillness," *Doubletake* 4 (Spring 1996): 89.

13. Wright Morris, *The Works of Love* (1952; Lincoln: University of Nebraska Press, 1972), back cover; hereafter cited in text.

14. Jack Rice Cohn, "Wright Morris: The Design of the Midwestern Fiction" (Ph.D. diss., University of California–Berkeley, 1970), 178–79, 230; hereafter cited in text.

15. G. B. Crump, *The Novels of Wright Morris: A Critical Interpretation* (Lincoln: University of Nebraska Press, 1978), 63.

16. Wayne Booth, "Form in *The Works of Love*," in *Conversations with Wright Morris: Critical Views and Responses*, ed. Robert E. Knoll (Lincoln: University of Nebraska Press, 1977), 56.

17. Roy K. Bird, *Wright Morris: Memory and Imagination* (New York: Peter Lang, 1985), 77.

18. Wright Morris, "The Writing of Organic Fiction: A Conversation between Wayne C. Booth and Wright Morris," in *Conversations with Wright Morris: Critical Views and Responses*, ed. Robert E. Knoll (Lincoln: University of Nebraska Press, 1977), 76.

19. Harold Rosenberg, "Portraits: A Meditation on Likeness," in *Portraits*, by Richard Avedon (New York: Farrar, Strauss, and Giroux, 1976), not paginated.

20. A more detailed version of this argument is found in my "Focus and Frame in Wright Morris's *The Works of Love*," *Western American Literature* 23 (1988): 99–112.

21. At this point in Morris's return to the past he wrote the odd, largely unsuccessful novel *War Games*. Apparently the publisher rejected it at that time, and it was not published until 1972. There is insufficient space to explore this novel in depth, beyond my brief discussion of it at the end of chapter 1, but interested readers may see my article "Dualism and Doubling in Wright Morris's *War Games*," *The Centennial Review* 37 (1993): 415–28.

22. Wright Morris, *The Huge Season* (New York: Viking, 1954), 3; hereafter cited in text.

Chapter Five

1. Wright Morris, "Man on the Moon," *Partisan Review* 1962): 241–49.

2. Wright Morris, *The Territory Ahead* (1957; Lincoln: University of Nebraska Press, 1978), 104; hereafter cited in text as *TA*.

3. Wright Morris, *A Cloak of Light: Writing My Life* (New York: Harper & Row, 1985), 180; hereafter cited in text as *Cloak*.

4. Wright Morris, *The Field of Vision* (New York: Harcourt, Brace and Company, 1956), 59; hereafter cited in text.

5. Sherrington's passage reads: "The brain is waking and with it the mind is returning. It is as if the Milky Way entered upon some cosmic dance. Swiftly the head-mass becomes an enchanted loom where millions of flashing shuttles weave a dissolving pattern, always a meaningful pattern though never an abiding one; a shifting harmony of subpatterns. Now as the waking body rouses, subpatterns of this great harmony of activity stretch down into the unlit tracks of the stalk-piece of the scheme. Strings of flashing and traveling sparks engage the length of it. This means that the body is up and rises to meet its waking day." Sir Charles Sherrington, *Man on His Nature,* 2d ed. (Cambridge: Cambridge University Press, 1951), 178; hereafter cited in text.

6. Wright Morris, "The Origin of a Species, 1942–1957," *Massachusetts Review* 7 (1966): 129.

7. Wright Morris, *Love among the Cannibals* (New York: Harcourt, Brace, 1957), 19; hereafter cited in text.

8. Wright Morris, *Ceremony in Lone Tree* (New York: Atheneum Publishers, 1960), 21; hereafter cited in text.

9. Jonathan Baumbach, "Wake Before Bomb," in *The Landscape of Nightmare: Studies in the Contemporary American Novel* (New York: New York University Press, 1965), 160, 163; hereafter cited in text.

10. Wright Morris, "The American Novelist and the Contemporary Scene: A Conversation Between John W. Aldridge and Wright Morris," in *Conversations with Wright Morris: Critical Views and Responses,* ed. Robert E. Knoll (Lincoln: University of Nebraska Press, 1977), 29.

11. That the Hyman Kopfman story recurs in Morris's work suggests its importance to Morris as an allegory pertinent to the American Dream; different versions of the story are found in the short story "The Safe Place" and in *War Games.*

12. Wright Morris, *What a Way to Go* (New York: Atheneum, 1962), 10; hereafter cited in text.

13. The most puzzling organ for Sherrington—as for Darwin—was the which seems to defy explanations from evolution. Sherrington writes: "The nd greatest problem vision faces is doubtless that attaching to it as part of er-mind relation. How is it that the visual picture proceeds—if that is ord—from an electrical disturbance in the brain?" He is perplexed g' by the brain behind the eye[.] Physics and chemistry there are ery question. All they say to us is that the brain is theirs, that which is theirs the seeing is not. But as to how? They vouch-

safe us not a word." Sir Charles Sherrington, *Man on His Nature*, 2d ed. (Cambridge: Cambridge University Press, 1951), 91, 109, 113–14.

14. Wright Morris, *Cause for Wonder* (New York: Atheneum, 1963), 223; hereafter cited in the text.

15. Marcus Klein, "Wright Morris: The American Territory," in *After Alienation: American Novels in Mid-Century* (Cleveland: World Publishing Co., 1962), 246.

16. Leon Howard, *Wright Morris* (Minneapolis: University of Minnesota Press, 1968), 33.

Chapter Six

1. Granville Hicks, "Wright Morris," in *Literary Horizons: A Quarter Century of American Fiction* (New York: New York University Press, 1970), 43.

2. Wright Morris, "How Things Are," in *The Arts and The Public*, ed. James E. Miller Jr. and Paul D. Herring (University of Chicago Press, 1967), 33–34; hereafter cited in text as "Things."

3. Wright Morris, *A Bill of Rites, A Bill of Wrongs, A Bill of Goods* (New York: New American Library, 1968), 152.

4. Wright Morris, "*One Day*: November 22, 1963—November 22, 1967," in *Afterwords: Novelists on Their Novels*, ed. Thomas McCormack (New York: Harper & Row, 1969), 12; hereafter cited in text as "OD."

5. Wright Morris, *The Fork River Space Project* (New York: Harper & Row, 1977), 124; hereafter cited in text.

6. Wright Morris, *One Day* (1965; Lincoln: University of Nebraska Press, 1976), 295; hereafter cited in text.

7. Cowie's reference to "cathedral" time is reminiscent of the "wise" Plotinus Plinlimmon's lecture on "Chronometricals and Horologicals" in Melville's *Pierre*. In his pamphlet Plinlimmon distinguishes between terrestrial and celestial time—and explains what adherence to one or the other signifies regarding human relationship to the world:

> "In short, this chronometrical and horological conceit . . . seems to teach this:—That in things terrestrial (horological) a man must not be governed by ideas celestial (chronometrical); that certain minor self-renunciations in this life his own mere instinct for his own every-day general well-being will teach him to make, but he must by no means make a complete unconditional sacrifice of himself in behalf of any other being or any cause, or any conceit." (248)

Plinlimmon presents the "practical" approach to time as it affects a solution indicative of the need of compromise for the sake of modern world; this compromise, however, necessitates wh called "bad faith." See Herman Melville, *Pierre, or the Ambiguities* (1852; New York: New American Library, 1964).

8. Wright Morris, "The Writing of Organic Fiction: A Conversation between Wayne C. Booth and Wright Morris," in *Conversations with Wright Morris: Critical Views and Responses*, ed. Robert Knoll (Lincoln: University of Nebraska Press, 1977), 100.

9. George Garrett, "Morris the Magician: A Look at *In Orbit*," *The Hollins Critic* 4 (June 1967): 1; hereafter cited in text.

10. Leon Howard, *Wright Morris* (Minneapolis: University of Minnesota Press, 1968), 39–40.

11. Wright Morris, *In Orbit* (New York: New American Library, 1967), 19–20; hereafter cited in text.

12. David Madden, "Wright Morris' *In Orbit*: An Unbroken Series of Poetic Gestures," in *The Poetic Image in Six Genres* (Carbondale: Southern Illinois University Press, 1969), 149; hereafter cited in text.

13. A. Carl Bredahl Jr., "Wright Morris: Living in the World," in *New Ground: Western American Narrative and the Literary Canon* (Chapel Hill: University of North Carolina Press, 1989), 130.

14. Wright Morris, *Fire Sermon* (New York; Harper & Row, 1971), 6; hereafter cited in text.

15. Wright Morris, *A Life* (New York; Harper & Row, 1973), 23; hereafter cited in text.

16. Raymond Neinstein, "Wright Morris: The Metaphysics of Home," *Prairie Schooner* 53 (Summer 1979): 150.

17. Craig Watson, "The Changing Eye: *The Fork River Space Project* by Wright Morris," *Great Lakes Review* 7 (Winter 1981): 3.

18. Wright Morris, "The Camera Eye," in *Time Pieces: Photographs, Writing, and Memory* (New York: Aperture, 1989), 17; the image is reproduced as Figure 1 in that book; hereafter cited in text.

Chapter Seven

1. Wright Morris, "The Camera Eye," in *Time Pieces: Photographs, Writing, and Memory* (New York: Aperture, 1989), 18; hereafter cited in text as "Eye."

2. Wright Morris, "Glimpse into Another Country" in *Collected Stories: 1948–1986* (New York: Harper & Row, 1986), 204.

3. Wright Morris, "In Our Image," in *Time Pieces: Photographs, Writing, ˩ Memory* (New York: Aperture, 1989), 8; hereafter cited in text as "Image."

4. Wright Morris, *Plains Song for Female Voices* (New York: Harper & ˀ80), 75; hereafter cited in text.

Ellen Serlen Uffen, "Wright Morris's Earthly Music: The Women of ' *MidAmerica* 12 (1985): 102.

ˢs photograph appears only in the original hardcover edition of
the Penguin and Godine paperbacks.

7. John Berger and Jean Mohr, *Another Way of Telling* (New York: Pantheon, 1982), 133.

8. Leroy Searle, "Images in Context: Photographic Sequences," in *Target III: In Sequence: Photographic Sequences from the Target Collection,* ed. Anne Wilkes Tucker (Houston: Museum of Fine Arts, 1982), 9, 19.

9. Marilyn Arnold, "Wright Morris's *Plains Song*: Woman's Search for Harmony," *South Dakota Review* 20 (Autumn 1982): 61.

10. Wright Morris, *The Works of Love* (New York: Knopf, 1952), 12–13.

11. Much of this section has appeared in other forms. See my "Wright Morris, Women, and American Culture," in *Women and Western American Literature,* ed. Helen Winter Stauffer and Susan J. Rosowski (Troy, N.Y.: Whitston, 1982), 212–29; and "Visual Artistry in Wright Morris's *Plains Song for Female Voices,*" *MidAmerica* 19 (1992): 116–26.

12. G. B. Crump, "Wright Morris: Author in Hiding," *Western American Literature* 25 (May 1990), 13.

13. Wright Morris, *A Cloak of Light: Writing My Life* (New York: Harper & Row, 85), 305; hereafter cited in text as *Cloak*.

14. That Morris is aware of this emphasis is apparent in his intimation that he considered revising *Will's Boy* because of "the easy way he [Will's Boy] accommodated intractable losses." This comment may be Morris's final word on the matter, because he includes this note in his brief "To the Reader" comments introducing *Writing My Life: An Autobiography* (Santa Rosa, Calif.: Black Sparrow Press, 1993), 5.

15. Wright Morris, *Will's Boy: A Memoir* (New York: Harper & Row, 1981), 2; hereafter cited in text as *WB*.

16. Richard Wilbur, "The House of Poe," in *Poe: A Collection of Critical Essays,* ed. Robert Regan (Englewood Cliffs, N.J.: Prentice-Hall, 1967), 99; hereafter cited in text.

17. As seen earlier, Morris employs such lighting in *The Fork River Space Project,* specifically as an aid to contemplation: "The light appeared to come through panels in the roof and had a curious subterranean dimness, as if filtered through water" (105).

18. Wright Morris, *Earthly Delights, Unearthly Adornments: American Writers as Image-Makers* (New York: Harper & Row, 1978), 10.

19. Wright Morris, "Origins: Reflections on Emotion, Memory, and Imagination," in *Conversations with Wright Morris: Critical Views and Responses,* e Robert E. Knoll (Lincoln: University of Nebraska Press, 1977), 165.

20. Three of these stories have achieved some distinction: "Victrol "Glimpse into Another Country" were included in both *Best American * ries and O'Henry *Prize Stories* annuals. "Fellow Creatures" was selec 1985 *Best* collection and later for *The Best American Short Stories of t*

21. Wright Morris, *Collected Stories: 1948–1986* (New Row, 1986), 268–69; hereafter cited in text.

22. I have dealt in greater depth with these stories, especially "Glimpse into Another Country," in "Myth and Melancholy: Wright Morris's Stories of Old Age," *Weber Studies: An Interdisciplinary Humanities Journal* 12 (Winter 1995): 36–47.

Chapter Eight

1. Two more stories published after *Collected Stories: 1948–1986* are "Uno Mas" in *New Yorker* 64 (6 February 1989): 28–31; and "What's New, Love?" in *American Short Fiction* 1 (Fall 1991): 98–105.

2. Ruthe Stein, "A Freeze-Frame on Eras Past," *San Francisco Chronicle,* 3 September 1992, B3-B4.

3. Wright Morris, *About Fiction* (New York: Harper & Row, 1975), 87.

4. Leslie Fiedler, *Love and Death in the American Novel,* 2d ed. (New York: Dell, 1966), 502.

5. Wright Morris, *One Day* (1965; Lincoln: University of Nebraska Press, 1976), 407.

6. Joe Flower, "Wright Morris Is Back," *Chicago Sun-Times Midwest,* 3 July 1977, 10.

7. Wright Morris, *God's Country and My People* (New York: Harper & Row, 1968), n.p.

8. Linda Ferguson, "A Morris Marathon," *Pacific Sun Literary Quarterly* 28 (November 1975), 17. (The other writer is Evan S. Connell.)

9. Lynn Waldeland, *"Plains Song*: Women's Voices in the Fiction of Wright Morris," *Critique* 24 (1982): 7.

10. Bruce Nixon, "The Rhythm of Time: Wright Morris at the San Francisco Museum of Modern Art," *Artweek* 23 (22 October 1992): 21; hereafter cited in text.

11. Mary Price, "Wright Morris: Three Photographs," *Raritan* 14, no. 2 (1994): 19.

12. Wright Morris, "The Camera Eye," in *Time Pieces: Photographs, Writing, and Memory* (New York: Aperture, 1989), 18.

13. Raymond I. Neinstein, "Wright Morris: The Metaphysics of Home," *Prairie Schooner* 53 (Summer 1979): 143–44.

14. Wright Morris, *The Territory Ahead,* (1958; Lincoln: University of Nebraska Press, 1978), 117–18.

Selected Bibliography

PRIMARY SOURCES

Novels

My Uncle Dudley. New York: Harcourt, Brace, 1942. Reprint, Lincoln: University of Nebraska Press, 1975.

The Man Who Was There. New York: Charles Scribner's Sons, 1945. Reprint, Lincoln: University of Nebraska Press, 1977.

The World in the Attic. New York: Charles Scribner's Sons, 1949. Reprint, Lincoln: University of Nebraska Press, 1971.

Man and Boy. New York: Alfred A. Knopf, 1951. Reprint, Lincoln: University of Nebraska Press, 1974. Reprinted (with *In Orbit*) as *Two for the Road*. Santa Rosa, Calif.: Black Sparrow Press, 1994.

The Works of Love. New York: Alfred A. Knopf, 1952. Reprinted in *Wright Morris: A Reader*. New York: Harper & Row, 1970. Reprint, Lincoln: University of Nebraska Press, 1972. Reprinted (with *The Huge Season*) as *The Loneliness of the Long Distance Writer*. Santa Rosa, Calif.: Black Sparrow Press, 1995.

The Deep Sleep. New York: Charles Scribner's Sons, 1953. Reprint, Lincoln: University of Nebraska Press, 1975.

The Huge Season. New York: Viking Press, 1954. Reprint, Lincoln: University of Nebraska Press, 1975. Reprinted (with *The Works of Love*) as *The Loneliness of the Long Distance Writer*. Santa Rosa, Calif.: Black Sparrow Press, 1995.

The Field of Vision. New York: Harcourt, Brace, 1956. Reprinted in *Wright Morris: A Reader*. New York: Harper & Row, 1970. Reprint, Lincoln: University of Nebraska Press, 1974.

Love Among the Cannibals. New York: Harcourt, Brace, 1957. Reprint, Lincoln: University of Nebraska Press, 1977.

Ceremony in Lone Tree. New York: Atheneum, 1960. Reprint, Lincoln: University of Nebraska Press, 1973.

What a Way to Go. New York: Atheneum, 1962. Reprint, Lincoln: University of Nebraska Press, 1979.

Cause for Wonder. New York: Atheneum, 1963. Reprint, Lincoln: University of Nebraska Press, 1978.

One Day. New York: Atheneum, 1965. Reprint, Lincoln: University of Nebraska Press, 1976.

In Orbit. New York: New American Library, 1967. Reprint, Lincoln: University
  of Nebraska Press, 1967. Reprinted (with *Man and Boy*) as *Two for the
  Road*. Santa Rosa, Calif.: Black Sparrow Press, 1994.
Fire Sermon. New York: Harper & Row, 1971. Reprint, Lincoln: University of
  Nebraska Press, 1979. Reprinted (with *A Life* and *The Fork River Space
  Project*) as *Three Easy Pieces*. Santa Rosa, Calif.: Black Sparrow Press, 1993.
War Games. Los Angeles: Black Sparrow Press, 1972. Reprint, Lincoln: Univer-
  sity of Nebraska Press, 1978.
A Life. New York: Harper & Row, 1973. Reprint, Lincoln: University of
  Nebraska Press, 1980. Reprinted (with *Fire Sermon* and *The Fork River
  Space Project*) as *Three Easy Pieces*. Santa Rosa, Calif.: Black Sparrow Press,
  1993.
The Fork River Space Project. New York: Harper & Row, 1977. Reprint, Lincoln:
  University of Nebraska Press, 1981. Reprinted (with *Fire Sermon* and *A
  Life*) as *Three Easy Pieces*. Santa Rosa, Calif.: Black Sparrow Press, 1993.
Plains Song for Female Voices. New York: Harper & Row, 1980. Paperback
  reprints, New York: Penguin, 1981; Boston: Godine, 1991.

Photographs and Photo-texts

The Inhabitants. New York: Charles Scribner's Sons, 1946. 2d ed., New York:
  Da Capo, 1972.
The Home Place. New York: Charles Scribner's Sons, 1948. Reprint, Lincoln:
  University of Nebraska Press, 1968.
God's Country and My People. New York: Harper & Row, 1968. Reprint, Lincoln:
  University of Nebraska Press, 1981.
Love Affair: A Venetian Journal. New York: Harper & Row, 1972.
Structures and Artifacts: Photographs 1933–1954. Lincoln, Neb.: Sheldon Memor-
  ial Art Gallery, 1975.
Photographs and Words, ed. James Alinder. Carmel, Calif.: The Friends of Pho-
  tography, 1982.
Picture America, with Jim Alinder. Boston: New York Graphic Society, 1982.

Short Stories

Real Losses, Imaginary Gains. New York: Harper & Row, 1976.
Collected Stories: 1948–1986. New York: Harper & Row, 1986. Paperback
  reprint, Boston: Godine, 1989.

~s and Criticism

* ·tory Ahead*. New York: Harcourt, Brace, 1958. Paperback reprints,
  · York: Atheneum, 1963; Lincoln: University of Nebraska Press,

A Bill of Wrongs, A Bill of Goods. New York: New American
  ~8. Reprint, Lincoln: University of Nebraska Press, 1980.

About Fiction: Reverent Reflections on the Nature of Fiction with Irreverent Observations on Writers, Readers, and Other Abuses. New York: Harper & Row, 1975.

Conversations with Wright Morris: Critical Views and Responses, ed. Robert E. Knoll. Lincoln: University of Nebraska Press, 1977.

Earthly Delights, Unearthly Adornments: American Writers as Image-Makers. New York: Harper & Row, 1978.

Time Pieces: Photographs, Writing, and Memory. New York: Aperture, 1989.

Autobiography

Will's Boy: A Memoir. New York: Harper & Row, 1981. Paperback reprint, Penguin, 1982. Reprinted in *Writing My Life: An Autobiography.* Santa Rosa, Calif.: Black Sparrow Press, 1993.

Solo: An American Dreamer in Europe: 1933–1934. New York: Harper & Row, 1983. Paperback reprint, New York: Penguin, 1984. Reprinted in *Writing My Life. An Autobiography.* Santa Rosa, Calif.: Black Sparrow Press, 1993.

A Cloak of Light: Writing My Life. New York: Harper & Row, 1985. Reprinted in *Writing My Life: An Autobiography.* Santa Rosa, Calif.: Black Sparrow Press, 1993.

Writing My Life: An Autobiography. Santa Rosa, Calif.: Black Sparrow Press. 1993. [This volume reprints the three memoirs *Will's Boy: A Memoir; Solo: An American Dreamer in Europe: 1933–1934;* and *A Cloak of Light: Writing My Life.*]

Readers

The Mississippi River Reader, ed. Wright Morris. Garden City: Doubleday Anchor, 1962.

Wright Morris: A Reader, ed. Granville Hicks. New York: Harper & Row, 1970.

SECONDARY SOURCES

Adams, Timothy Dow. *Lightwriting and Lifewriting: Photography in Autobiography* (forthcoming). See chapter entitled "Wright Morris: The Mirror without a Memory: *Will's Boy* and *A Cloak of Light.*"

Albers, Randall K. "The Female Transformation: The Role of Women in Tw Novels by Wright Morris." *Prairie Schooner* 53 (Summer 1979): 95–1 A defense of Morris from critics who think of him as a "calumnia the female."

Aldridge, John W. "Wright Morris Country." In *Conversations with W ris: Critical Views and Responses,* edited by Robert E. Knoll, 3 University of Nebraska Press, 1977. Morris continues tradition of writing about the whole of American exper also evidence of a "dark strain" in his work since the

Alinder, James. "Introduction." *Wright Morris: Photographs and Words,* 7–11. Carmel, Calif.: The Friends of Photography, 1982. Brief overview of Morris's career as a photographer.

————. "You Can Go Home Again." *Modern Photography,* March 1978, 116–25, 193. Brief introduction—with small portfolio—to Morris as a photographer by the curator of the *Structures and Artifacts* exhibition at the Sheldon Gallery.

Arnold, Marilyn. "Wright Morris's *Plains Song*: Woman's Search for Harmony." *South Dakota Review* 20 (Autumn 1982): 50–62. Fine close reading of the novel, focused on Sharon's reconciliation with Cora and the sexuality Sharon rejected as a young woman.

Baumbach, Jonathan. "Wake Before Bomb: *Ceremony in Lone Tree.*" In *Landscape of Nightmare: Studies in the Contemporary American Novel,* 152–69. New York: New York University Press, 1965. Analysis of Morris's "comic despair," his use of acts of violence to indicate social impotence, and Boyd as "conscience."

Bird, Roy K. *Wright Morris: Memory and Imagination.* New York: Peter Lang, 1985. Excellent revised dissertation, emphasizing Morris's deliberate intrusions into his photographs and texts and his careful merging of memory and imagination, technique and raw material.

Booth, Wayne C. "Form in *The Works of Love.*" In *Conversations with Wright Morris: Critical Views and Responses,* edited by Robert E. Knoll, 35–73. Lincoln: University of Nebraska Press, 1977. An attempt to help readers experience the relationship between Morris's "spare style" and his storytelling in *The Works of Love.*

————. "The Shaping of Prophecy: Craft and Idea in the Novels of Wright Morris." *American Scholar* 31 (Autumn 1962): 608–26. A review of Morris's career as a novelist in the light of the most recently published *What a Way to Go.*

————. "The Two Worlds in the Fiction of Wright Morris." *Sewanee Review* 65 (Summer 1957): 375–99. The formative, influential essay that explains Morris as a Platonic dualist attempting in his novels to escape the everyday world through heroism, the imagination, and love.

Bredahl, A. Carl. "Wright Morris: Living in the World." In *New Ground: Western American Narrative and the Literary Canon,* 126–34. Chapel Hill: University of North Carolina Press, 1989. Interesting discussion of the energy in Morris's images of sexuality and penetration in *In Orbit,* in contrast to the passive, nostalgic verticals and horizontals of *The Home Place.*

Jack. "Wright Morris's West: Fallout from a Pioneer Past." *Denver ·terly* 10 (Winter 1976): 63–75. Morris as a writer who deals with ·ex questions about the nature of readers' responses to Western ·s and ideas; incisive comparisons with other writers.

"The Photography of Wright Morris: A Portfolio." In *Conver-*

sations with Wright Morris: Critical Views and Responses, edited by Robert E. Knoll, 121–39. Lincoln: University of Nebraska Press, 1977. As a photographer, Morris is interested in culture, not nature; his work, like that of Evans, Atget, and others, attempts "to suggest absolutes beyond" artistic intentions.

Cantie, Philippe. "Lettre et icone dans l'incipit de *The Inhabitants.*" *Caliban* 29 (February 1992): 1–12. Discussion of the significance of Morris's different photographic versions of a Connecticut Meeting House.

Carabine, Keith. "Some Observations on Wright Morris's Treatment of 'My Kind of People: Self-Sufficient, Self-Deprived, Self-Unknowing.' " *MidAmerica* 8 (1981): 115–34. In contrast to Sinclair Lewis, Morris creates carefully observed characters with whom he closely empathizes, as seen in his portrayal of Bud Momeyer in *Ceremony in Lone Tree.*

Coates, Christopher. "Image/Text: Wright Morris and Deconstruction." *Canadian Review of American Studies* 22 (1991): 567–76. Examination of the tension Morris creates between photos and texts in the light of Derrida's "rupture" between "signified" and "signifier."

Coleman, A. D. "Novel Pictures: The Photofiction of Wright Morris." In *Light Readings: A Photography Critic's Writings, 1968–1978,* 242–46. New York: Oxford University Press, 1979. An appreciation of Morris's phototexts upon the publication of *God's Country and My People,* which Coleman sees as the final installment of a trilogy.

Crump, G. B. *The Novels of Wright Morris: A Critical Interpretation.* Lincoln: University of Nebraska Press, 1978. Essential study of Morris's dualities of immanence and transcendence; the most thorough study of Morris's fiction, through *A Life.*

———. "Wright Morris: Author in Hiding." *Western American Literature* 25 (May 1990): 3–14. Focus on the "image of the hidden child" in Morris's novels in relation to the three volumes of autobiography.

———. "Wright Morris's *One Day*: The Bad News on the Hour." *MidAmerica* 3 (1976): 77–91. An excellent reading of *One Day* as among the most important of Morris's novels, linking character psychologies to the ultimate meaning of the Kennedy assassination; Morris's views of contingency, consciousness, and choice are akin to those of existentialism.

Daverman, Richard. "The Evanescense of Wright Morris's *The Huge Season.*" *MidAmerica* 8 (1981): 79–91. Carefully detailed defense of Morris' "purposeful ambiguity" in this carefully structured, complex novel.

Dyck, Reginald. "Revisiting and Revising the West: Willa Cather's *My Á*· and Wright Morris' *Plains Song.*" *Modern Fiction Studies* 36 (Spring 25–37. *Plains Song* as "a willful misreading" of Cather that he' to see deliberate "omissions and contradictions" in *My Ánton*'

Eisinger, Chester E. "Wright Morris: The Artist in Search for An *tion of the Forties,* 328–41. Chicago: University of Chic

Perceptive discussion linking Morris's quest in his early work for personal identity to his need to define America and comprehend patterns in American life.

Evans, Walker. "Photography." In *Quality: Its Image in the Arts,* edited by Louis Kronenberger, 169–211. New York: Atheneum, 1969. Evans briefly and appreciatively discusses one of Morris's chair photographs, seeing in it "all the heartbreak of the century."

Fullerton, Adelyn. "Myth, the Minotaur, and Morris's *The Field of Vision.*" *West Georgia College Review* 16 (May 1984): 1–8. Careful analysis of Morris's intricate use of myth, tracking the thematic importance of minotaur and labyrinth images and clarifying the bullfight arena as a complex "mythic location."

Garrett, George. "Morris the Magician: A Look at *In Orbit.*" *Hollins Critic* 4 (June 1967): 1–12. Celebration of *In Orbit* for its intricate design and energy as "a comedy of doom and destiny."

Gohlke, Frank. "Bare Facts: The Photography of Wright Morris." *Hungry Mind Review* 3 (Fall 1986): 10–11. Photographer Gohlke's sensitive appreciation of Morris as having affinities with Thoreau in his search for the essences of things and experiences.

Guettinger, Roger J. "The Problem with Jigsaw Puzzles: Form in the Fiction of Wright Morris." *Texas Quarterly* 11 (Spring 1968): 209–20. Repetition, pattern, and reformulations of character and idea in four of Morris's novels between 1956 and 1963.

Hall, Joe. "Three Consciousnesses in Wright Morris's *Plains Song.*" *Western American Literature* 31 (Winter 1997): 291–318. The three shapes of consciousness are acceptance of the past, rejection of the past, and a form of transformation allowing people to understand the past to enlighten the present. Cora's wielding of the hairbrush is redemptive because it helps Sharon to understand "luminous silence" and to accept the "nonconscious" mysteries of life.

———. "Wright Morris' *The Field of Vision*: A Re-reading of the Scanlon Story." *Journal of American Culture* 14, no. 2 (1991): 53–57. Argues that critics have misread Scanlon's role: it is Scanlon whose story entails the risk Boyd only talks about and who embodies Lehmann's evolutionary theories of human possibility.

Halter, Peter. "Distance and Desire: Wright Morris' *The Home Place* as 'Photo-Text.' " *Etudes Textuelles* 4 (October-December 1990): 65–89. Arguably the best essay on *The Home Place,* treating text and images as equal partners, and on the tension between "distance and desire, separation and identification" in Muncy's (and Morris's) responses to the rural environ-

t D. "Wright Morris's *Ceremony in Lone Tree*: A Picture of Life in merica." *Western American Literature* 11 (November 1976):

199–213. Insightful reading of *Ceremony* as combining themes from American frontier, gothic, and novel of seduction traditions.

Hicks, Granville. "Introduction" to *Wright Morris: A Reader*. New York: Harper & Row, 1970, ix–xxxiii. Appreciative introduction to Morris and to a judicious selection of some major moments in Morris's fiction. Hicks surveys Morris's life and fictional effects under the headings "Places," "People," "Things," "Shapes," "Words," and "Ideas."

————. "Wright Morris." In *Literary Horizons: A Quarter Century of American Fiction*, 7–47. New York: New York University Press, 1970. Ten reprinted appreciative reviews of Morris's books from *The Works of Love* to *A Bill of Rites, A Bill of Wrongs, A Bill of Goods*.

Hollander, John. "The Figure on the Page: Words and Images in Wright Morris's *The Home Place*." *Yale Journal of Criticism* 9 (Spring 1996): 93–108. Brief appreciation of Morris's photo-text practice in relation to his use of Henry James.

Howard, Leon. *Wright Morris*. Minneapolis: University of Minnesota Press, 1968. (University of Minnesota Pamphlets on American Writers, No. 69.) Very helpful, if dated, appreciation of Morris as a writer who focuses on the artist's search for *meaning* in America. Sees his former student Morris as knowledgeable, sympathetic to the comic human condition, and honest.

Hunt, John W., Jr. "The Journey Back: The Early Novels of Wright Morris." *Critique* 5 (Spring-Summer 1962): 41–60. Early argument for the importance of Morris's "first phase"; discussion of the development of themes and patterns in the first five novels, as Morris searched for ways to articulate meaning and to make an escape from the past through versions of transformation.

Hunter, Jefferson. "The Work of Wright Morris." In *Image and Word: The Interaction of Twentieth-Century Photographs and Texts*, 56–63. Cambridge, Mass.: Harvard University Press, 1987. Somewhat authoritarian but useful brief discussion of photo-text "collaboration"; narrowly considers *The Home Place* a "consistent work of illustrated fiction."

Jacobson, Joanne. "Time and Vision in Wright Morris's Photographs of Nebraska." *Great Plains Quarterly* 7 (Winter 1986): 3–21. Morris's means in his Midwest images of revealing processes of perception rather than simple acceptance or denial of time's transgressions.

Klein, Marcus. "Wright Morris: The American Territory." In *After Alienat American Novels in Mid-Century*, 196–246. Cleveland: World Publ 1964. Klein's argument is that Morris is one of a few writers w alienation as a literary stance was exhausted, "accommodat selves to social realities. It is essentially Morris's comic visio his characters to live in precarious balance between social sonal freedom.

Knoll, Robert E., ed. *Conversations with Wright Morris: Critical Views and Responses*. Lincoln: University of Nebraska Press, 1977. Useful exchanges between Morris and friendly critics.

Lewis, Linda M. "*Plains Song*: Wright Morris's New Melody for Audacious Female Voices." *Great Plains Quarterly* 8 (Winter 1988): 29–37. Examines the significance of Morris's shift from male to female audacity in his novels; compares Cora to Hecate and Margaret Laurence's Hagar Shipley, and Sharon to the archetypal daughter of the middle border.

Madden, David. "Character as Revealed Cliché in Wright Morris's Fiction." *Midwest Quarterly* 22 (Summer 1981): 319–36. Examination of Morris's deliberate reinvigoration and transformation of clichés in his style and creation of character.

———. "The Hero and the Witness in Wright Morris' *The Field of Vision*." *Prairie Schooner* 34 (Fall 1960): 263–78. Arguable thesis that the formulaic relationship between the Morris hero and his witness is *the* most important theme in Morris's novels.

———. "Morris' *Cannibals*, Cain's *Serenade*: The Dynamics of Style and Technique." *Journal of Popular Culture* 8 (Summer 1974): 59–70. Madden examines the effect in the classroom of studying a popular work and a serious work in tandem and finds both surprising similarities and an improved sense of discovery in students.

———. *Wright Morris*. New York: Twayne, 1964. The first full-length study of Morris; still important for the work through *Cause for Wonder*.

———. "Wright Morris' *In Orbit*: An Unbroken Series of Poetic Gestures." *Critique* 10 (Fall 1968): 102–19. Reprinted in *The Poetic Image in Six Genres*. Carbondale: Southern Illinois University Press, 1969. Superb essay, putting *In Orbit* into perspective in Morris's canon, appreciative of both the novel's "poetic immediacy" and Morris's comic but "frightening" commentary on the disorderly American scene.

Miller, Ralph N. "The Fiction of Wright Morris: The Sense of Ending." *MidAmerica* 3 (1976): 56–76. Morris as pessimist, interested in illustrating the effects of social entropy.

Neinstein, Raymond I. "Wright Morris: The Metaphysics of Home." *Prairie Schooner* 53 (Summer 1979): 121–54. An excellent examination of most of the Nebraska works, including discussion of the photo-texts—superb on the tensions between prose and photograph, author and character, nostalgia and nausea, and the expectations of viewer and reader.

nic, Gerald. "A Ripening Eye: Wright Morris and the Field of Vision." *idAmerica* 1 (1974): 120–31. Discussion of the roles of photography visual perception in shaping Morris's view of the relation between d present, using *The Field of Vision* and *Ceremony in Lone Tree* as evi-the maturation of Morris's "visual metaphor."

ative Capability in Wright Morris' *The Home Place*." *Word and*

Image 4 (January-March 1989): 163–69. Although Morris has similarities to the FSA photographers, Nye sees him also as having affinities with
those who used photography to "defamiliarize" objects in fresh acts of
perception; ultimately his "romantic aesthetics of presence" supports
postmodern theories of the "disappearing subject."

Phillips, Sandra S. "Words and Pictures." In *Wright Morris: Origin of a Species,*
23–32. San Francisco Museum of Modern Art, 1992. Rich biographical
account, focusing on Morris as a maker of photo-texts, "an indirect Midwestern way to tackle intimate emotion."

Power, Mark. "Introduction." *Time Pieces,* by Wright Morris. Washington, D.C.:
Corcoran Gallery, 1983. [Exhibition catalog.] Succinct, perceptive introduction to Morris as a "romantic classicist" in his photographs and
photo-texts. The catalog illustrates 14 of the 53 photo-texts in the Corcoran show.

Price, Mary. "Wright Morris: Three Photographs." *Raritan* 14, no. 2 (1994):
19–28. *Window, mirror,* and *clue* as guides to understanding of two corn-
cob photographs and a mirror image photograph. Suggests that the photographs constrict experience, in contrast to Morris's *content,* which sometimes seems to posit death as release, freedom.

Quantic, Diane Dufva. *The Nature of the Place: A Study of Great Plains Fiction.* Lincoln: University of Nebraska Press, 1995. Morris and others as writers connecting reality to literary myths and contradictory Plains images. The final
chapter argues compellingly for a distinctive "Great Plains literary style."

Szarkowski, John. "Wright Morris the Photographer." In *Wright Morris: Origin
of a Species,* 9–21. San Francisco: San Francisco Museum of Modern Art,
1992. Appreciative analysis of Morris's subtleties, interests, and complexities, by an important champion of Morris's photography.

Trachtenberg, Alan. "The Craft of Vision." *Critique* 4 (Winter 1961): 41–55.
The first essay—and still a crucial one—to link Morris's fiction seriously
to his practice as a photographer.

———. "Wright Morris's 'Photo-Texts.'" *Yale Journal of Criticism* 9 (Spring
1996): 109–119. Perceptive appreciation and analysis of Morris's photographs as "endlessly generative" of narrative texts, in contrast to
Walker Evans's more culturally "historical" approach.

Uffen, Ellen Serlen. "Wright Morris's Earthly Music: The Women of *Plains
Song.*" *MidAmerica* 12 (1985): 97–110. Good discussion of "Plains" as
metaphor, Cora as crucial center, and the significance of Cora's role a
type of Earth Mother of the Plains."

Waldeland, Lynne Maret. "The Deep Sleep: The Fifties in the Novels o
Morris." In *Silhouettes on the Shade: Images from the 50s Reexam*
by Joseph I. Mammola, 25–43. Muncie, Ind.: Ball Sta
[1973]. Morris's novels of the 1950s as urging responsib
the social withdrawal of some other prominent Americ

————. "*Plains Song*: Women's Voices in the Fiction of Wright Morris." *Critique* 24 (1982): 7–20. Appreciative reading of *Plains Song* as a "feminist novel."

Waterman, Arthur E. "Wright Morris's *One Day*: The Novel of Revelation." *Furman Studies* 15 (May 1968): 29–36. Morris's method in novels probing the meaning of American experience hidden within everyday life. *One Day* reflects contemporary American culture by leaving the characters' points of view deliberately inconclusive, in need of further transformation.

Watson, Craig. "The Changing Eye: *The Fork River Space Project* by Wright Morris." *Great Lakes Review* 7 (Winter 1981): 1–11. Perceptive analysis of Morris's evolution toward "ocularity" as the subject of his penultimate novel, linking his fiction to his photography, to ideas about memory and emotion, and to relations between perceptual and conceptual vision.

Westerbeck, Colin S., Jr. "American Graphic: The Photography and Fiction of Wright Morris." *Views: The Journal of Photography in New England* 6 (Spring 1985): 5–11. Reprinted in *Multiple Views: Logan Grant Essays on Photography, 1983–89,* edited by Daniel P. Younger, 271–302. Albuquerque: University of New Mexico Press, 1991. The best essay linking Morris's photography to his fiction, finding in *The Home Place,* for example, a strategy of deliberate counterpoint, relating "absence to presence" in both narrative and visual terms; rich readings of several photographs.

Wilson, James C. "Wright Morris and the Search for the 'Still Point.' " *Prairie Schooner* 49 (Summer 1975): 154–63. Traces Morris's attempt to reconcile his characters' two worlds (of reality and timeless dream) in novels from *The Field of Vision* to *Fire Sermon* and *A Life.*

Wydeven, Joseph J. "Consciousness Refracted: Photography and the Imagination in the Works of Wright Morris." *MidAmerica* 8 (1981): 92–114. Morris's photography in three categories: images of "the thing itself," "equivalents," and "metaphotographs."

————. "Dualism and Doubling in Wright Morris's *War Games*." *Centennial Review* 37 (1993): 415–28. Character doubling in Morris's work in relation to his need to recover his mother.

————. "Focus and Frame in Wright Morris's *The Works of Love*." *Western American Literature* 23 (1988): 99–112. The importance of photography to *The Works of Love*; the effect of Morris's imagistic technique as similar to viewing a photograph album.

—. "Images and Icons: The Fiction and Photography of Wright Morris." *Under the Sun: Myth and Realism in Western American Literature,* edited ?arbara Meldrum, 176–203. Troy, N.Y.: Whitston, 1985. The pertinence ?f myth to Morris's novels and photographs.

?? and Melancholy: Wright Morris's Stories of Old Age." *Weber* ?nterdisciplinary Humanities Journal 12 (Winter 1995): 36–47. stories, especially "Glimpse into Another Country."

———. "Photography and Privacy: The Protests of Wright Morris and James Agee." *Midwest Quarterly* 23 (1981): 103–15. Before Sontag, Agee's and Morris's arguments regarding the potential intrusiveness of photography as incorporated, respectively, in *Let Us Now Praise Famous Men* and *The Home Place*

———. " 'Turned on the Same Lathe': Wright Morris's Loren Eiseley." *South Dakota Review* 33 (Spring 1995): 66–83. Morris's literary debt to Eiseley, including his homage to Eiseley in "The Origin of Sadness."

———. "Visual Artistry in Wright Morris's *Plains Song for Female Voices*." *MidAmerica* 19 (1992): 116–26. Morris's use of visual effects, including photography, to support theme in *Plains Song*.

———. "Wright Morris, Women, and American Culture." In *Women and Western American Literature*, edited by Helen Winter Stauffer and Susan J. Rosowski, 212–29. Troy, N.Y.: Whitston, 1982. Morris's approach to female characters; comparison of *Plains Song* to *The Works of Love*.

Interviews

Bleufarb, Sam. "Point of View: An Interview with Wright Morris." *Accent* 19 (Winter 1959): 34–46.

Carlisle, Olga, and Jodie Ireland. "Wright Morris: The Art of Fiction CXXV." *Paris Review* 33 (Fall 1991): 52–94.

Golightly, Bill. "Wright Morris: An Interview." *Society for the Fine Arts Review* 5 (Fall 1983): 5–7, 20.

Knoll, Robert E., editor. *Conversations with Wright Morris: Critical Views and Responses*. Lincoln: University of Nebraska Press, 1977. Includes Morris in conversation with John W. Aldridge, Wayne C. Booth, Peter Bunnell, and David Madden.

Kovacsi, Gabor. "An Interview with Wright Morris." *Plum Creek Review* (Spring 1965): 36–40.

Nemanic, Jerry, and Harry White. "Interview." *Great Lakes Review* 1 (Winter 1975): 1–29.

Pfeil, Fred. "Querencias and a Lot Else: An Interview with Wright Morris." *Place* [*Neon Rose*] 3 (June 1973): 53–63.

"Wright Morris's Field of Vision: A Conversation." *Black Warrior Review* 10 (Fall 1983): 143–55.

Bibliography

Boyce, Robert L. "A Wright Morris Bibliography." In *Conversations with Morris: Critical Views and Responses,* edited by Robert E. Knoll, Lincoln: University of Nebraska Press, 1977. Indispens... 1975.

Index

The Author

Joseph J. Wydeven received his B.A. from Indiana University, his M.A. from DePaul University, and his Ph.D. in American Studies and English from Purdue University, where he wrote a dissertation on Wright Morris. He has published a number of articles and book chapters devoted to Wright Morris, as well as essays on James Gould Cozzens, American Indian art, and teaching. He has served as a Humanities consultant, received grants from the National Endowment for the Humanities and the Nebraska Committee for the Humanities, and earned the Sears-Roebuck Excellence in Teaching and Campus Leadership Award. He is professor of English and Humanities and dean of the College of Arts and Sciences at Bellevue University, where he has long been involved in pedagogical and curricular efforts. He currently oversees the university's general education reform.

The Editor

Joseph M. Flora earned his B.A. (1956), M.A. (1957), and Ph.D. (1962) in English at the University of Michigan. In 1962 he joined the faculty of the University of North Carolina, where he is professor of English. His study *Hemingway's Nick Adams* (1984) won the Mayflower Award. He is also author of *Vardis Fisher* (1962), *William Ernest Henley* (1970), *Frederick Manfred* (1974), and *Ernest Hemingway: A Study of the Short Fiction* (1989). He is editor of *The English Short Story* (1985) and coeditor of *Southern Writers: A Biographical Dictionary* (1970), *Fifty Southern Writers before 1900* (1987), and *Fifty Southern Writers after 1900* (1987). He serves on the editorial boards of *Studies in Short Fiction* and *Southern Literary Journal*.